Dead End

DEAD END

Suburban Sprawl and the Rebirth of American Urbanism

BENJAMIN ROSS

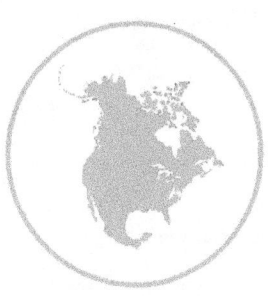

OXFORD
UNIVERSITY PRESS

OXFORD

UNIVERSITY PRESS

Oxford University Press is a department of the University of Oxford.
It furthers the University's objective of excellence in research, scholarship,
and education by publishing worldwide.

Oxford   New York
Auckland   Cape Town   Dar es Salaam   Hong Kong   Karachi
Kuala Lumpur   Madrid   Melbourne   Mexico City   Nairobi
New Delhi   Shanghai   Taipei   Toronto

With offices in
Argentina   Austria   Brazil   Chile   Czech Republic   France   Greece
Guatemala   Hungary   Italy   Japan   Poland   Portugal   Singapore
South Korea   Switzerland   Thailand   Turkey   Ukraine   Vietnam

Oxford is a registered trademark of Oxford University Press
in the UK and certain other countries.

Published in the United States of America by
Oxford University Press
198 Madison Avenue, New York, NY 10016

Library of Congress Cataloging-in-Publication Data
Ross, Benjamin.
Dead end : suburban sprawl and the rebirth of American urbanism / Benjamin Ross.
pages cm
Summary: "A witty, readable, and highly original tour through the history of America's suburbs and
cities to uncover the human impulses that keep sprawl spreading"— Provided by publisher.
ISBN 978-0-19-936014-7 (hardback); 978-0-19-026330-0 (paperback)
1. Suburbs—United States.   2. Cities and towns—United States—Growth.
3. Urbanization—United States.   4. Traffic flow—United States.
5. Land use—Planning.   I. Title.
HT352.U6R67 2014
307.740973—dc23
2013044046

9 8 7 6 5 4 3 2 1
Printed in the United States of America
on acid-free paper

Contents

17. On Track toward Livable Cities   **199**

Introduction

Escape from the Suburbs

The place where I grew up might have been a museum of suburbia.

Albertson Downs was five blocks of Cape Cod houses built by Levitt and Sons just after the Second World War. The subdivision rose on small lots near the Long Island Railroad, 17 miles from Times Square, as the Levitts were perfecting their techniques of suburban development. A few years later and a few miles to the east, they would burst onto the national stage with Levittown, the vast expanse of tract housing that pioneered assembly-line construction.

Historic highways were close at hand. A thousand feet to the south, on the other side of a horse farm, sat a strip of broken asphalt. What we knew as the Old Motor Parkway was a remnant of the world's first limited-access roadway. A mile to the east was the southward jog of the Northern State Parkway. The parkway's creator, the master highway-builder Robert Moses, had here suffered a rare defeat. In 1929, after an epic battle, the heirs of the previous century's robber barons compelled him to divert his road around their great estates.

On a street full of children, we played ball in the roadway. We fed the horses sugar cubes through the pasture fence. Fathers walked to the train station each morning and went into New York. Mothers stayed home and kept house. By the station stood a supermarket and a drugstore, their doors next to the sidewalk and parking off to the side.

By the time we reached high school, our world was changing. The horse farm made way for houses; the supermarket and drugstore closed; mothers went to work. A civic association, never much more than the organizer of July Fourth fireworks, was defunct. Life in the suburbs seemed boring and oppressive. We waited eagerly for the weekend and the opportunity to escape to what everyone called "the city."

What was it that we sought to flee? What was the city that we yearned for? These worlds were not defined by municipal boundaries; they were kinds of places, almost different states of mind.

What we fled is sprawl. The term, coined years earlier by specialists, came into wider use as I grew up in the 1950s. Sprawl is suburbs spread helter-skelter across the land, inhabited in isolated pods. Houses are in one place, factories and offices in another, stores in a third. Stringing them together are wide highways where no one walks. For the simplest errand, there is no choice but to get in a car.

The city of our desire was no abstraction. It was where grandparents lived and where fathers worked. It had neighborhoods with corner stores, bustling shopping districts, skyscraper downtowns. It was full of people and of life. Its streets were not barren suburban highways. They were natural, connected, and truly human.

For my parents' and grandparents' generations, leaving the city was an escape from crowded streets and sooty air. Half a century has passed, and the suburban oasis they moved out to has proved a mirage.

They left the city to escape congestion and found traffic jams. They fled factory smoke, only to breathe auto fumes. They sought peace and quiet; they got nerve-wracking commutes.

Cities had been feared for their infectious diseases. Now suburbs are in need of medical attention. Automobile crashes cause carnage on the road; lack of movement on foot brings obesity and diabetes.

Suburbs were where children could be raised in safety and ease. Away from the dangers of city streets, they would have room to play and freedom to roam. Instead, we have play dates and "helicopter parents," children robbed of spontaneity and parents hovering constantly above them. Street play is proscribed; in places, even sidewalk games are against the law.

After a century, the outward migration is running up against physical limitations. The automobile, a necessity of suburban travel, runs on oil that is ever more expensive to extract. The time, cost, and bother of long-distance commuting surpasses the limits of toleration. And with the wasteful use of energy on cars, houses, and lawns comes the disaster of global warming.

Even before I was born, experts saw that suburban growth was on a path that could not be sustained. As new subdivisions spread across the land, the first warnings reached the public. Just after my tenth birthday in 1959, the *New York Times* raised the alarm in front-page articles. "Cars Choking Cities as 'Urban Sprawl' Takes Over," one headline warned.

It took longer to understand why we, like young suburbanites elsewhere, yearned so strongly for the city. In 1961 Jane Jacobs published her classic *The Death and Life of Great American Cities* and demolished the theories that justified the suburb. Jacobs denied that people and things need to be sorted out, with each kind given a place of its own. She celebrated the vitality and diversity of urban neighborhoods.

Within a decade, the city Jacobs loved reasserted itself. The destruction of neighborhoods by urban renewal ground nearly to a halt, bogged down in heavy opposition. A massive freeway revolt confronted the powerful highway lobby. Across the country, it rubbed interstate highways off maps, and subways were built instead. The profession of land-use planning was in turmoil, searching for new ideas to replace old and discredited concepts.

As the seventies began, the forces gathered against sprawl grew even stronger. A rising environmental movement smashed cars, saved trees, and became a political power. On the suburban fringe, a wave of protest against development toppled local power structures. Towns, counties, and even states enacted laws for growth control. Sprawl, it seemed, was being tamed.

Jane Jacobs was not the only self-educated woman to challenge the orthodoxies of the 1950s. Rachel Carson's *Silent Spring*, published a few months after *Death and Life*, revealed the hazards imposed on nature and human life by spraying with synthetic pesticides. The chemical and agrobusiness interests Carson challenged were as potent as the highway lobby, yet the environmental movement achieved fundamental change. DDT was banned; rivers no longer smell; the air is easier to breathe.

The movement Jacobs helped inspire won victories too. The destruction of cities by redlining, urban renewal, and expressway building was largely checked. Urban life has regained appeal, and cities that declined for decades grow again.

Yet lively, stable, and economically diverse neighborhoods remain hard to find. Decay and gentrification keep nibbling away at what escaped the wrecking balls of the mid-twentieth century. Builders hasten to transform old factory districts into city neighborhoods. But with their wide streets, condos, and chain stores, the new urban quarters still seem less appealing than places built a century and more ago.

Meanwhile, ugly suburbs still spread outward, consuming rural land and carrying the failings of their predecessors to new extremes. Cheap townhouses, tony high-rise apartments, and pretentious McMansions scatter across the landscape, entangled in an ever-expanding web of highways and parking lots.

The house I grew up in is no more, torn down a few years ago to build something bigger. My classmates have moved on, some still in suburbs and others seeking urban places. And today's suburban children are denied the pleasures of our generation. They see their friends when parents arrange it; they rarely walk to school. If a lively city is nearby—sometimes there's just a clump of office buildings—it's hard to reach without a car.

These suburbs have their advocates. Sprawl, they contend, is how people choose to live. The automobile creates a freedom to move about that is unprecedented in human history. City dwellers, crammed into apartments, dream of escaping to a spacious home of their own.

These arguments are not frivolous, but they never appealed to me. I went to school in Cambridge, Massachusetts, where I walked to stores, to restaurants, and across the river to Fenway Park. When I graduated I worked in Cambridge and commuted by bicycle. A new job in the suburbs gave me no choice but to drive, but my two feet and the Boston subway still carried me after five o'clock.

I moved to Washington, DC in 1981. Three years later the Metro arrived where I had settled, outside the city in Montgomery County, Maryland. From the first day on, I took the train to work, but there were few other reasons to ride it. Lively streets were still scarce in Washington. Two more decades would have to pass before a quilt of walkable neighborhoods emerged, one flowing into another as in Boston and New York.

My walk to the subway took me down a street with no sidewalk. When I asked to have one built, county bureaucrats sent me on a paper chase. I discovered a tiny sidewalk-building budget and an ever-growing mountain of requests. The waiting list was ideal fodder for an organizer—I had plenty of experience from my years in Cambridge—and soon the county council, flooded with letters of complaint, raised the budget to a reasonable level.

In 1996 I was asked to be president of the Action Committee for Transit, founded ten years earlier to promote a light rail line. The group's field of action already took in the whole range of transit issues, and it soon widened to include development around the stations. I came to grapple directly with the forces of sprawl, and I saw how hard it is to overcome them.

I puzzled over questions with import far beyond my own suburb. Why is our nation still addicted to sprawl, so long after experts raised the alert? What is the compulsion that keeps us building what so many revile? Why are urban streets, so much in demand, so rarely supplied? Why do attempts at cure so often worsen the disease? How can we break free of our addiction, and create the cities we desire?

This book is a quest for answers to these riddles. The inquiry must start with a search for the roots of sprawl, roots buried deep in history.

1

The Strange Birth
of Suburbia

"The mutant spawn of a socialist commune." Of all the imprecations that a blanket of McMansions on a once-wooded hillside might provoke, this is surely among the least likely to escape beholders' lips. Yet it is what the aggrieved onlookers see.

The American suburb has a most peculiar parentage. The neighborhood of crescent streets and cul-de-sacs was born from a nineteenth-century experiment in social engineering. What now are hallmarks of conformity—enforced exclusion of commerce, rules for setbacks and lot sizes, the meddlesome homeowner association—were created by the dissidents of another era, abolitionists, sexual pioneers, seekers of spiritual enlightenment.

A century and more has passed, and these long-forgotten origins still shape the landscape of subdivision and strip mall. An inherited system of belief limits the use of private land and makes owners yield to neighbors' preferences. From this doctrine of collectivism comes today's suburban scheme of governance, with its zoning codes, deed covenants, and preservation rules. Landowners are told how big to build a house, where to dry their wash, and even what color to paint the door.

This terrain is rife with pettiness and paradox. A Michigan woman is threatened with jail for growing vegetables in her yard. A rabbi in Chicago strives to make his synagogue's environs Vietnamese. A California city specifies which breeds of goats its citizens may keep. In Maryland, barbecues are banned from "public use space" because they would encourage the public to use the space.

Such everyday oddities betray a profound confusion of beliefs and rules, the legacy of suburbia's tangled past. Ardent defenders of property rights insist on telling neighbors how to use their land. Trailer parks and parking lots are hailed as landmark architecture. Zoning proscribes what historic preservation requires. New neighborhoods may not resemble the most admired old ones.

Ideas and history are what make sprawl, as much as brick, shingle, and asphalt. Our ideological inheritance is at the root of what makes change so slow. It insists that what exists is the natural and immutable order of things, and without breaking free of it we can barely even imagine other ways to live. Even when we seek something different, all we know how to ask for is more of the same.

Our story begins in the second quarter of the nineteenth century. Cities then were small and crowded, their size limited to the distance one could walk. As the industrial revolution advanced, machines and people flooded in. Workers toiled long hours in the "satanic mills" and went home to horrific slums. A wave of ferment followed. Why, it was asked, did progress bear such bitter fruit? And how could things be bettered?

The answer, for many, was to leave the old cities and build towns of a new kind, organized on collective principles. In Europe, where these ideas first arose, the good land was already taken and the theories stayed mostly on paper. The United States, with its empty western territories and its openness to new thinking, had room for reformers to put their plans into practice. Over the course of the quarter-century, well over a hundred utopian colonies sprang up, sprinkled from the Atlantic coast to the frontier.

These settlements drew inspiration from a French thinker, Charles Fourier, who laid out detailed plans for ideal communities he called phalansteries. Albert Brisbane, a young American studying in Europe, came across Fourier's writings and brought them home. Brisbane did not lack for erudition—in Berlin, he learned philosophy from Hegel—and he managed to attract the interest of leading American thinkers.

The phalanstery aimed for spiritual enlightenment along with social harmony. Workplace and residence were housed together in a single structure, divided into sections serving body, soul, and intellect. Private property did not disappear; investors financed the community and shared its revenue with workers in a fixed ratio. Capital's share was divided in proportion to the money each put in. Wages were inverse to the enjoyment of the work, and heavy manual labor paid best.[1]

These agricultural communes were launched with much enthusiasm but scant calculation, and they found it hard going. Abstract theory was not easy to translate into practice, and intellectuals made mediocre farmers. Most settlements foundered within months, and even those that managed to sustain themselves rarely prospered.

A few did survive for years. The best remembered is Brook Farm, founded outside Boston in 1840 by the circle of New England intellectuals that included Ralph Waldo Emerson, Nathaniel Hawthorne, and Henry David Thoreau. Seeking transcendence more than sustenance—its residents "dove into the infinite, soared into the illimitable, and never paid cash," a clear-eyed teenaged onlooker would later recall—Brook Farm in 1844 adopted an eclectic version of Fourierism.[2]

By the time Brook Farm expired in 1846, the flaws in Fourier's economic blueprint were obvious, and his remaining followers pursued their ideals by other means. Watered-down utopias sprang up outside New York, featuring individually owned houses and outside employment. These colonies pursued different strands of utopian thought, but they moved in geographic parallel—on a heading toward today's suburbia.

One group narrowed its vision to economic reform. An "Industrial Home Association," aiming to protect its members against the power of capital and land monopoly, settled Mount Vernon north of New York. By now the new railroads had made commuting possible, at least for those who could afford the fares. By 1852, three hundred houses were going up on quarter-acre lots around a train station.[3]

Elsewhere the intellectual ferment continued. Horace Greeley, radical publisher of the *New York Tribune*, was among investors in the Long Island community of Modern Times. The residents—abolitionists, feminists, and transcendentalists—lived with no laws or jails and rejected the institution of marriage. The settlement was soon a magnet for cranks and eccentrics, and it became notorious for its unconventional ideas. Things calmed down during the Civil War, and the town, wishing to escape its reputation, changed its name to Brentwood.[4]

Some Fourierists still soldiered on. Albert Brisbane remained active in the city, writing a column in the *Tribune* and organizing. He came to grief in 1855 when the police—egged on by Greeley's upstart rivals at the *New York Times*—raided a meeting of an alleged Free Love Society and briefly jailed the organizers.

One orthodox colony remained: the North American Phalanx in Red Bank, New Jersey. Even it was riven by internal disagreements, and in 1853 there was a split. The minority, less attached to communalism, attracted new adherents whose striving for spiritual and artistic elevation overshadowed the egalitarian aspects of their philosophy. Under the leadership of a wealthy New York merchant, Marcus Spring, they undertook to build their own colony on the nearby coast.

Spring was an intellectual as well as a businessman. He and his wife had accompanied the transcendentalist Margaret Fuller on her trip to Europe a few years earlier. To design the new community—known to history as the Raritan Bay Union—he engaged a leading architect of the day, Alexander Jackson Davis. For himself Spring built a fine private house alongside the imposing communal structure, and other wealthy members could erect individual homes as well. Davis took advantage of this assignment to exchange visits with a young architect of his acquaintance who lived across the bay in Staten Island, Frederick Olmsted.[5]

From Raritan Bay Union sprang the settlement that laid down a pattern for the suburbia to come. There Davis had designed a three-sectioned house for New York merchant Llewellyn Haskell. The two men joined together again to create a new community in South Orange, New Jersey, an hour by train and ferry from New York. Davis was enamored of the beauty of Orange Mountain, and the land, unsuitable for agriculture, was cheap. An architect of genius, he took full advantage of the situation—the property, which Haskell dubbed Llewellyn Park, possessed extraordinary views across Newark all the way to the harbor and city of New York.

Llewellyn Park was built for the upper middle class rather than the wealthy. To limit maintenance expense, formal gardens were omitted and the forest growth largely retained. Davis laid out curving streets, then a novelty, to follow the terrain. Homes were set back from the street, within the woods, on lots of an acre or larger. Departing from the prevailing custom—developers of the time subdivided land into lots but did not build—Davis designed the first residences himself in a consistent style, Gothic revival, which stood on the architectural avant-garde of the moment. The park-like naturalism of the design, although it drew on precedents from London and Manchester, was an innovation in its openness and its adaptation to the landscape.

Haskell and Davis were attempting only a partial retreat from Fourierist communalism. The imposing common edifices that had reached an apogee at Raritan Bay Union shrank into a few rustic buildings and a planned but never built Lyceum. A large park occupied a rugged and picturesque portion of the land, maintained by a self-governing association that all property owners were required to join. Covenants attached to each deed made mandatory the set-backs and minimum lot sizes, banned commercial activities, and required payment of assessments to the association.[6]

Llewellyn Park retained a tone of social and political innovation. The son of antislavery leader William Lloyd Garrison was among the first residents. Another early purchaser was Theodore Tilton, editor of a widely read abolitionist magazine. Tilton, in 1871, would write of the Paris Commune that "the central idea of communism is the same that George Washington spent seven years in killing his fellow-countrymen to achieve—the same which Alexander Hamilton wrote into a constitution which survives to this day." [7]

Along with radical politics came sexual experimentation, more discreet than at Modern Times but hardly invisible. As a newspaper recounted a May Day celebration, the high point of the community's life:

> In the center of the green, the May Pole was erected. It was a tall tulip tree, stripped of the bark, and the top of it was clasped by a garland of flowers and ribands, as in the old heathen days, when Priapus was a god, and all the people did him reverence...

Just how the celebrants honored the Greek god of the phallus can only be guessed today, but what they thought of Victorian morality is beyond doubt.[8]

The institutional structure that undergirded Llewellyn Park's physical layout—a structure replicated countless times in the ensuing 160 years—stood only a short step removed from its socialist forerunners. In an experiment in communal living, it was only natural to exclude profit-making commerce and establish a governing body. With separately owned structures taking the place of a single edifice, setback and lot size covenants were essential to the achievement of a common vision; these rules were far less onerous than the regulations of a phalanstery.

Still, the direction such a colony was headed in could be sensed. For two critics on the left, writing in 1848, "abolition of the distinction between town and country" ranked first among the useful concepts to be found in Fourier's writings. But his followers, they observed, had been "compelled to appeal to the feelings and purses of the bourgeois."

The pamphlet where these remarks appeared, under the title of *The Communist Manifesto*, has rarely been accused of excessive timidity. Yet in this matter Karl Marx and Friedrich Engels were, if anything, too mild in their judgment. A partial retreat is the most difficult of maneuvers, and at Llewellyn

Park the retreat from socialism turned into a rout. This offspring of the pha-lanstery soon developed an appeal that was quite exclusively bourgeois. By the end of the 1880s Llewellyn Park was a bastion of suburban wealth. It boasted Thomas Edison as a resident and was emulated by a growing number of purely capitalist real estate operators.

The modern suburb, far removed from these origins, still conserves their ideological heritage. Each Llewellyn Park property owner, Theodore Tilton wrote in 1864, "possesses the whole park in common, so that the fortunate purchaser of two or three acres becomes a virtual owner of the whole five hun-dred."9 Here in germ is the belief of today's suburban homeowner that prop-erty rights include a veto over building on neighbors' land—an understanding shared by even the most ardent defenders of private property.

Historians of architecture see Alexander Jackson Davis' invention of the lay-out of the modern suburb as the key to Llewellyn Park's longevity—it remains little changed today—and its long-lasting influence. But what enabled this style of land use to persist and multiply was an equally innovative institutional structure. A trait that played no small role in the failure of Fourierist social-ism—the imposition of a predesigned structure highly resistant to change—endowed capitalist suburbs with market appeal and resilience.

A single man, Frederick Olmsted, was largely responsible for perpetuat-ing the organizational and architectural heritage of Llewellyn Park. Olmsted gained fame through his design of New York's Central Park, an assignment he and Calvert Vaux won in an 1858 competition. The architectural firm the two men established is best remembered for its parks, civic jewels of New York, Boston, and other cities, but real estate promoters engaged it too for the design of park-like suburbs.

The first of these assignments was Riverside, built after the Civil War on 1600 acres of prairie outside Chicago. Here the layout took another step toward the modern suburb. Divided into 2250 lots of about a half-acre each, the community was centered around a small commercial district at the rail-road station. Houses were set back at least 30 feet from the winding roads and surrounded by trees and well-kept gardens. Olmsted's design adorned the community with numerous parks; however, these were slow to appear, and it soon emerged that the developers were of dubious character. They went bank-rupt in the Panic of 1873, but Riverside filled out and remains a prosperous enclave today.10

In the two decades that followed, Olmsted and Vaux designed fifteen more railroad suburbs. All followed the architectural and institutional model of

Llewellyn Park and Riverside. Houses were set back on curved streets, commerce was excluded from residential districts, and the entire edifice rested on a structure of legal covenants that the Olmsted firm soon systematized. Most of these subdivisions endure to this day as wealthy neighborhoods of single-family homes, among them such prestigious suburbs as Chestnut Hill in Massachusetts, Druid Hills near Atlanta, and Tarrytown Park, New York.[11]

Only the affluent could afford to live in communities that met these high standards. For Olmsted, whose crowning achievements were parks open to the entire population, this was a matter of regret. His intent in employing legal covenants was to ensure the fulfillment of his artistic vision and then protect it from unwanted commercial intrusions that, he recognized, the very success of his creations would attract. As years went by and neighborhoods matured, the covenants and homeowner associations proved effective indeed in accomplishing their purpose—so effective that they attracted imitators who cared little for Olmsted's artistic and social ideals.

As Llewellyn Park and its progeny grew into havens for the wealthy, it could be seen that the covenants excluded more than unwanted architectural intrusions. They excluded people—people whose incomes fell short of what became the community standard. By the 1880s, subdividers began to make this explicit, setting a minimum cost for the houses that went up on the lots they sold. After a few more years, developers of large tracts would carefully apportion their land into zones of differing status, with a sliding scale of prescribed construction costs.

Toward the end of the 1880s, a new wave of railroad suburbs arrived. In organization and layout they followed the pattern of Llewellyn Park, but they were planned and marketed on a frankly elitist basis. "Park" might still be the name, but a members-only country club and its golf course took the place of public open space. At Short Hills in New Jersey and the Chicago suburb of Kenilworth, developers screened prospective purchasers by judging their social graces in a personal interview. The subdivisions of this era include such renowned bastions of privilege as Bronxville and Tuxedo Park in New York's Westchester County.[12]

The pattern set by upscale railway suburbs would later become the suburban norm, but in the years after the Civil War these enclaves constituted only a tiny part of urban expansion. What enabled cities to spread far beyond their historic limit, the distance of a reasonable walk to work, was the new technology of the street railway. Even when pulled by horses, streetcars could carry commuters into former countryside. In the 1890s electric power expanded their range. The fare, usually a nickel on electric lines, was low enough that clerks and artisans could commute, and urban growth became a movement of the masses.

Streetcars quickly became big business. Real estate speculation often promised bigger profits than the transit line itself, so operators would buy up farms and extend the tracks beyond the limits of existing settlement. The land was sold to subdividers, a mix of large and small promoters, who sold off the lots and left construction to the purchaser. There were a multitude of small-scale builders and contractors, and future residents erected many houses themselves.

The communities built around streetcar lines have come to be known as streetcar suburbs. Today most of them are thought of as urban neighborhoods. Some older cities like Boston and San Francisco are, outside their downtowns, made up almost entirely of streetcar suburbs.

The streets that carried the tracks are, naturally enough, the main axes of streetcar suburbs. Along them commercial activity is strung out in a thin line. Side streets are straight, parallel, and closely spaced, with long blocks, an arrangement that offered rapid access to the streetcar and maximized the number of saleable lots. There are regional variations in the type of structure—small single-family bungalows predominate in Chicago and the Midwest, Baltimore and Philadelphia have brick row houses, wooden two-, three-, and even six-family houses are common in New England—but sub-dividers everywhere created small lots to squeeze in more homes and make them affordable.[13]

While all classes had lived in proximity in the old walking cities, residents of the new streetcar suburbs soon found themselves sorted by income level. One cause of this separation was transportation. Sam Bass Warner's classic study of Boston, *Streetcar Suburbs*, shows how the more affluent segment of the city's middle class, with steady downtown jobs, moved to outer suburbs where streetcars ran only toward the city center. Artisans, salesmen, and fac-tory workers were confined to inner suburbs, where development was more advanced and the population was dense enough to justify crosstown transit. The desire of homebuyers to live near people like themselves reinforced this social sorting, as did the natural conservatism of small builders. The build-ers could be sure that houses would find buyers if they resembled what had already been sold on the same block.[14]

The streetcars, like the suburbs, assumed the social status of their occu-pants. In Henry James' 1886 novel *The Bostonians*, the well-born, socially con-scious Olive Chancellor considers how to move about her city:

> She would have taken the public conveyance (in her heart she loathed it) to the South End. Boston was full of poor girls who had to walk about at night and to squeeze into horse-cars in which every sense was displeased; why should she hold herself superior to these?

Social prestige attached, as we will see again and again, to the mere presence of an upscale clientele, quite apart from the intrinsic merit of what they purchased. Olive, accompanying a visiting cousin to hear a speech on women's rights, thought it best to hire a carriage. That vehicle, it turned out, offered little more comfort than the horse-car; she found herself "bouncing and bumping over the rail-way tracks very little less, after all, than if their wheels had been fitted to them."[15]

A more affluent ridership could make streetcars—especially the electrically powered kind—attractive even to the wealthy residents of restricted railroad suburbs. By 1910 a Portland, Oregon real estate promoter would advertise that "the fact that the Broadway car line, for its entire course, runs through a restricted residence district insures a desirable class of fellow passengers." When Senator Francis Newlands set out in 1891 to create the expensive Chevy Chase neighborhood outside Washington, DC, he made sure there was access by both streetcar and railroad. The streetcars, running straight up Connecticut Avenue through affluent Cleveland Park, were soon full of passengers; the railroad followed a less direct route and never carried anything but freight.[16]

By the end of the 1880s, older streetcar suburbs were changing as the city grew past them, and the evolution began to trouble both subdividers and homeowners. One had sold, and the other had bought, a cut-rate version of the rural ideal of Olmsted and Vaux, and part of the package was the reflected social glory of expensive railroad enclaves. Even the architectural ornaments on streetcar suburb houses were usually knockoffs of recent fashion among the more affluent. But in crowded neighborhoods close to the city, social pretensions rested on precarious foundations. As a district evolved, it became more than just a bedroom suburb for downtown. There came new land uses, and new residents, of lower social status. The remaining vacant lots grew too expensive for peers of the first wave of buyers, who were outbid by builders of crowded rental housing for workers and the lower middle class.[17]

Olmsted had identified the problem two decades earlier. A growing population attracted "butchers and bakers and tinkers and dramsellers and the followers of other bustling callings," who could easily find places for their businesses along streets laid out in a grid. The new residents who accompanied these enterprises might fill small lots with "ill-proportioned, vile-colored, shabby-genteel dwelling houses." Olmsted had architectural remedies for this problem in curving streets and large lots, but few streetcar-line subdividers had the means to implement them. It was the legal device he had long championed—the restrictive covenant—that offered hope of a quick and easy cure. Real estate promoters, who wanted mostly to hold off deterioration of the neighborhood just long enough to sell all the lots, found covenants especially attractive.[18]

Homebuyers initially resisted limits on their right to use property as they saw fit. For new landowners, an important appeal of the suburbs was the chance to escape subordination to a landlord. Moreover, the effect of restrictions was to prevent changes in land use that would raise property values. The buyer of a restricted lot was trading money for social status. As time passed, upwardly mobile city dwellers came to find this an attractive exchange. By the end of the 1890s, covenants were in wide use, sometimes even in less expensive neighborhoods.[19]

A breakthrough in the use of covenants came with the upscale Baltimore community of Roland Park. George Kessler, a well-regarded planner of parks and boulevards who had assisted Olmsted in the design of Central Park, laid out the first phase of this development in 1891. He banned business establishments outside of a designated commercial center, set back houses 30 to 40 feet from the street, and specified a minimum price of house construction. The second phase of development was designed in 1898 by the Olmsted firm itself. Olmsted's sons, who now ran the firm, promoted the separation of social classes without their father's hesitations. They added more restrictions, including a developer veto over the design of each house.[20]

Roland Park was a commercial success, and it attracted imitators across the country. The most prominent of these was Jesse Clyde Nichols, whose real estate business began in 1905 with a ten-acre plot next to the Kansas City Country Club. Within three years, Nichols and his backers gained control of more than one thousand acres and arranged for streetcars to reach their property. They laid out the new development, dubbed the Country Club District, with wide curving streets. Stringent covenants, including minimum house prices graded by neighborhood, enabled Nichols to boast of "1000 acres restricted." After he made direct contact with the developers of Roland Park in 1912, he copied their system of architectural review and established homeowner associations to enforce these and other rules.

Nichols, a careful follower of land-use trends, is credited with many innovations in suburban development. He devised covenants that were effectively

Sign advertising J. C. Nichols' Country Club District.
(Courtesy of the State Historical Society of Missouri, J. C. Nichols Company scrapbooks.)

immortal, overcoming long-standing legal doctrines that limited the lifetime of restrictions on real estate. He was also among the earliest designers of residential suburbs for the automobile. His subdivisions intentionally discouraged walking so that buyers would feel insulated from the city. Blocks were enlarged and sidewalks shrunk; by 1921 pedestrians were rare enough in the more affluent sections that sidewalks could be eliminated there entirely. And in 1923 he opened a regional shopping center, the best known of all his firsts. Earlier planned suburbs had neighborhood stores at railroad stations and streetcar lines; Country Club Plaza was conceived on a grand scale to draw shoppers by car from the entire metropolis. Located at a highway junction and surrounded by parking lots, it was the prototype of the modern shopping mall.[21]

Nichols' leadership in trade associations gave the Country Club District immense influence. With deep insight into social and economic trends joined to an intellectual bent uncommon among real estate promoters, he laid out his ideas in well-publicized talks at public meetings as well as closed sessions among developers. Nichols first attended the National Conference on City Planning in 1912 and was soon elected to its General Committee. He also served on the City Planning Committee of the National Association of Real Estate Boards, which in 1919 initiated annual meetings of "Developers of High-Class Residential Property." Within a few years the Country Club District was inspiring other expensive suburbs, such as Houston's River Oaks, designed from the start for access exclusively by automobile.[22]

The developers understood what their buyers sought—the defining characteristic of their market segment was "high class" rather than high price. The property they offered was, to be sure, conveniently placed and attractive to the eye, but these were secondary attributes, chosen to elevate social status as much as for their intrinsic worth. A planner of Palos Verdes Estates, a famous subdivision laid out near Los Angeles by Frederick Olmsted Jr. in the 1920s, explained it this way:

> The type of protective restrictions and the high class scheme of layout which we have provided tends to guide and automatically regulate the class of citizens who are settling here. The restrictions prohibit occupation of land by Negroes or Asiatics. The minimum cost of house restrictions tends to group the people of more or less like income together as far as it is reasonable and advisable to do so.[23]

The rules set down by these developers include many of today's suburban norms, sometimes taken so much for granted that the original purpose is hard to discern. Here Thorstein Veblen's classic analysis of status-seeking, *The Theory of the Leisure Class*, offers guidance. The core of Veblen's theory is that the visible display of unproductive expenditure—what he called conspicuous waste or conspicuous consumption—elevates social standing whereas routine useful labor degrades it.

Conspicuous waste is easy to observe in the suburbs. Houses must be set back from the street. Covenants (and later zoning ordinances) require large front lawns, space that gets far less use than the backyard. Chickens provide food and are often proscribed; pets serve no productive function and are allowed. The dog in particular is a suburban favorite; Veblen explained that it is an especially honorable beast:

> The dog has advantages in the way of uselessness as well as in special gifts of temperament.... He is the filthiest of the domestic animals in his person, and the nastiest in his habits. For this he makes up in a servile fawning attitude towards his master, and a readiness to inflict damage and discomfort on all else.[24]

Wealth and habits of consumption were not, of course, the only attributes of a desirable neighbor in early-twentieth-century America. Race was an unavoidable issue in a country resegregating after the Civil War and Reconstruction. Developers of expensive real estate were rarely willing to sell property to blacks, but for a long time they hesitated to include racial restrictions in their deed covenants. They did not want to risk invalidating the entire structure, under legal doctrines that allowed covenants to limit the use of property but not its sale. Only in the early 1900s, when covenants gained easier acceptance in the courts, did racial clauses become commonplace. Blacks were by far the most severely affected, but they were not alone in their exclusion—Jews were a frequent target, covenants drafted on the West Coast often kept Asians out, and sometimes even Italians, Greeks, and Slavs were proscribed.[25]

Along with these covenant-controlled developments, the years after the First World War brought yet another burst of speculation in unregulated building lots. As in the previous generation, transportation controlled urban form, but now the automobile had arrived to rival the streetcar. This new means of transport freed subdividers from earlier constraints, and the layout of their new suburbs showed the effect.

Henry Ford's introduction of the Model T in 1908 made the car an option for the masses, and by 1920 there was one auto for every thirteen Americans. The rapidly expanding automobile industry, its national clout complemented by the local influence of car dealers, gas station owners, and road builders, joined with real estate interests to lobby for better roads. By the early 1920s well-paved highways were fanning out from the cities. Traffic engineers, already seeking to separate automobiles from pedestrians, were developing the concepts that matured into today's interstates.

The first highway built for cars, Long Island's Motor Parkway of 1908, was a private enterprise intended for racing and "pleasure driving" by wealthy estate owners. But road-building quickly became a public undertaking. Road Acts of 1916 and 1921 began the policy of federal aid to state highway builders. State gasoline taxes, first enacted in Oregon in 1919 and in effect ten years later in all forty-eight states, yielded a steady flow of funds. City dwellers, whose local taxes maintained the streets that drivers used, paid indirectly through the gas tax for the spread of suburbs. Streetcars, meanwhile, remained in private hands, wasting away as subsidized competition sapped their revenues and rapacious owners starved them of investment.

Houses no longer had to cluster along streetcar lines and could spread across the countryside. Real estate promoters were quick to take advantage of the opportunity, selling land to buyers with meager financial resources. Vast expanses of mostly empty lots soon surrounded Los Angeles and Detroit, the fastest-growing cities. Here and there someone built a house, but most of the new owners could barely afford a shack.[26]

The twin forces of rising incomes and easy mortgage credit set off a suburban land bubble in the early 1920s. Speculation was, as usual, accompanied by fraud. One Florida developer was Charles Ponzi of Boston, remembered today as perpetrator of a pyramid investment scheme, who sold property "near Jacksonville" that was actually 65 miles away. (Ponzi, for all his other faults, appreciated the value of urban density—he cut his land up into twenty-three lots per acre.) The boom in Los Angeles peaked in 1923, but in Florida the mania progressed until 1926. Demand began to falter in the spring, and then two autumn hurricanes delivered the coup de grace. The flow of money through Miami banks in 1928 was one-seventh of what it had been three years earlier.[27]

Since the last years of the nineteenth century, covenants had been widely used to exclude undesirable people, buildings, and activities from new subdivisions. But these private contracts worked only imperfectly and incompletely. Older neighborhoods still lacked their protection. In principle, landowners could establish restrictions at any time, but in practice covenants had to be imposed in advance by the subdivider because a large group of homeowners could never agree on the details of the rules. And even when in place, covenants were hard to enforce. Individuals had little incentive to undertake expensive legal action against violators, and homeowner associations sucked up time and money that were hard to come by in less affluent neighborhoods. Homeowners and real estate developers desired more comprehensive and more effective controls. This was something only the power of government could achieve.[28]

The call for action was not unanimous. What covenants and zoning offered homebuyers was permanence—assurance that in future years they would be surrounded by people and buildings of the same quality as when they moved in. Stopping change was not in everyone's interest. The subdividers of large tracts, who maximized the value of the initial sale with promises of permanence, benefited most. They spearheaded the push for government regulation as they had for deed covenants. Small-scale speculators, who dealt in property already subdivided and hoped to profit from new and denser uses, led the opposition.

Los Angeles took a first step toward the systematic separation of land uses in 1908. The Los Angeles Realty Board, dominated by developers of upscale restricted neighborhoods, urged zoning on the city with the support of affluent homeowners. A pair of ordinances created seven industrial districts and defined nearly all of the city's remaining territory as residential districts. There businesses were allowed only when the City Council granted an exception. Other cities soon followed this example. In 1913 Wisconsin, Minnesota, and

New York authorized cities, when property owners so requested, to establish districts where nonresidential uses were banned. The Illinois legislature passed a similar law that died when the governor, on being advised that it was unconstitutional, used his veto.[29]

Early zoning laws often proscribed unwanted races along with unwanted land uses. In 1910 a Baltimore ordinance kept blacks from any block where more than half the residents were white. Birmingham, Atlanta, Richmond, St. Louis, and other municipalities soon enacted racial zoning as well. Blacks could of course sleep in white neighborhoods when they were household help living on their employers' property—and the Atlanta ordinance also permitted black homeowners to house white servants. This bow to constitutional doctrine showed how hollow was the promise of "separate but equal." A black man who presumed, in that time and place, to hire whites as domestic help would be lucky to see another sunrise.

Such maneuvers were too transparent even for the conservative judges of the day. In a 1917 case that gave the National Association for the Advancement of Colored People its first legal victory, a unanimous Supreme Court struck down racial zoning. Louisville's zoning ordinance, the court held, violated the white landowner's constitutional right to sell property to blacks. Racial segregation would have to rely on private contracts.[30]

Zoning codes could no longer divide races, but they could still separate uses, and soon the nation's largest city had one. The skyscrapers that would dominate New York's skyline had just appeared, and many feared these giant buildings would shut off light and air and congest traffic. Meanwhile, the spread of garment manufacturers into the upscale shopping district on Fifth Avenue was annoying retailers. Their customers were now forced to mix on sidewalks with immigrant workers. "Gentlemen, you are like cattle in a pasture, and the needle trades workers are the flies that follow you from one pasture to another," storeowners were told at a private luncheon. Such rhetoric lacked mass appeal, so the merchants promoted zoning with other arguments. Their well-funded publicity campaign warned of a grab bag of evils from truck traffic to overcrowding to high rents.

The city's major real estate and commercial interests joined retailers and municipal reformers to seek the separation of land uses, and action came quickly. In 1914 the city gained authority to impose zoning, and two years later a detailed ordinance was in place. Its underlying principle, as the framers conceded, was to freeze in place the existing land use. This entailed not a full spatial separation along the lines of upscale suburbs but a pattern similar to streetcar suburbs—midblock parcels were restricted to residential use, with commerce allowed on the avenues that carried through traffic. The code also placed limits on tall buildings, imposing gradual setbacks of higher stories to allow light and air to enter. From this rule came the terraced skyscrapers that have long defined New York's skyline.[31]

New York's adoption of a zoning code triggered a frenzy of activity in cities large and small. The landowning public clamored for separation of land uses, and developers of restricted communities joined in the call for government control. Machine politicians joined municipal reformers in the embrace of zoning—it was easy to see that variances, exceptions, and rezonings would open up a cornucopia of patronage and graft.[32] By 1920 zoning ordinances were in place in 904 cities, including 82 of the 93 municipalities with populations over 100,000. Given further encouragement by a model ordinance issued by Secretary of Commerce Herbert Hoover in 1924, a wave of regulation rolled on through the decade.[33]

The zoning movement quickly advanced beyond the isolation of residential uses to the exclusion of apartment houses from residential areas. The middle and upper classes did not like apartments. The most varied objections were raised. They were ugly; they gave off noise and smoke. They were simply not the way Americans should live. But most of all, zoners objected to the people who lived in apartments. The flavor of the tenement seemed to attach to even the most luxurious buildings. Residents were prone to disease and immorality. Tenants were "a class of nomads," said Harvard University president Charles Eliot, "that have no stable footing in the town."[34]

Many cities were already manipulating their fire and building codes to keep apartments out; with zoning they could reach the same end more directly. Berkeley, California, was the first to take this path. Its zoning ordinance, adopted in 1917, enforced a rigid separation of uses that went far beyond contemporaries. At a time when other cities were merely separating residential uses from commercial and industrial ones, Berkeley established a multitude of zones—twenty-seven in all. One-family, two-family, and apartment houses each had their own assigned districts, and homes were kept out of industrial areas as industry was from residential areas. Almost immediately, the exclusion of multifamily residences from single-family districts became a standard zoning rule.[35]

But zoning, despite all its advantages, was not a complete replacement for the older restrictive covenants. For one thing, racial zoning had been ruled out by the Supreme Court. Not only did new subdivisions continue to include racial covenants in their deeds, but also homeowners in existing neighborhoods added them. Less affluent homeowners sought to raise their status by imitating "high-class" suburbs. In the racist atmosphere of the early 1920s, with a revived Ku Klux Klan flourishing in both the North and the South, it was not hard for neighbors to come to consensus on racial exclusion.[36]

Control over the appearance of buildings was another reason for private agreements. The legal doctrines justifying zoning did not, until later modified, allow restrictions that were based on aesthetics. Upscale subdivisions like Roland Park and the Country Club District needed covenants to impose architectural review of house designs. And even for purposes that zoning could accomplish, private restrictions might be piled on top. Deed covenants offered a permanence that zoning, subject to the vagaries of the political process, could not ensure.[37]

Just one large American city, Houston, has never passed a zoning law. While restrictive covenants once covered almost every acre of the city, most became inoperative because only wealthier neighborhoods could afford to enforce them. Beginning in the 1920s, the developers of River Oaks led the city's business elite in repeated efforts to enact a zoning ordinance. But smaller property owners, black and white, wanted no limits on their chances to profit from changes in land use, and successive referendums went down to defeat.

In the end, though, landowners are constrained in Houston much as they are elsewhere. Minimum lot sizes were enacted in 1940, effectively banning construction of row houses in middle- and lower-income neighborhoods. Setbacks from the property line were required for buildings of all kinds, and stringent minimum parking requirements followed a few years later. After yet another failure at the polls, the pro-zoning forces turned to the state legislature in 1965. The city was empowered to enforce private deed restrictions, and a simple majority of the property owners in a subdivision can put in place new covenants that are enforceable against dissenters. This, for all practical purposes, is zoning, minus only the ability of the population as a whole to override the exclusionary wishes of a single neighborhood.[38]

By now, restrictive covenants and zoning had created a new form of land tenure. A landowner's property rights no longer end at the lot line but extend beyond it to the entire neighborhood. When Theodore Tilton wrote in 1864 that "the fortunate purchaser of two or three acres becomes a virtual owner of the whole five hundred," he was describing a single community of fifty-odd residences. Six decades later, the doctrine of common ownership was second nature to suburban Americans.

The regime of covenants and zoning obliterated a basic principle of nineteenth-century real estate law: that owners of land could build as they liked absent special circumstances. Free trade in land, which had earlier displaced feudal landholding in Europe, now gave way to the new suburban land tenure. The collectivist spirit of the new system was a sharp departure from the individualism of American legal and economic thinking. Sacred doctrines of freedom of contract and freedom of movement were set aside; people and buildings would henceforth be separated according to fine gradations of social status.

New systems of government arose to oversee the intertwined property rights of suburbia. Homeowner associations allowed only landowners to vote, reverting to a constitutional arrangement obsolete since the days of Andrew Jackson.[39] With zoning, the new property regime gained the support of law enforcement and tax revenue.[40] Owners of nearby homes enjoy a right that, even when much weaker in form, often amounts in practice to a veto over new construction. This right attaches to property and not citizenship; "public" input into decisions comes (sometimes de jure and almost always de facto) from landowners rather than the entire population.[41]

The path from the invention of suburban land tenure to its general acceptance was anything but straight. The sentiments that brought wide acceptance were almost polar opposites to those that had given it birth. Dissidence gave way to conformism. Manual labor, once rewarded, was disdained. Deed covenants devised by abolitionists now enforced racial segregation.

Did suburban land tenure arise by mere happenstance, engendered by the odd conjuncture of an unlikely collection of people and ideas? Or was its emergence the inevitable consequence of suburban growth?[42] The new doctrine reflected a reality of real estate—the enjoyment of one's land depends greatly on what one's neighbor builds—and it was propelled forward by powerful social and economic forces. Yet it could be propelled because it was already there, embodied in wood, brick, pavement, and grass. For the practical men and women who sold lots and built houses, Llewellyn Park and Roland Park were compelling examples that no abstract theory could have matched.

What would have happened had not the socialistic impulse of lapsed Fourierists first put the modern suburb into concrete form and the artistic genius of Frederick Olmsted kept it alive in the public eye? To such questions, history can offer no sure answer.

2

Planners and Embalmers

The system of landholding based on restrictive covenants and zoning would have momentous consequences for the future growth of American cities. Yet no grand plan had conceived it. Stepwise changes, each justified on narrow grounds, had accumulated into a dimly understood whole. Only in retrospect could it be seen how far the new order departed from received economic doctrines and accepted legal precedents. The creators of suburban land tenure had never articulated any underlying rationale, but without a clearly stated justification for the rejection of past jurisprudence, the entire structure stood on shaky legal foundations.

A new doctrine was needed to underpin the altered governance of land use. Such a doctrine must necessarily begin by explaining for what purpose the established rights of property owners had been curtailed. But those who undertook this task came immediately up against an obstacle: honesty was not an option. In a country founded on the rejection of aristocracy, the maintenance of status distinctions was not a proper purpose of government. Americans in their private lives might obsess over social rank, but as an explicit object of public policy the entire subject was out of bounds. Other motivations must stand in for status.

One early favorite was appearance. Wealthy suburbs were indeed attractive, and their history lent support to this line of thought. The first devisers of residence-only covenants, men like Alexander Jackson Davis and Frederick Olmsted Sr., were unquestionably devoted to artistic goals. And the order that zoning imposes on neighborhoods surely contributes to aesthetic harmony.

But intrusive government regulation could not be justified on artistic grounds alone. Beauty is, after all, a matter of taste. And art is the fruit of individual creation, rarely improved by bureaucratic supervision. Americans are a people disinclined to let officials tell us what to do, unless compelled by depression or war. Almost nowhere would government intrusion be less welcome than in the appearance of one's house.

A more promising candidate was property values. Here there was no need to be shy. If status is America's dirty secret, money-making is its pride. Zoning's partisans were quick to take this tack.

They were so quick, in fact, that they neglected to sort out whether zoning would make real estate prices go up or down. Harland Bartholomew, whose consulting firm wrote zoning ordinances for dozens of cities, claimed that zoning was needed to keep property prices up. Prices rose in restricted suburbs, he argued, and fell in those that allowed "promiscuous" mixed-use development. This had a certain plausibility; the most expensive suburbs were indeed highly restricted.[1]

But zoning had its main effect not in elite enclaves but in streetcar suburbs where the masses lived. Here zoning brought *lower* property values. Sam Bass Warner's later research into Boston suburbs shows that the introduction of mixed uses increased the price of land. Zoning proponents understood this and saw it as an advantage. They argued that holding property prices down improves neighborhoods by filling them with single-family houses. When apartment buildings are allowed, speculators buy up land and keep it empty in the hope of selling to a developer later.[2]

Advocates could list other benefits. Factory smoke and odors were kept out of residential neighborhoods. Large buildings brought traffic congestion. Most of all, though, and coming closest to the truth, owners of single-family homes were protected from change. "The protection of the homes of the people is probably the primary purpose of use districting," wrote Robert Whitten, who helped write the New York zoning law and then drafted Atlanta's separate-but-equal rules and ordinances for Dallas, Providence, and other cities and suburbs.[3]

These arguments, and others like them, were used to good political effect. But they did not add up to an overarching theory of land-use regulation. For that, control proponents turned to an economic doctrine in wide fashion in the 1920s: the idea that the destructive anarchy of the market must be tamed through planning. This was a widely held belief, from the extremes of Vladimir Lenin and Benito Mussolini to the sober center of Herbert Hoover. Hoover, the dominant American political figure of the decade, controlled domestic policy-making as secretary of commerce even before he became president. The planners, in his conservative vision, were not government bureaucrats but industry assembled into trade associations. Government's role was to encourage the organization and modernization of the private sector. Housing was a segment of the economy particularly in need of such transformation.

Comprehensive city planning was not a new idea; it was a prominent item on the agenda of Progressive-Era municipal reformers. Cities, without question, were plagued with poverty, pollution, and overcrowding. Planning was the solution. Calculate the city's needs, measure its physical and human resources, and bring destructive chaos under control by scientifically matching resources to needs.

Advocates had been writing earnest reports since the first years of the century, and in 1909 they organized on a national scale. A National Conference on City Planning and the Problems of Congestion was held in Washington. Practical experience was not lacking among the attendees; such men as Frederick Olmsted Jr. and George Kessler were succcessful designers of parks, boulevards, and upscale suburbs. But the ambition to map out entire cities had as yet produced only paper studies that lacked the force of law.[4]

The conference met annually, its attendance and influence growing as theorists and consultants were joined by the entrepreneurs who built expensive suburbs. Edward Bouton, the creator of Roland Park, attended the first year, and developers and real estate agents arrived in numbers in 1912. As the developers saw it, the private sector was already doing what the planning movement wanted for the entire community. High on their agenda was zoning. It would give their projects protection beyond the limits of the land that could be assembled under a single ownership.[5]

From the beginning, the city planners had observed the spread of land-use restrictions with great interest. The congestion that the title of their first gathering warned against was an excess not of automobiles but of people, and zoning promised to outlaw excessive human density. Beyond that, the zoning movement had a natural appeal to planning enthusiasts. Many of them were veterans of the Progressive-Era municipal reform movement and its fight against urban machine politics. The animus of reformers often extended beyond the political machines to the immigrants whose votes they relied on. Zoning, with its exclusionary thrust, could protect the Anglo-Saxon middle class against new arrivals.[6]

More important, perhaps, land-use regulation offered a means to advance planning from report-writing into reality. A central thrust of progressivism was the substitution of rational principles for politics; the planners were in a position to supply those principles. The planners thus endorsed the idea of zoning with enthusiasm, and they added an appeal for delineation of the zones on a basis that was scientific rather than political.[7]

Rushing to jump on the zoning bandwagon, planners sometimes placed expediency ahead of rigor. Many had first encountered urban problems as supporters of Henry George's single tax movement in the 1880s, and some still held to his theories. The premise of the single tax was that urban problems are caused by too little development. George recommended taxing only land, and not structures, to create incentives for more building. For not a few of his followers, one of the single tax's benefits was that covering the ground with single-family houses would keep apartments out. Zoning undoubtedly did serve the aim of excluding apartments, but its basic thrust of limiting development went directly against George's theories. Nonetheless, there were many single taxers among the leading zoning advocates, and they gave no sign of seeing any inconsistency. What mattered, their actions said, was having a plan.[8]

Cities that adopted zoning were slow at first to take up the planners' offers of help. They might well hire a planning consultant to write the ordinance— two dozen firms, Harland Bartholomew's being the biggest, offered their services. But of the cities that had zoning ordinances in the late twenties, fewer than one in five had a written plan. And even where there was a plan, there was little desire for the more systematic kind of planning that the profession's leaders advocated.[9]

Still, zoners had a compelling reason to adopt the agenda of the planning enthusiasts—to ensure that the rules were constitutional. Judges of the day were deeply hostile to restraints on the rights of private property. The Supreme Court had even thrown out a New York statute that said bakers could not work more than ten hours a day. Zoning laws limited owners' ability to use their land, and they would be struck down if they merely protected private parties like the Fifth Avenue merchants. They could be justified only as a means of protecting the general welfare—something that could be demonstrated by deriving them from a comprehensive city plan.

At the 1914 national planning conference, a Cincinnati attorney named Alfred Bettman laid out the legal logic. For zoning to pass muster, he said, "It is…necessary to show that the particular residential-district ordinance or statute under discussion has behind it a motive other than an aesthetic motive, has a motive related to safety or comfort or order or health." Before adopting a zoning ordinance, he advised, cities should undertake "some scientific study of the city's plan, so that the residential-district ordinance may bear a relation to the plan of the city, and the plan should be devised with a view to the health or the comfort or the safety of the people of the city."[10]

Here was a mandate that could loosen the pursestrings of stingy city fathers. The way was open for planning to grow from a cause into a remunerated profession.

Bettman had good reason to warn that zoning laws stood on fragile constitutional footing. Jurists were far from unanimous in their opinion of the matter. By 1925 the highest courts of nine states had upheld zoning. But the temper of the judiciary was hostile to government interference in the economy. The Supreme Court, dominated by a bloc of highly conservative justices, regularly struck down social legislation.

The high court spoke in a case from Euclid, Ohio. In 1922, this Cleveland suburb enacted a code that placed most of its territory in residential zones. One affected landowner was the Ambler Realty Company, which ten years earlier had purchased a sixty-eight-acre tract in anticipation of industrial development. On half of Ambler's land, only one- and two-family homes were allowed.

Ambler, joined by other aggrieved property owners, filed suit in federal district court. Their attorney was Newton Baker, former mayor of Cleveland and secretary of war in the Woodrow Wilson administration. Baker argued that Ambler had the right to develop its land for industrial purposes. Judge Dale Westenhaver, his former law partner, agreed, and the ordinance was ruled unconstitutional as a taking of property without compensation.

The city appealed to the Supreme Court. After hearing arguments from both sides, the closely divided justices called for a rehearing. At this point Alfred Bettman filed a crucial "friend of the court" brief, offering the arguments laid out in his 1914 speech. Zoning was an exercise of the police power, government's inherent right to suppress public nuisances and keep order. Bettman's reasoning won the day, and in November 1926 a 6-to-3 decision upheld zoning.

The case moved quickly beyond the specifics of Ambler's property; from the beginning, the principle of zoning was at stake. And the main principle was the exclusion of people, the people who lived in apartment houses. "In the last analysis," Judge Westenhaver wrote perceptively in his opinion, "the result to be accomplished is to classify the population and to segregate them according to their income or situation in life." The Supreme

Court saw the issue similarly. The village's power to keep out factories was not really in doubt, it observed: "The serious question in the case arises over the provisions of the ordinance excluding from residential districts apartment houses, business houses, retail stores and shops, and other like establishments."

The court's answer to this question left no doubt about whether it was permissible to segregate the population "according to their income or situation in life." Looking at apartments very much from the single-family owner's point of view, it wrote that

> …the development of detached house sections is greatly retarded by the coming of apartment houses, which has sometimes resulted in destroying the entire section for private house purposes; that in such sections very often the apartment house is a mere parasite, constructed in order to take advantage of the open spaces and attractive surroundings created by the residential character of the district. Moreover, the coming of one apartment house is followed by others, interfering by their height and bulk with the free circulation of air and monopolizing the rays of the sun which otherwise would fall upon the smaller homes, and bringing, as their necessary accompaniments, the disturbing noises incident to increased traffic and business, and the occupation, by means of moving and parked automobiles, of larger portions of the streets, thus detracting from their safety and depriving children of the privilege of quiet and open spaces for play, enjoyed by those in more favored localities—until, finally, the residential character of the neighborhood and its desirability as a place of detached residences are utterly destroyed. Under these circumstances, apartment houses, which in a different environment would be not only entirely unobjectionable but highly desirable, come very near to being nuisances.[11]

The Supreme Court decision put new wind in planners' sails. Zoning was constitutional unless it was arbitrary and unreasonable, and in finding that the Euclid ordinance passed that test the court stressed how the subject had "received much attention at the hands of commissions and experts." The message was reinforced two years later by the case of *Nectow v. Cambridge*, in which the court overturned a zoning decision because no benefit to the city as a whole had been shown. Towns seeking to zone their land would be well advised, if they wanted their rules to stand up, to put the experts to work and produce paperwork that would pass muster in court.

Hoover's Commerce Department reinforced the push from the Supreme Court. In 1924 it issued a model state enabling act for zoning, whose drafters included many planning enthusiasts. The act provided that zoning maps "shall be made in accordance with a comprehensive plan." What that plan might entail was spelled out four years later, when the committee issued a model act for city planning. Many states adopted these texts without change.

The 1928 model act situated zoning as one element of a "master plan" that encompassed parks, streets, public buildings, and utilities. The plan would be drawn up by a commission conceived, in the high style of municipal reform, as a nonpolitical body of experts resistant to the pressures of venal politicians. The plan might extend into unincorporated areas beyond a city line, and there was even a hopeful bow to regional planning. So far the act fulfilled all the hopes of the planning movement.

But the enabling act was not the product of planners alone. Key provisions were worked out in advance through negotiations between the American City Planning Institute and the National Association of Real Estate Boards. The realtors, chastened after the mid-1920s collapse of the real estate bubble, wanted to control the supply of new lots. They sought to block competition from cut-rate subdividers, who did indeed often leave behind messes that others would have to clean up. Where realtors' interests were at stake, the final document fell short of planning enthusiasts' hopes. The realtors were not troubled by the nonpolitical planning commission; the "experts," they foresaw, might be found among their own ranks. But they killed a requirement that developers set aside land for parks. And, most important, cities could adopt land-use restrictions immediately, without waiting for the comprehensive plan.

The people who staffed the new planning bureaucracies had much useful work to do. Although they might, in practice, have little influence on the zoning of the areas already built up, subdivision control empowered them to shape the rapidly growing new suburbs. Without question, unplanned suburbs had evils in need of correction: uncontrolled rainwater runoff, badly built streets, groundwater polluted for lack of sewers. Still, as a historian of planning has recognized, the overall effect was to "encourage cities to portray in long-range plans the conditions of the present rather than the changes required." New subdivisions would avoid past mistakes, but the rigid zoning structure prevented future adjustment if their design was later found lacking. Planners might dream of molding the city of the future. They found themselves embalming the city of the present.[12]

Planners did look to the future; subdivision controls required it even if zoning did not. When they did, transportation was at the center of their concerns. And the transportation they privileged was the automobile.

Automobiles, as writers recognized, had a cachet other transportation lacked. The hero of F. Scott Fitzgerald's *The Great Gatsby* wooed Daisy Buchanan in a yellow Rolls Royce. Sinclair Lewis, in his 1922 bestseller *Babbitt*, veered from fiction into sociology:

> In the city of Zenith, in the barbarous twentieth century, a family's motor indicated its social rank as precisely as the grades of the peerage determined the rank of an English family.

For the title character, Lewis tells us, driving was a sacred recreation, second only to (of course) golf. "His motor car was poetry and tragedy, love and heroism."[13]

On suburban roads drivers found little in their way, but on busy city streets others were there first with long-established rights. Children played in the roadway; pushcarts and newsstands lined curbs. Pedestrians were accustomed to crossing the pavement at their own convenience. Streetcars unloaded their passengers in the middle of the road. Collisions with cars exacted a rapidly rising toll of deaths, and in the early 1920s a broad popular movement for safer streets arose with the aim of taming auto traffic.

Motorists and carmakers fought back, and the traffic tamers went down swiftly to defeat. From the beginning, cars were able to chase competitors off the street with their sheer mass. Then the auto manufacturers' lobby, with Herbert Hoover doing its bidding, rewrote the rules of the road. Those on foot became subordinate to cars, responsible for avoiding collisions with them. "Safety" campaigns belittled pedestrians who resisted the new order as jaywalkers, a new word coined from *jay*, which meant a country bumpkin, and shamed them into compliance by public ridicule. The ownership of space was here at issue more than safety. Motorists were free to plant their feet on the pavement to leave a parked car—but a pedestrian who stood on the same spot was an interloper on the roadway.[14]

Planners, in this conflict, were enthusiastic allies of the auto interests. For many among them, the prestige of the automobile was reason enough to prefer it to walking and mass transit. But there were other motivations too, motivations that were easier to speak out loud. To decentralize the cities, as most saw it, was a positive good; cars allowed suburbs to spread, while rail lines, especially underground or elevated ones, would only bring more people downtown. For Edward Bassett, the preeminent zoning expert of the time, the greatest danger of unregulated growth was the congestion caused by new subway lines.

New suburban roads, moreover, could be laid out in a logical pattern, while the tangle of existing trolley lines resisted planners' science. And automobile manufacturers were not shy in lobbying for better roads, while streetcar operators often saw transit improvements as threats to existing monopolies.

The creators of the new regulated city thus tended to the automobile just as they tended to the single-family home. Planners dreamed of highway networks fanning out across the countryside, of overpasses, of double-decked streets, of superhighways. Elevated railways, detested for their noise and pollution, were torn down, and in their place rose elevated highways, even noisier and dirtier once they filled with traffic.

The planners tended most to what was known as pleasure driving. Pleasure driving, the least productive use of a vehicle, had special prestige, just as the dog was most honorable of domestic animals. A particular favorite was the parkway, a road surrounded by parks and nature. Its allure was so great that Thomas MacDonald, the master highway builder who long headed the Bureau of Public Roads, was moved in 1924 to issue an unneeded caution. Fearing an angry public reaction against the desecration of "pleasure parkways," he urged against their conversion to utilitarian arteries.[15]

The planning profession, driven by its scientific pretensions and encouraged by automotive lobbies, outsourced the design of roads to specialists. As Harland Bartholomew later put it, the design of highways was "a scientific process or an engineering matter, just as the design of sewer and drainage systems." Traffic engineers could determine the proper width of streets in much the same way that sanitary engineers calculated the diameter of sewer pipes.[16]

As they assembled their recipes for regulated subdivision, planners began with a well-stocked intellectual cupboard. It was furnished from two principal sources: the Garden City of turn-of-the-century England; and the American City Beautiful. But the practical planners of the new generation applied these doctrines selectively at best, and not rarely in ways that undid their intent.

The City Beautiful movement aimed to bring the beauty of classical architecture to the central cores of American cities, creating a republican version of the grandeur of European capitals. Its principal figures were Charles McKim (who had grown up in Llewellyn Park), Frederick Olmsted Jr., and Daniel Burnham. "Make no little plans," said Burnham, "they have no magic to stir men's blood," and their ideas played out on a vast scale. First the Chicago

World's Fair of 1893, and then a comprehensive plan for the city of Washington in 1902, won widespread praise and imitation.[17]

The classicism of the City Beautiful was still in vogue in the 1920s among architects and builders of public buildings, but the new city planning profession had moved on. Zoning rules, the Supreme Court had ruled, must contribute demonstrably to "public health, safety, morals, or general welfare." Planners had the job of making these demonstrations. They were now technocrats, collecting facts and using them to calculate the future course of the metropolis.

Attention thus turned from old downtowns to new subdivisions. Parks remained a central concern; they served definable functions of fresh air and recreation. But otherwise planners lowered their sights. Instead of designing grand boulevards, they engineered the movement of traffic. Landmarks gave way to separated uses. What stirred suburban blood, after all, was keeping big things out.[18]

A second source of inspiration was the Garden City of Ebenezer Howard. An English social reformer, Howard imagined slums and crowded cities replaced by new towns set among farms and fields. Self-sufficient communities of thirty thousand residents would feature a mix of industry, commerce, and homes, kept efficient and sustainable by common ownership of land. In 1903 his followers undertook to build a first example, Letchworth, north of London. They entrusted the design of Letchworth to the architect Raymond Unwin. He had made a name as advocate and designer of better working-class housing, and in 1909 he published a book titled *Town Planning in Practice*.

The Garden City, in origin more functional than artistic, remained in fashion among American planners in the twenties. But in their version, many of the precepts laid down by Howard and Unwin were abandoned. No clear boundary was set between town and country; city planning boards had neither the power to create permanent agricultural belts nor the desire to do so. The egalitarianism that was a main feature of the Garden City was gone; municipal planners created few homes for workers. Where the main point of Howard's concept had been to replace oversized cities with self-contained communities of manageable size, the Americans found themselves endlessly expanding those cities through the addition of new suburbs. On this last subject Unwin himself had experienced a change of heart when charged during the war with creating new housing for workers. On a visit to the United States, he found himself admiring J. C. Nichols' Country Club District.[19]

Street layout was a topic to which Unwin gave much thought. He rejected the practice, then widespread, of laying out straight streets in a rectangular grid. Instead, he tried to focus residential life on courtyards and narrow

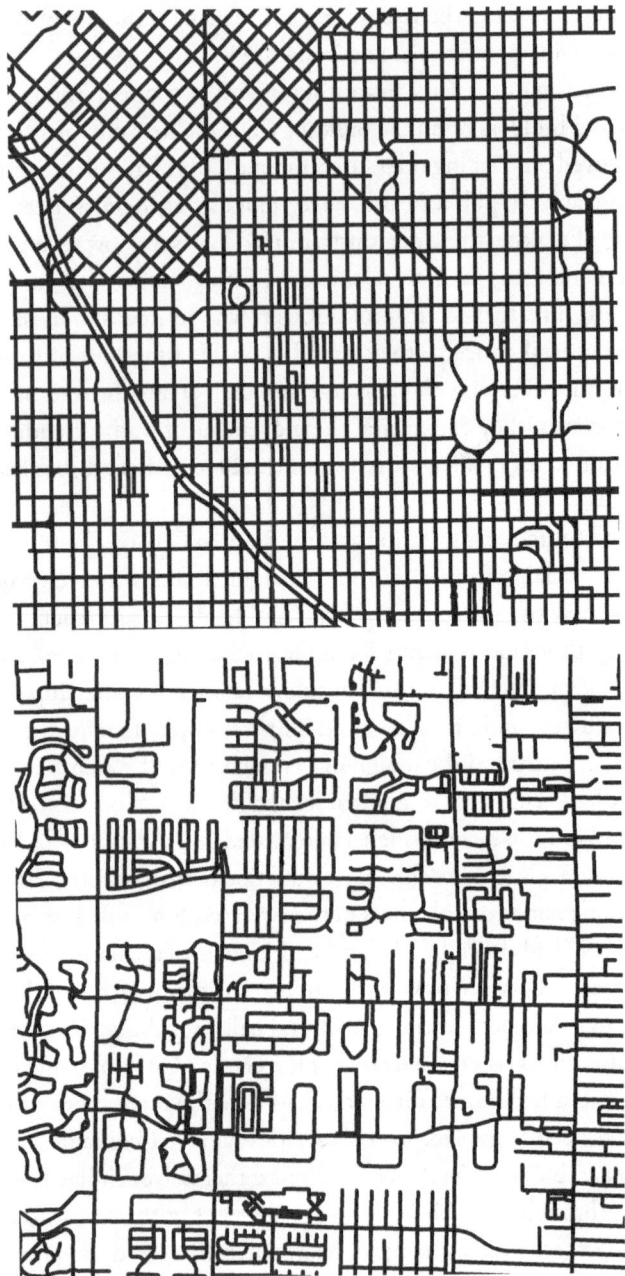

Grid and superblock street layouts. Examples from Denver, Colorado (above), and Palm Beach County, Florida (below).

dead-end streets. The American planners took up some of these ideas with enthusiasm. They replaced the street grid with a hierarchy of roads. Through traffic was removed from residential streets and channeled onto arterials. The favored road layout was the "superblock," bounded by wide highways and lacking internal connections.

But similar concepts were applied toward very different ends. Unwin, when he accepted the suburb, had concluded that traffic congestion is unavoidable. His purpose, in pushing cars out of neighborhoods onto arterials, was to relocate the congestion. Americans sought instead to move automobiles ever faster on ever-bigger roads. Unwin narrowed residential streets and placed footpaths where automobile traffic was shut off. American superblocks repelled pedestrians, their wide internal streets often lacking sidewalks altogether.[20]

It did not take long for practices to gel into a doctrine, taught in the universities that were beginning to grant degrees in planning and practiced in the bureaucracies of cities large and small. Among its chief tenets were separation of land uses, low density, and the fastest possible movement of automobiles. It loved parks, abhorred grid streets, and tried not to think about people who couldn't afford to buy a house.[21]

The human congestion of the founding years of their profession had abated—New York's Lower East Side lost more than half its population between 1910 and 1930—but planners still sought to empty out cities. Their new orthodoxy owed less to earlier theorists than to high-end suburban developers, the first clients of the leading figures in the field.[22]

Regardless of scientific pretension, status remained the lodestar of land-use regulation. A town might allow a supermarket yet judge the same land unsuitable for a discount store. Motels were banned where hotels and country inns were welcome.[23]

This point was driven home by a craze miniature golf in the early 1930s. Golf courses were a permitted use in residential zones, modeled as they were after Jesse Nichols' Country Club District. Owners of unbuilt house lots, put out of work after the crash, spied a loophole in the law and opened putt-putt operations on land not otherwise usable to earn a living. A loud outcry soon ensued. Planners, in their wisdom, determined that the miniature sport was not the noble game of golf at all. It was a commercial recreation unfit to coexist with homes.[24]

Planners had set out in a burst of optimism and idealism, in search of a better and more beautiful city. They had, they would admit, made compromises along the way. They recognized that narrow interests of real estate developers and suburban exclusionists might often outweigh the broader public interest. But their work, they insisted, still served its original mission. And public opinion agreed. Planning, as a profession and as a theory, retained an aura of idealism from its progressive birth.

Even critics of the planning orthodoxy accepted many of its premises. What faults were recognized were chalked up to the insufficient application of the planners' concepts, not to any error in the ideas themselves. Lewis Mumford, in 1927, came before the city planners' annual conference to denounce "the domination of purely financial values." But Mumford shared the hostility to dense cities that united planners and suburban developers. Crowded skyscrapers and packed subways were the problem; the solution was "countryside and city developed together."[25]

What made this theory so attractive to progressive thinkers? One source of its appeal was American culture's idealization of the open land. America was the refuge of "huddled masses yearning to breathe free." A ban on huddling in apartment houses fulfilled the promise of the lamp beside the golden door. It bore no animus against the poor and tempest-tossed.

Critics of the decade's business-dominated politics felt an inchoate but deeply rooted distrust of the metropolis. For municipal reformers, from whose ranks the first planners derived, loathing of political corruption easily spilled over into a dislike of the immigrant-filled cities that bred Tammany Hall and its ilk. Other progressives might not share that bias, but for reasons of their own they were no enthusiasts of urban life.

Rural populism, no longer an organized movement, was still an influence. In 1920 it was only twelve years since its champion William Jennings Bryan had been the Democratic Party's candidate for president. Bryan did not merely voice the economic interests of rural farmers; he celebrated their way of life. "Burn down your cities and leave our farms, and your cities will spring up again as if by magic. But destroy our farms and the grass will grow in the streets of every city in the country," he declaimed in the famous "cross of gold" speech that won his first presidential nomination.

The urban Left as well had an inherited suspicion of city living. The oppressive working and living conditions of the early industrial revolution had led a young Karl Marx to endorse the "abolition of the distinction between town and country." These urban ills were still far from fully cured, and any scheme for getting rid of tenements could win a hearing. Marx had not idealized the countryside—he spoke of "the idiocy of rural life"—but his followers' ears were open to promises, made by new towns and old suburbs alike, that the advantages of town and country would be combined.

Still, it was not the substance of planning that excited 1920s progressives most. It was the new land-use rules' rejection of the ruling doctrine of laissez-faire. Government, in one sphere at least, was actively interfering in economic life and was even purporting to direct it.

The Supreme Court's approval of zoning came as a rare breath of fresh air from judges willing to strike down even the mildest reform legislation—even more so because the opinion was written by Justice George Sutherland. That deeply conservative jurist had led the court in holding that a minimum wage for women in the District of Columbia was an unconstitutional interference with the right of contract. By affirming the permissibility of government interference with property rights, *Euclid v. Ambler* set a welcome precedent that might bring a future reversal of judicial fortunes.

More broadly, the wide vistas of the city planners' ambitions encouraged—one might even say seduced—believers in economic planning. The profession claimed a steadily expanding scope, encompassing new topics and new territory. Practitioners were soon called "planners," without any limiting modifier. Indeed, it was hard to see how one could with any specificity direct the growth of a city, unless one also directed to some degree its economy. The model planning law of 1928 fed these hopes in an optional section on regional planning, with vague but enticing hints of regional government and statewide planning.

A contradiction lay at the heart of the planners' agenda. One plans for the future because it may be different from the present. But the aim of zoning, which they administered and justified, was to embalm the present.

A lapse of time must necessarily pass before the consequences of that embalming would emerge. Events conspired to prolong the interval. When the planning apparatus came into full flower with the 1928 model planning act, the real estate bubble of the 1920s had already burst. Depression and war followed; private-sector construction did not fully resume until 1946. The problems that turned up in the twenties could be blamed very plausibly on the haphazard and unscientific drafting of early zoning ordinances. Whatever the question, planners could answer with new rules and tighter controls. Only in the 1950s, with the maturing of zoned subdivisions, could the fruit of their work be tasted. By then the compromises that accompanied the birth of the profession were long forgotten.

As official doctrine had it, the planners were scientific optimizers, the Master Plan was their grand design, and zoning was a tool they employed to bring that design to fruition. But the reality was otherwise. Land-use restrictions were an end in themselves, and the primal urge that caused them to multiply was status-seeking. Planning was pasted over the midsection of the zoning code, a fig leaf hiding its unmentionable reproductive organs.

3

Government-Sponsored Sprawl

A s the newly professionalized city planning agencies settled into a routine at the end of the 1920s, the unequal balance of power between planners and real estate developers was about to shift. The depression shut down privately financed building, and the New Deal soon stepped into the breach. Now the bureaucrats in federal agencies, and in the local governments they financed, were the ones with the money. Where planners had once evangelized builders, the builders now needed to convince planners. To that end they employed, along with instruments of suasion, the potent tools of lobbying and political pressure.

Reversal of roles brought only a partial reversal of policy. Public housing, once barely discussable in polite company, was now a major goal of government. But planning theories devised in a more conservative era dictated the design of government-sponsored housing and how it was inserted into the surrounding landscape. And real estate lobbyists, fearful of government-sponsored competition, kept the new housing projects under constant criticism and succeeded in denying their benefits to all but the certifiably poor.

Meanwhile, builders and reformers reached a modus vivendi over homes for the middle class. Government support for private construction mushroomed, untroubled by controversy, while political battles raged over public housing. Federal intervention thus accelerated the trends of the preceding

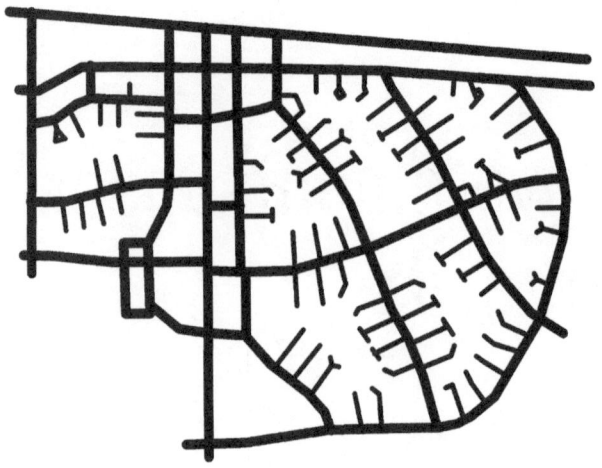

Street map of Radburn.

half-century. It made the automobile-dependent lifestyle, earlier a mark of exclusivity, accessible to clerks and factory workers. Home ownership became far more widespread, but the housing market remained segregated by income and race.

New York's City Housing Corporation, set up before the crash to take the profit motive out of housing, showed the way for later New Deal programs. Its work was made possible by a state law that offered tax advantages in exchange for a limitation on investors' returns. A gallery of reform luminaries graced its board of directors, among them Eleanor Roosevelt, the Ethical Culture leader Felix Adler, and assorted philanthropists and settlement-house directors. Building began with a financially successful and innovatively designed row house project in Queens. This was followed in 1929 by the new town of Radburn, near Paterson, New Jersey, which pointed the way to the car-centered suburbia of the future.

Radburn consciously imitated the Garden City, but in the hands of American planners Ebenezer Howard's concept mutated into a somewhat denser approximation of an upscale suburb. Individual ownership replaced common property, under a private government whose authority rested on deed covenants. Roads, laid out in an irregular pattern, divided the community into superblocks a quarter-mile across. Single-family homes were set on cul-de-sacs within the superblocks. Children had playgrounds, and pedestrians came off the streets too. Footpaths, set behind the houses in commonly owned parkland, crossed the roadways through tunnels.[1]

Aiming to integrate pedestrians and motorists, Radburn wound up pioneering the future of automotive sprawl. Its winding roads and dead ends discouraged through car traffic as intended, but they also made it all but impossible to get anywhere by walking along the street. Radburn compensated with its footpaths, but for-profit imitators found it easier to forget altogether about those on foot. The layout of superblocks and cul-de-sacs would come to shape the car-centric American suburb.

The crash of 1929 brought building to a near halt, and it put existing homeowners at risk too. The house-building boom of the 1920s had been financed with short-term loans, the only form of credit then available. When the balloon mortgages came due, banks were loath to lend. Delinquent mortgages added more fuel to the fire of financial crisis.

With both banks and borrowers in need of relief, one of the first undertakings of the New Deal was the Home Owners Loan Corporation. President Franklin Roosevelt proposed a law to establish the HOLC in April 1933, just a month after taking office, and he signed it two months later. Within two years it had issued more than a million loans. It refinanced one-tenth of all the nonfarm houses in the United States with long-term, fixed rate mortgages at low interest rates.

The HOLC was a stopgap, but its influence lingered for decades. It perfected and popularized the long-term mortgage. These self-amortizing loans freed borrowers from the overhanging threat of a balloon payment that required them to return to the credit market. Home ownership became more affordable and more stable, laying a foundation for the suburban boom after the Second World War.

Equally important was the HOLC's pioneering effort to create a uniform system of appraisal. Systematic procedures were needed to manage the vast number of loans the agency issued. Even after the HOLC expired, its system of valuing real estate endured, the basis for a large-scale inflow of private capital that made it easier to finance homes.

The HOLC appraisal methods did vast damage. Recognizing that the value of a house depends on its surroundings, the agency established four categories of neighborhoods. Its ratings reflected the housing market's established pecking order of social status. Newly built subdivisions automatically scored higher than older ones, and traditional urban layouts, such as houses built close to the street, were downgraded. Old streetcar suburbs lacked access to funds that flowed into newer developments built for the automobile.

Appraisers judged a neighborhood's ethnic character along with its buildings. A place with even an "infiltration of Jews" was ineligible for the highest rating, and African American districts were grouped with areas of prevalent poor maintenance or vandalism and given the lowest grade. Color-coded maps displayed the results of this evaluation, with the lowest category shown in red. For years afterward these maps were used by private banks for lending decisions, giving rise to the term *redlining*.[2]

The HOLC was effective at rescuing homeowners and stabilizing banks, but it did little to encourage new construction. Unemployment was the central problem of the depression, and many of the lost jobs were in the building industry. The Roosevelt administration, moreover, was under political pressure to do something about private-sector jobs in addition to its government employment programs. The result in June 1934 was the creation of the Federal Housing Administration.

The new agency had a mission of reviving house construction by insuring mortgage loans made by private banks. Where commercial banks had previously demanded 50% down payments, the FHA required only 20%, and that figure was soon reduced to 10%. Three-year balloon mortgages gave way to loans that amortized over twenty or even twenty-five years. Not only were the terms more generous, but government guarantees also brought interest rates down by two or three points. These incentives worked; housing starts jumped from 93,000 in 1933 to 332,000 in 1937 and 619,000 in 1941.

The FHA began life with the enthusiastic support of developers, and it did not disappoint them. Staffed largely with executives from real estate and financial businesses, its policies closely tracked the agenda of the large-scale suburban developers. Its guidelines and controls retained the HOLC appraisal system—it is unclear whether the same maps were used—and went far beyond it to shape the design of new housing and new communities. The ostensible purpose of the guidelines was to ensure that only economically viable loans were issued, but in practice their scope was much broader. The FHA imposed the style of subdivision pioneered by the "high-class" developers as a national norm. This was a major item on the agenda of the real estate developers, because the willingness of local politicians to grant exceptions undercut their efforts to enforce such controls through zoning.

"If a neighborhood is to retain stability," the FHA's underwriting manual said, "it is necessary that properties shall continue to be occupied by the same social and racial classes." The agency denied insurance to new housing

Wall built at the behest of the Federal Housing Administration to separate black and white neighborhoods in Detroit.
(Courtesy of Library of Congress, Farm Security Administration collection.)

in towns that lacked zoning or passed ordinances that allowed the density of existing neighborhoods to increase. As a further bulwark against change, it recommended—and often insisted on—restrictive covenants covering race, house design, and maintenance. In one section of Detroit, it refused to insure houses because blacks and whites were living too close together and only relented when the developer built a concrete wall to separate the races.

While the agency by law was to finance both apartments and single-family houses, its policies had a strong suburban bias. Neighborhoods that were crowded or contained older buildings were disfavored. Lending commitments, even for apartment buildings, were concentrated in the periphery of metropolitan areas; the recommended setting for rental development was "what amounts to a privately owned and privately controlled park area." Loans for new one-family houses carried much more favorable terms than those for multifamily buildings or rehabilitation of existing homes.

FHA design standards specified minimums for lot sizes, front and side setbacks, and the width of the house. Some traditional home styles, such as Baltimore's sixteen-foot row houses, were entirely ineligible. Front yards were to be lawns, with a limited presence of trees and shrubs. Grid street plans were strongly discouraged in favor of superblocks penetrated by cul-de-sacs and curving streets. Field staff, a historian of the building industry reports, adhered to these rules "with messianic fervor."

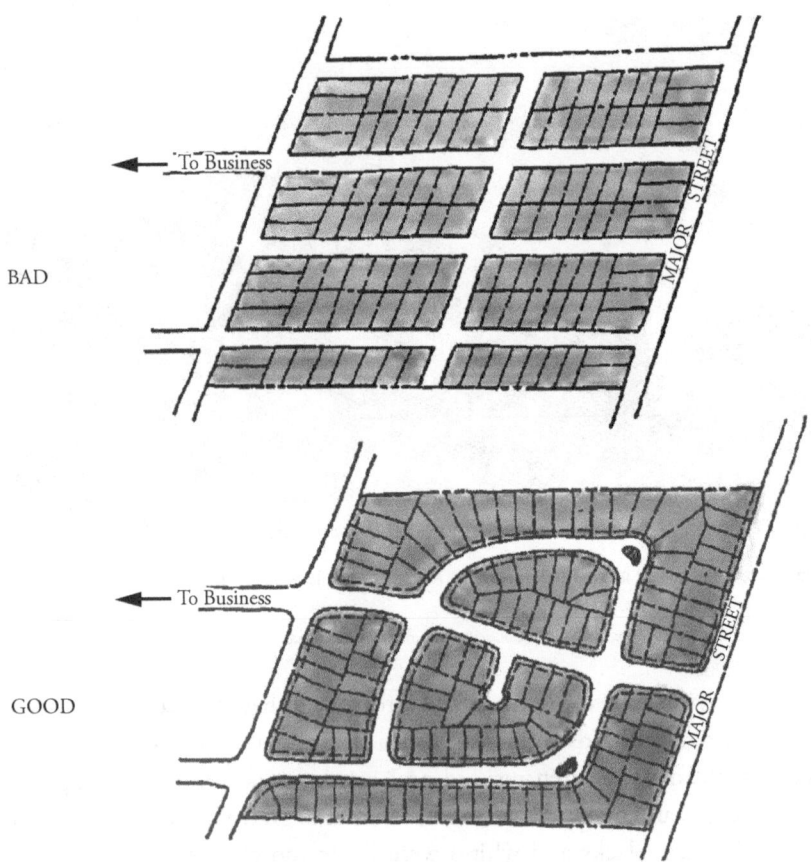

Good and bad street layouts according to the Federal Housing Administration.
(From Planning Profitable Neighborhoods, 1938.)

Developers who laid out entire communities and built the houses were privileged with commitments to approve loans before the houses were built. The FHA did not make construction loans, but its promise of mortgages made private financing much easier to get. The stated purpose of the preference for large-scale operations was to reduce construction costs through mass production and raise standards. Another reason for this policy, surely, was the dominant role of the big builders in the trade associations that influenced the agency's actions.

FHA guidelines were presented as mere recommendations, different in nature from the New Deal regulations that businessmen found so oppressive. In reality they were nearly mandatory; financing was all but unobtainable for builders who failed to conform. New development was frozen in the status-driven and automobile-centered pattern laid down by developers, zoners, and planners of the preceding decades. What we now know as sprawl was here.[3]

The New Deal concerned itself too with housing for the less affluent, a problem swept under the rug in the 1920s. Government, free from the ideological inhibitions of previous generations, built inexpensive dwellings. There was even an innovative effort to build new towns along the Garden City model of Ebenezer Howard and Raymond Unwin; three communities were created before congressional conservatives killed the program.[4]

The public housing program began in 1934 and was continued by the Housing Acts of 1937 and 1949. On one level, it was a success. Within four years 130,000 new apartments sprang up, and by 1962 more than two million people were living in a half-million public housing units. Housing projects filled a real need; as late as 1950 New York had one hundred thousand apartments without private toilets and nearly a quarter-million homes without central heating. Long waiting lists for vacant units demonstrated that tenants found the projects far superior to available alternatives.

Still, as the waiting lists demonstrated, the supply of public housing fell far short of the demand. This was largely the result of limited funding, a problem that the more politically popular FHA did not face. The United States built less publicly owned housing than other industrial countries. And public housing had defects—most, but not all of them, the result of compromises made to pass the legislation—that led to the decay and eventual destruction of much of what did get built.

For one thing, income limits restricted public housing to the poor. The most stable residents were often forced to leave as their conditions improved. These limits were imposed at the insistence of the private real estate industry, fearful of government-sponsored competition even as FHA subsidies were essential to its own prosperity. The program was further handcuffed with intermittent bans on building on vacant land. A slum housing unit had to be destroyed for every new apartment built. And, because public housing was exempt from property taxes, local officials had reason to put it where taxes would be least—on low-value land in undesirable areas.

Fears that public housing would bring minorities into homogeneous neighborhoods added to the long-standing dislike of apartment buildings, stirring up opposition among homeowners. Local governments held a veto over the placement of projects, and public housing easily became a political football. In New York City, where renters had the power of numbers, giant public and cooperative apartment complexes rose on empty land in the outer boroughs. But in Detroit, a city of single-family homes, the powerful auto workers union was abandoned by its members on the housing issue. A conservative Republican running on an anti-public housing platform overwhelmed the labor-backed candidate for mayor in 1949, and the city built no more projects outside the worst sections of the central city.

Republicans, when they regained the presidency in 1953, did not end public housing as some of their supporters would have liked, but the Dwight D. Eisenhower administration was careful to avoid any disturbance of the racial status quo. Public housing was kept out of suburbs and concentrated near downtown. The projects brought more low-income residents to old neighborhoods that were already filling with the poor as a consequence of redlining and zoning. These former streetcar suburbs became the decaying inner city.

On top of the injuries imposed by economic and racial segregation came self-inflicted wounds, the consequence of planning doctrines. Housing authorities ripped up street grids, placing apartment towers in superblocks devoid of commerce. Theories born in affluent suburbs, when applied in the conditions of poverty, quickly showed their defects. Crime flourished, sending many projects into decline. In the 1960s new rules let welfare recipients into housing first intended for the working poor, and the downward spiral accelerated.[5]

The end of the Second World War brought boom years to the American economy. Consumers had savings to spend, accumulated during a wartime of long work hours, union wages, and shortages of consumer goods. In no sector of the economy was there more pent-up demand than for housing. Returning GIs, newly married and with children on the way, crammed into tiny apartments or doubled up. The federal government responded as it had to the unemployment of the thirties—with more suburbanization. In 1944, even before the war ended, congress established a Veterans Administration mortgage program modeled on the FHA.

Construction flourished. Single-family housing starts in 1946 were 50% higher than in 1941, and in the next four years they nearly doubled again. Shifts in industry structure accompanied the growth. Subdividers were now builders as well, selling completed houses instead of leaving construction to the lot buyer. Large firms emerged, building cheaply with techniques of mass production borrowed from factories.

New Deal reforms had created a far broader housing market. Unions raised wages and stabilized employment, while the FHA and VA offered mortgages to workers with income but no wealth. Builders, with a strong push from the FHA, responded with neighborhoods that were priced for economy but designed as stripped-down versions of the previous generation's upscale suburbs. House lots were bigger than in streetcar suburbs. Subdivisions were cut into superblocks, with interior streets that curved and dead-ended. Sidewalks, if built at all, led uselessly to unwalkable arterials. The highways, given little thought, were soon lined with ugly commercial strips. New housing was nearly unreachable without a car.

The largest and best known of the new suburbs was Levittown, named for the family that built it. Its 17,400 houses, set on former potato farms 25 miles east of New York City, offered cut-rate entry to the middle class. They bore the trappings of higher status inside and out, but the Levitts did not build for the long term. Buyers got brand-name washing machines but no sewers, and rules requiring owners to mow their lawns were enforced only so long as new dwellings were on sale nearby.

The structures went up on an assembly line, with twenty-seven crews marching down a street to carry out successive tasks. Four-room Cape Cods were priced at $7990 and ranches at $9500, underselling competitors by a wide margin. Across the country, large-scale builders were soon imitating Levittown's widely publicized success.[6]

By many means, government policy in the postwar years reinforced the automobile orientation of the new suburbs. Construction of new subway lines had slowed after the First World War, and the depression halted it almost completely. The New Deal's vast public works programs poured federal money into highways; streetcars, owned by private monopolies that reformers detested, were ineligible for aid. The only major rail projects to win support were subways in Chicago and on New York's Sixth Avenue.

Streetcars had been losing customers since the twenties, and they lost speed as they got stuck behind cars. Where they mixed with car traffic, drivers wanted them and their passengers off the road; where they didn't, the powerful automobile lobby coveted their right of way. Faced with tax-supported competition from the roads, street railways were no longer able to make a profit. By the end of sixties streetcar tracks were largely gone. Buses, bumpy and usually infrequent, filled the gap, patronized for the most part by those unable to drive by reason of age, poverty, or infirmity.[7]

As rail transit decayed, the country invested massively in new roads. In the postwar years, there was no federal transit funding at all, and local budgets had similar priorities. Los Angeles built its famous network of freeways;

expressways cut through New York; and other cities imitated them. Suburban arterials grew wider and straighter, and many states followed the prewar examples of Pennsylvania and Connecticut by connecting their major cities with toll-financed limited access highways.

But this was only the beginning. President Eisenhower in 1954 brought together highway proponents, previously divided over whether to pay for new roads with tolls, a gas tax, or general revenues. Francis du Pont, whose family had owned the controlling interest in General Motors, was put in charge of the Bureau of Public Roads, and Gen. Lucius Clay, a GM board member, headed a study of highway needs. In 1956, Clay's committee recommended a vast network of toll-free superhighways financed by increasing the federal gasoline tax. Congress agreed and launched construction of a 41,000-mile system with 90% of the cost paid by the federal government.

The new roads were called the interstate highway system, but they served local commuting as much as long-distance travel. The damage done to cities was twofold. By subsidizing long-distance commuting, expressways accelerated the stampede to the suburbs and sucked life out of urban neighborhoods. Beltways around cities, justified as bypasses to divert through traffic past congested downtowns, rapidly became crowded rush-hour routes. Meanwhile, the new highways devastated neighborhoods, tearing down what lay directly in their path and spreading a pall of noise, soot, and fumes over what remained standing.

If one man was the face of the expressway era, it was Robert Moses. A master builder with an almost countless collection of official titles, he remade New York City. He was an advocate for road-building on the national stage and a consultant who devised elaborate highway networks for other cities. He built parks, highways, and housing projects, going from big to bigger, rolling over almost anyone and anything that got in his way.

Moses' career epitomized the trajectory of urban reform in the mid-twentieth century. After starting as a municipal reformer and enemy of political patronage, he grew close to Governor Al Smith and was put in charge of a new Long Island State Park Commission. He pushed aggressively forward to create a chain of parks centered at Jones Beach, opened to New York's masses by new parkways. The parkways were blocked at first by the political influence of wealthy estate owners, who preferred to keep the public far from their homes. But Moses cut a deal with the Nassau County Republican machine, letting local politicians skim profits from real estate development at parkway exits. Work then proceeded according to his designs—except for the route of

Robert Moses in 1933 at the opening of Bethpage State Park. The park boasts a championship golf course that was later the site of the U.S. Open.
(Courtesy of New York State Archives.)

the Northern State Parkway, forced onto a southward detour that kept it away from the largest estates.

Moses' vision was distinctly elitist. Even his greatest achievements were very much for, not by, the public, and he held a narrow idea of what that public was. The poor were effectively excluded from Jones Beach. Moses vetoed a plan to extend the Long Island Railroad to the shore, and the parkways were built—when two-thirds of New York's population could not afford a car—with bridges too low for buses to pass through. As his powers grew, he punched highways and redevelopment projects through crowded New York neighborhoods with the same imperious disdain he had shown to Long Island farmers.

Buoyed by popular acclaim for his parks, and loved by mayors and governors with a thirst for getting public works built, Moses won one construction task after another. As the years passed, his credit with the public declined, but by now control of jobs and contracts gave him immense political clout. His powers grew apace. By the 1950s he ran the parks of both city and state; he oversaw highways, bridges, and tunnels throughout the city; he had built one of the world's largest hydroelectric projects at Niagara Falls; he headed New York's slum clearance committee; and without any formal position he controlled the city's public housing. Objecting in 1959 to free Shakespeare plays in Central Park on the grounds that the audience should pay for damage to the grass, he ignored the views of the mayor who was his nominal superior and declined even to return phone calls. Only after a long battle by director Joseph Papp did he agree to the building of the Delacorte Theater for free performances.

The toll bridges and tunnels under Moses' control had grown into a vast money-making machine, and he dominated the spending of even greater sums in federal and state transportation budgets. Subways and commuter trains were falling apart, yet he remained rigidly devoted to the automobile. Not a mile of new rail line was started in New York City between 1933 and 1965. Between 1955 and 1965 alone, the city added 439 miles of highways, and even greater plans were in the works.[8]

It was not just grand engineering works that put postwar America on rubber tires. Actions on a much smaller scale reinforced car dependence. Hidden in obscure engineering standards and in the fine print of zoning codes, new mandates rewove the fabric of local streets and neighborhoods by granting the automobile primacy over pedestrians and transit riders.

The highway engineers applied the means of science, but they used them to serve ends imposed from without. When city engineers first observed congested car traffic in the early 1920s, they were struck by the danger of speeding automobiles and the ability of streetcars to move greater numbers of people. The scarce space of city streets could be used most efficiently, many thought, by placing limits on automobiles. Carmakers and their allies in government road-building agencies saw this as a threat. They reacted as they did to another challenge that faced them in the same years, the poisonous nature of leaded gasoline, by seizing control of the science.

A new profession of highway safety was created under industry control. Studebaker Corporation funded the first traffic research institute in 1926, soon yielding its place to the carmakers' trade association. In 1930 a professional society, the Institute of Traffic Engineers, was formed. Ernest Goodrich, ITE's president, was a civil engineer who had long called for the removal of streetcars from city streets; his deputy was Miller McClintock, the chief of the industry-supported institute. In the hands of this new profession, even local streets were designed above all to move automobiles. Practitioners aimed, in the words of a 1955 textbook, "to achieve efficient, free, and rapid flow of traffic; yet, at the same time, to prevent traffic accidents and casualties." Efficiency was measured by the movement of vehicles; a car and its driver were equal to a streetcar full of passengers. Pedestrians were at best an afterthought, and more often an obstacle.[9]

At the request of federal and state highway officials, ITE in 1942 issued its first *Traffic Engineering Handbook*. The prescriptions of this manual aimed at traffic speed and driver comfort. Lanes were to be 12 feet wide for mixed car and truck traffic and 11 feet for cars alone. For parking lanes on urban streets, 13 to 15 feet were recommended. These guidelines were devised for through streets, but by the 1950s the group had recommendations for subdivisions too. On interior streets, it encouraged curves and dead ends with few access points to the perimeter highway—anyone on foot was sent the long way around. Pavement widths were stipulated as 26 to 36 feet, a far cry from Raymond Unwin's 16 to 20 feet, and sure to induce fast driving. In 1965 the minimum street width was hiked to 32 feet.

By the sixties ITE was giving lip service to pedestrians, but it still designed its standards for cars. Dead ends proliferated, rarely completed with pedestrian cut-throughs. The guidelines merely encouraged sidewalks; most suburbs ignored the exhortation and allowed developers to leave them out. For roads and intersections, however, ITE handbooks were often enforced as if written on stone atop Mount Sinai.[10]

As streets widened, parking lots proliferated. Until the invention of the parking meter in 1935, on-street parking was free everywhere. Downtown parking quickly became scarce, and roadways filled with drivers circling in search of parking spaces. Zoning authorities added minimum parking rules to their ordinances, requiring new buildings to accommodate visiting cars off the street.

As is common in zoning matters, status motivations lie hidden behind the stated rationales for parking minimums. Large-lot subdivisions where curb space is plentiful are rarely exempted. Indeed, early off-street parking rules, which mandated one space per house, could shrink the supply of parking. A one-car garage furnishes one space, but that space goes to waste when the owner is away from home. Its driveway eliminates a curb space that was usable twenty-four hours a day.

Curbside parking was disfavored because it was déclassé, suggestive of old neighborhoods with no garages and cars lining the roads. A 1969 planning text says that homeowners often object to on-street parking "from the purely aesthetic standpoint." Aesthetics, here, is best understood as a euphemism. Parking is still allowed on driveways, and any given car is no better-looking there than on the street. But one's own BMW in the driveway is entirely different from someone else's Toyota at the curb.[11]

In 1946 a survey found that parking mandates were imposed in only 17% of cities. Just five years later, 71% had them in effect or on the way. Parking requirements were calculated to handle the most cars that might ever visit a building, with nothing spilling over onto the street. The ITE eventually chimed in with inflated guidelines, based on measurements of the number of cars parked in places where alternatives to driving are nonexistent.

Parking, available without limit, was provided free to the driver. This was a vast government program promoting the automobile, its cost hidden because it was paid with private rather than tax money. Not only was the car directly subsidized, but parking requirements changed the city, discouraging walking and transit use. With land gobbled up by parking lots, commercial districts were less dense and less walkable.[12]

By the late 1930s it was evident that growth had spread past the legal boundaries of many cities and decline had set in within. Downtown retailers and their landlords, losing customers to stores closer to suburban homes, grew concerned when city neighborhoods slid downhill—something once welcomed as a natural process that cleared the way for expansion of the business district. Declining neighborhoods were afflicted with "blight," an ill-defined condition that sometimes meant simply that the residents were not wealthy enough to be good customers. Planners had long debated cures for slums; now they saw blight as nearly as great a threat. Many thought the remedy was to clear whole districts and rebuild them from the ground up, in accordance with their theories. Government would plan, but rebuilding, all but a few left-wingers thought, should be carried out by private owners.[13]

To rebuild large areas at one time, land owned by many parties must be assembled under a single owner. In the course of the 1940s, many states established redevelopment authorities empowered to use eminent domain for this purpose. A few prominent projects, among them New York's Stuyvesant Town and Pittsburgh's Golden Triangle, began quickly. But there was a problem: blight was worth more in the marketplace than developers would pay for the land beneath it. If "slum clearance" was to go forward, subsidies were needed. The federal government, in the 1949 housing act, stepped forward with these funds.[14]

By now the original rationale for the program had disappeared. Planners of the 1920s and 1930s aimed at decongestion—getting rid of poverty by destroying slums and pushing people out of overly crowded neighborhoods. Removal of housing was a positive good. As late as 1944, when Robert Moses put forward an expressway plan for Baltimore that would have destroyed the homes of 19,000 residents, he argued that "the more of them that are wiped out the healthier Baltimore will be in the long run."[15]

But in the postwar years the city was shrinking on its own. Slum clearance got a new purpose—to bring the middle class back downtown—and the Housing Act of 1954 gave it a new name, "urban renewal." As before, however, the rebuilding would be done by private capital. For renewal to yield a profit, the new structures had to be bigger than what they replaced. The economic logic of the program led not to decongestion but to high-rises.

The federal program began slowly, delayed by court battles and the discovery that few municipalities really had the citywide plans that the law required before land could be condemned. Only in the mid-fifties did it gain momentum. Demolition of urban neighborhoods then moved ahead rapidly, propelled by the backing of powerful financial and real estate interests and greased by machine politicians who saw opportunities to sell their friends valuable real estate at below-market prices.[16]

Urban renewal was a disaster for cities. Livable working-class neighborhoods were torn down along with genuine slums. Low-income residents thrown out of their homes had nowhere to go; the Republican congress of 1954 slashed already small public housing programs while doubling the appropriation for urban renewal. And accompanying the carnage of slum clearance was the destruction of homes in the path of interstate highways and the ongoing damage that the interstates, once built, did to their surroundings.

What replaced the old neighborhoods only multiplied the damage. Architectural fashion had changed since the first talk of slum clearance—modernism, with its disdain for adornment, displaced the classicism of the City Beautiful. But the designers of the new urban quarters turned to their inherited planning principles. Cars came before people, and conspicuous waste was the mark of status. The doctrines of suburban subdivision were applied in the middle of cities.

The areas targeted for renewal were old streetcar suburbs and even older city neighborhoods, with their closely spaced and easily walkable street networks. (Grid streets, in themselves, were seen as a sign of blight.) The dense fabric of houses and stores vanished. In its place came sterile towers surrounded by parking lots, divided into superblocks by high-speed arteries that repelled pedestrians. Windswept plazas imitated the uselessness of front lawns. Suburban sprawl, with fewer trees and less grass, had come to the city.[17]

One thing was clear about slum clearance almost as soon as it got going. It did not get rid of slums.

Philadelphia's Yorktown urban renewal project, a low-density suburban-style neighborhood ten blocks from City Hall.
(Courtesy of Special Collections Research Center, Temple University Libraries.)

Northern cities were seeing a massive population turnover. As white renters and the married children of homeowners moved out into suburban subdivisions, a flood of impoverished blacks arrived from the South. Ethnic transitions in urban neighborhoods had never been free of friction; this one was explosive.

Segregated neighborhoods, their boundaries fixed by thirty years of racial covenants, remained in place even after a 1948 Supreme Court ruling made those restrictions legally unenforceable. "Respectable" real estate agents still refused to sell to blacks. Changing the ethnic composition of a neighborhood violated brokers' ethics codes and was grounds for expulsion from the indispensable multiple listing services. Blacks who did move into an all-white area were often targets of violence. Civil rights groups struggled against these practices; antidiscrimination laws were passed locally and, in 1968, nationally. But enforcement faltered in the face of local resistance. The expanding black population was housed, in its vast majority, by the conversion of all-white neighborhoods to all-black.

Racial turnover was commonly brought about by the ugly process of *blockbusting*. In an all-white neighborhood near the boundary, a single house would be sold to a black, or an apartment rented—sometimes it was enough to pay a black mother to walk down the street with a stroller. Real estate operators, eager to cash in, spread panic among white residents. Homeowners would sell quickly and cheaply. The speculators turned around and sold or rented to blacks, who were forced by their lack of housing options to pay higher prices.

White neighborhoods, often helped along by local real estate agents, banded together to keep blacks out. The reasons for opposition to change are easy to understand. Conversion often brought crowding; new black residents of single-family neighborhoods, struggling to pay mortgages, would take in boarders, or investors would convert homes to boarding houses. In an era of disappearing blue-collar jobs and rising crime rates, the arrival of lower-income tenants raised fears of lawlessness. Sensationalist media fanned these fears with reporting on the crime- and drug-ridden neighborhoods that black buyers were fleeing. Demographics shifted rapidly once a "tipping point" was passed; refugees from urban renewal joined new arrivals from the South to create an immense population pressure. Three or four years after the first black family moved in, a neighborhood would be entirely African American.

Class resentments mixed with racial prejudice in the resistance of white residents. The racial borderlines ran through old neighborhoods where federal lending guidelines had discouraged reinvestment. Houses were old and had low market values; owners feared that after selling out they would be short of funds to buy elsewhere. White supporters of fair housing laws often lived in wealthier sections where single-family houses were protected from change by zoning, covenants, and high real estate prices.[18]

Although times were prosperous and unemployment low, crime and welfare dependency rose. Riots in 1965, 1967, and 1968 heightened racial tensions, and *inner city* became a shorthand expression that meant poor, black, and dangerous. Homeowner resistance to racial change exploded onto the national scene as a *white backlash* that Republican politicians would exploit for decades to come.

Once housing discrimination was outlawed in 1968, the FHA and banks were forced to begin lending in cities. A final explosion of blockbusting ensued. The practice then faded away; there was no money to be made once blacks no longer paid higher prices than whites.[19]

The 1968 housing law tried to solve the problems of public housing projects, by then widely recognized. New varieties of subsidized low-income housing were authorized, smaller buildings that could be sited in suburbs as well as cities. The Richard Nixon administration—which gained great political advantage by stirring up white backlash—at first vigorously promoted the dispersal of low-income housing into the suburbs. By the end of the decade public housing of all kinds was violently unpopular. The entire program expired in

1973 when a presidential order halted construction of subsidized housing for the poor and middle class.[20]

The racial crisis left a strong imprint on the politics of land use, as racism reinforced the already ingrained belief in the importance of the social pecking order. In the white urban neighborhoods that remained, the instinct to resist change congealed into a fierce determination, often given political form by civic associations. The long-standing suburban antipathy to the city persisted, made more intense by school busing orders that left suburban towns alone and integrated schools within the city's legal boundaries. Public transit, already disdained as the vehicle of the less affluent, was now feared as a carrier of black criminals.

Elite opinion and the mass media did much to promote these trends by portraying urban issues, in which race, class, and economics were intertwined, as purely racial. It was much easier for affluent integrationists to pin the blame for center-city problems on the racism of others than to set blockbusting battles in the broader context of zoning and transportation. Their own suburbs, a wider look might show, perpetuated a system of social sorting that pitted blacks against whites in decaying urban neighborhoods. Race, in a backward way, thus joined property values, beauty, and sanitation as a code word for status-seeking.

4

Ticky-Tacky Boxes

The project of remaking the world in the image of the Country Club District of Kansas City never lacked for skeptics. Living, breathing, complex cities had their lovers.

These early lovers were few in number. They did not build, they made no laws or ordinances, and often they barely knew what it was they loved. The men and women who made things happen hardly noticed them. But in the realm of culture they rode high.

The first to be infatuated with the city were artists. In the course of the nineteenth century, a little world of impoverished poets, writers, musicians, and painters began to float around the less expensive districts of great cities. For the bohemians, as they became known, self-expression and rejection of the conventional were high virtues; aesthetic experiment was joined to spiritual and sexual exploration. In Paris and London, where they gathered, their art and their lives were soon celebrated. They burst onto the Parisian scene in 1830 and are still remembered through Puccini's opera.

New York, in the middle of the 1800s, already possessed its own artistic demimonde, but it was one that languished in obscurity. The city's bohemia flitted from here to there until the end of the century, when it found a place to settle down and flourish. It came to pass, as O. Henry recounted it in 1910, somewhat by happenstance:

> To quaint old Greenwich Village the art people soon came prowling, hunting for north windows and eighteenth-century gables and Dutch attics and

low rents. Then they imported some pewter mugs and a chafing dish or two from Sixth Avenue, and became a "colony."[1]

It wasn't just art people. Greenwich Village wished as passionately for the overthrow of the economic order as for the overturning of the old aesthetics. Leftist writers like Max Eastman and John Reed flocked there. The marriage of artistic self-expression to radicalism created an American formula—European bohemia was mostly apolitical—and it is a formula that still endures.

This was a proudly urban combination. Municipal reformers from old New York and Boston families might disdain the cities and their new immigrant populations. For young radicals who flocked to Greenwich Village from small-town America in the years around the First World War, crowded streets and tenements were something to embrace. The juxtaposition of slum and salon was among the chief enticements—for refugees from the stultifying uniformity of small town and suburb, the intellectual and political ferment of the Jewish Lower East Side was an exhilarating change.[2]

Still, a contradiction was buried in the Greenwich Village synthesis of politics and art. Radicals and bohemians both rejected middle-class conformism, but to different ends. One sought to level hierarchies; the other erected its own ranking system to replace the conventional scale. One rejected affluence; the other wished everyone could enjoy it. Bohemian outrage against the bourgeoisie had, perhaps, more in common with aristocratic disdain than with proletarian revolt. Its ethos was akin to the knightly values Veblen identified with the leisure class, disdaining the humdrum, domestic, and routinely productive to exalt self-expression, instinct, and authenticity.[3] The working class aspired, in no small part, to what the Village spurned; what would happen if workers' demands were met? A thin line separated comradeship from condescension.

Greenwich Village and its urban sensibility found a resonance. By the twenties, artistic enclaves had grown up in other cities—in Chicago's Towertown, on San Francisco's Russian Hill, in the French Quarter of New Orleans—and expatriate American writers established a colony in Paris.[4] Nonconformism was their credo, and it hardly escaped notice that uniformity was the governing principle of the emerging suburbia. Writers need not treat urban themes— no one would turn to Ernest Hemingway or F. Scott Fitzgerald to understand the daily routine of city streets—and they might sometimes abandon the city for rural retreats. But by the way they lived they affirmed that urban diversity ranked above suburban homogeneity.

Jesse Nichols was still perfecting his subdivision techniques in Kansas City, yet he and his kind were already in the crosshairs of the arbiters of culture. Sinclair Lewis, a political radical if not a bohemian, fired the heavy artillery. His *Babbitt* was a comic portrait of the suburban conformist of 1922. A firm Republican, of course, and a strict Presbyterian, George F. Babbitt had a clear credo:

> The ideal of American manhood and culture isn't a lot of cranks sitting around chewing the rag about their Rights and their Wrongs, but a God-fearing, hustling, successful, two-fisted Regular Guy, who belongs to some church with pep and piety to it, who belongs to the Boosters or the Rotarians or the Kiwanis....

For the real estate promoters of the time, conformism was the very essence of a successful business strategy. So it was only fitting that Sinclair's protagonist was a realtor, sponsor of a "high-class restricted development." The principles of suburban land use were as self-evident as the canons of the Republican Party and the Rotary Club. Babbitt was, we are told, ignorant of "all landscape architecture save the use of curving roads." America might not be perfect, he was willing to concede, but that was because "we've got a lot to do in the way of extending the paving of motor boulevards."

The educated American middle class, eagerly buying up houses in the Country Club District and its imitations, recognized the man who sold those homes. Readers jumped at the chance to think of themselves as better than him. *Babbitt* was a bestseller, and the name entered the language. Even George F. Babbitt himself, ever a reflection of his surroundings, looked down on the crass materialism he saw in others. He was not, he insisted, one of those who "don't see the spiritual and mental side of American supremacy."[5]

American culture continued in the 1930s to value urban life as American life did not, but it did so in a different way. Bohemianism gave way to economic radicalism, the ordinary man and woman were no longer disdained, and the suburb was made immune from criticism by its very ordinariness.

The New Deal brought the previously excluded into the American mainstream, and the largest group of the excluded was city dwellers—the Catholic and Jewish immigrants and their children. But political inclusion was not matched with cultural recognition. Socially conscious writers and artists favored rural themes—the California migrants of John Steinbeck's novels, the impoverished countryside of Dorothea Lange's photographs, the lumberjacks and fishermen of Rockwell Kent's paintings, the Appalachia of folk singers. New Deal culture welcomed city people, yet the city itself was still somehow less than fully accepted.

New housing tracts rolled outward after the Second World War, and the suburbs quickly came again under critical fire. Not until the sixties would the bombardment be heavy enough to slow the juggernaut of sprawl development, but a steady sniping came from two sides. The academic and literary establishment, turning away from radicalism, still assailed the stifling conformism of the Levittowns of the world. And urban bohemias, by their very existence, questioned the premises of suburbia.

It was indeed an age of conformity, but bohemia maintained itself and even slowly grew. Alongside it, and often overlapping, a new gay subculture emerged among men made conscious of their sexuality by wartime service. Greenwich Village was more than ever a magnet, now not just the home of artists, writers, and activists, but the birthplace of a musical style, folk music. Chicago's Towertown had lost its special character, but the French Quarter of New Orleans remained, protected since 1936 by an amendment to the state constitution. New centers of cultural and sexual dissent sprouted in decrepit corners of big cities: North Beach in San Francisco, Venice in Los Angeles, and elsewhere.

Places like Greenwich Village and the French Quarter were no longer slums. Union wages and postwar prosperity lifted their working-class population out of poverty. The artistic and intellectual "colonies," still minorities, grew in numbers and attracted newcomers who were settled and stably employed. But artistic self-expression remained closely allied to youth and urban poverty. The beatnik, a new edition of an old style, brought rejection of suburban conformism to a new level. Where earlier bohemias had been poor out of necessity or out of devotion to art, poverty was now a preference. For the beats, lack of money was a point of pride.[6]

The beats were no model for established writers and scholars; it was a time when intellectuals were moving from the fringe of society into the mainstream of affluence. Even so, the rise of postwar conservativism drew liberals' attention to the plague of conformism. The seat of this malady was easy to locate— in the dull, undifferentiated suburbs. Social science was now the rage, so the criticism took the form of academic studies as well as fiction. A new literary form, the best-selling work of sociology, brought this message to a wide public.

William Whyte's *The Organization Man*, a detailed study of a new Chicago suburb, was on the bestseller list for a year after its 1956 publication.

Houses in Daly City, California, the suburb that inspired Malvina Reynolds's "Little Boxes."
(Courtesy of Adrian M. Hayes.)

Whyte described his subjects in sympathetic detail, yet the book was read as a deeply critical work. Suburbia was a sink of conformism, dominated by a generation of bureaucrats who worked in large corporations.

Vance Packard's *The Status Seekers*, a more popularly written book, was a number-one bestseller in 1959. Rigid stratification, it warned, was destroying the openness of American society. No treatment of this topic could pass over the pecking order of real estate. "A great deal of thought, on the part of builders, has gone into finding symbols of higher status," Packard explained, and he went on to give a lengthy catalogue of those symbols. The "rather frightening, headlong trend toward social stratification by residential area" particularly bothered him: "Even more oppressive than the uniformity of these new one-layer town developments is the synthetic, manipulated quality of the community life found in many of them."[7]

Many readers of these works were living the life they were warned against, and others were surely thinking of moving to the suburbs. Some, no doubt, wanted only to learn how to acquire the status symbols and move ahead in the organization. Still, the criticism stuck. A foundation was in place for debates to come.

It was in 1962 that the two strands of discontent, the intellectual and the countercultural, came together in a folk song. The sight of houses covering a hillside in Daly City, just outside San Francisco, inspired Malvina Reynolds to compose "Little Boxes." She saw Daly City from the highway, passing through on her way from one bohemia to another. In South Berkeley she lived down the street from an anarchist commune. Her destination was a political meeting in the countercultural outpost of La Honda, where writer Ken Kesey would soon host the LSD parties made famous by Tom Wolfe's *The Electric Kool-Aid Acid Test*.

"Little Boxes," a minor hit after Pete Seeger rerecorded it in 1963, is remembered on the Left to this day. Its target, or at least its intended target, is the wealthy suburban establishment:

> *And the people in the houses*
> *All went to the university,*
> *Where they were put in boxes*
> *And they came out all the same,*
> *And there's doctors and lawyers,*
> *And business executives,*
> *And they're all made out of ticky tacky*
> *And they all look just the same.*
> *And they all play on the golf course*
> *And drink their martinis dry....*

But these short verses, examined closely, are full of ambiguity. As much as "Little Boxes" is on target as cultural metaphor, its lyrics are bad sociology. The tract houses of Daly City were San Francisco's Levittown, built for the working class. Doctors, lawyers, and business executives resided elsewhere, in bigger homes on larger lots. And, even more to the point, they lived in houses that didn't look like those boxes in Daly City.[8]

Someone who listened to "Little Boxes," but not too closely, might hear a song about the sameness of houses rather than the conformism of people. And ears were open to hear that song. In the folk scene of the sixties, as in the Greenwich Village of a half-century earlier, feelings of cultural superiority were buried beneath the Leftism. The satirist Tom Lehrer sang to the same audience, and he knew its weaknesses. "The nicest thing about a protest song," he observed, "is that it makes you feel so good." In "The Folk Song Army" he portrayed a certain type of listener:

> *We all hate poverty, war, and injustice,*
> *Unlike the rest of you squares.*

Is the enemy the boxes or the people in them? Do we seek a better world or to be better than the neighbors? These might be fine distinctions when the antidote to suburban sterility was the music of Malvina Reynolds and the drugs of Ken Kesey. But the "Folk Song Army," like generations before it, would grow older, and soon it would buy real estate.

After a while the counterculture faded from view. But it hardly went away; the memory of the sixties was absorbed into the mainstream of commercialism. While many survivors strove to maintain the ideals of their youth, among some aging hippies and more of their camp followers egalitarianism gradually faded into the snobbery of nonconformity. In an older house, built by an earlier generation, they could stand out from those conformists in new suburbs full of boxes made of ticky-tacky. Never mind that the neighbors were those doctors, lawyers, and business executives. At least the houses didn't all look just the same.

5

Jane Jacobs versus the Planners

Cities in the 1950s were visibly in trouble. Factories closed, downtown stores lost customers, office jobs moved to the suburbs, and residential neighborhoods, with rare exceptions, went downhill as they aged.

That something was going wrong was not in doubt. But established opinion, loath to admit mistakes, placed the blame on natural processes. The housing economist William Grigsby summed up the era's conventional wisdom in words that the next half-century would prove spectacularly wrong:

> With a few notable exceptions, the *residential* real estate market works only once. It creates, alters, maintains, and improves, and eventually discards assets, but seems incapable of providing for their replacement on the site.[1]

The antidote for this supposed market failure was urban renewal. City neighborhoods were rebuilt with separated land uses, superblocks, high-speed roadways, and barren plazas. The solutions for other urban problems were similar: to make cities even more like the suburbs that were strangling them. The cure for traffic jams was more roads. To bring shoppers back downtown, store buildings were torn down and replaced with parking lots.

The technocrats who prescribed these remedies were quick to reject any questioning of their science by the untrained masses. Their discipline was, or so they claimed, akin to engineering. It was not a matter of taste or social convention but the logically determined response to the facts. On this façade of objectivity rested the jobs of credentialed planners, and much more. An edifice of authorities and agencies, along with the politicians who sponsored them, was tightly linked with the developers and contractors who profited from government-subsidized land and large-scale construction.

Critics there were of this commercial juggernaut, but for the most part they shared its basic doctrines. Apostles of the automobile, a Le Corbusier and a Frank Lloyd Wright, dominated the architectural avant-garde. Planners did realize that the new interstate highways would hollow out cities, but even the profession's dissidents were slow to question basic principles.[2] No antidote could be devised for what was poisoning the cities until the underlying causes of the malady were diagnosed.

Jane Jacobs was the one who dared to say the emperor was naked.

She arrived in New York from Scranton, Pennsylvania, fresh out of high school in 1934, and quickly fell in love with the city. She got a job as a secretary and moved with her sister to Greenwich Village, where she would spend the next thirty-four years. Frequent walks took her through Manhattan's extraordinarily specialized business districts, and her acute and readable observations soon made her a magazine writer. She married and with her husband bought a three-story building on Hudson Street. They paid a thousand dollars less than the price of the cheapest house in Levittown.

In 1952 she talked herself into a job at *Architectural Forum*, where she was sent to report on the gathering wave of urban renewal. She didn't like what she saw. The "renewed" neighborhoods were empty of life. A short walk outside showed what was missing—streets full of little stores, children playing, people hanging around. Yet these were the blocks, the planners told her, that were next to be demolished.

Substituting for an editor who took ill, she gave a talk at Harvard in 1956 to an all-star audience of architects and planners. Word of her unconventional views spread, and William Whyte, author of *The Organization Man* and an editor at *Fortune* magazine, had her turn the talk into an article. "Downtown Is for People" brought her ideas to a larger audience. Then came a grant from the Rockefeller Foundation that allowed her to work full time on a book. In January 1961 she completed the manuscript of *The Death and Life of Great American Cities*.[3]

Where others had started from the defects of cities and sought ways to correct them, Jacobs began by asking what makes cities succeed. The simplest level

Jane Jacobs with petitions opposing urban renewal in Greenwich Village, 1961.
(Courtesy of the Library of Congress, World Telegram & Sun collection.)

was a single street. Watching her own block in Greenwich Village day after day, she perceived a complex pattern of order among disorder, what she called the ballet of the sidewalk. The dancers were young and old, shopkeepers and strangers, they lived on the block, they worked nearby, they were visitors from the suburbs. All did their part in making the street a safe, welcoming place. Together they made it truly urban.

Jane Jacobs stood on her Hudson Street sidewalk, an Archimedes whose lever was her power of seeing the everyday things that others missed. She reasoned from one observation to another until she overturned the world of city planning. "Eyes on the street" were what made cities safe. To keep those eyes there all day, uses must be densely mixed, not sorted and thinned out. The street needs attractive uses that draw people onto the sidewalk, with variety that maintains their interest. The streetcorner is especially valuable, the site of human encounters both habitual and unexpected.

She summarized her findings in four principles:

1. The district, and indeed as many of its internal parts as possible, must serve more than one primary function, preferably more than two.
2. Most blocks must be short; that is, streets and opportunities to turn corners must be frequent.
3. The district must mingle buildings that vary in age and condition, including a good proportion of old ones so that they vary in the economic yield they must produce. This mingling must be fairly close-grained.
4. There must be a sufficiently dense concentration of people, for whatever purposes they may be there.

This turned the received doctrines of city-building on their head. Density is good, monotony bad. Automobiles yield to those on foot; superblocks make way for grid streets. Permanence brings decay. And enforced separation of land uses, the principle on which all else rested, is not just unnecessary but actively destructive.

These ideas did not merely dispute the design principles of urban renewal; they challenged the very essence of the planning enterprise. Cities, as Jacobs saw them, are not engineering problems. They are frames for the spontaneous flowering of the human spirit.[4]

Conventional planners were quick to find fault. Jacobs, they alleged, spoke for literary bohemians and not for ordinary folk. It was true that Greenwich Village benefited from an unusual mixture of people and activities. Bars where longshoremen drank in the afternoon were hardly out of the ordinary in those years, but few such establishments could boast the evening literary clientele of Hudson Street's White Horse Tavern. Such complaints issued from the establishment, but not just from there. Herbert Gans, an early opponent of urban renewal, chided Jacobs for failing to understand that the middle class did not share the tastes of intellectuals, artists, and tourists.[5]

This objection was off the mark. Jacobs' ideas rested on a wider inquiry; she put Hudson Street directly under her microscope simply because she lived there. Before she ever organized her own neighborhood, she protested urban renewal in the bohemian-free precincts of East Harlem. Even Hudson Street was a place mostly of shopkeepers and blue-collar workers. The 1950 census, taken a few years after she moved in, counted in her fourteen-block neighborhood 149 apartments that had no kitchen and shared a bathroom in the hall.[6]

For that matter, Jacobs was not the first to point out the sterility of housing projects. Another independent thinker, George Orwell, saw the same

thing two decades sooner. His 1937 account of the life of the English working class, *The Road to Wigan Pier*, condemned public housing without pubs
and corner stores as "monstrously inhuman." In Orwell's judgment, the
new homes were barely better than the Dickens-era slums of Liverpool and
Manchester. Orwell knew that workers are not bohemians—no book could
be clearer on that point. *Wigan Pier* is still remembered for the scorn it pours
on "that dreary tribe of high-minded women and sandal-wearers and bearded
fruit-juice drinkers who come flocking towards the smell of 'progress' like
blue-bottles to a dead cat."[7]

The claim that only intellectuals like diverse and lively streets is still heard
today, but it has long since lost all plausibility. The passage of time has made
clear how widely this taste is shared. Greenwich Village, like other places, has
fallen victim to its own desirability. The house Jane and Bob Jacobs bought for
$7000 was put on the market in 2009 for $3.5 million.

Death and Life did have its shortcomings, even if they were not what its detractors complained about.

For one thing, the book says almost nothing about transit. You walk,
you drive, occasionally you take the bus. The subway, so central to the life of
Manhattan, does not make an appearance until page 467. For all Jacobs' ability
to see what others overlooked, the subway was so much part of the landscape
that she failed to perceive its importance to New York. The further development of public transportation, she wrote, should come only after the revitalization of neighborhoods.[8]

This was, for the most part, a harmless error. In San Francisco, where some
desired to freeze the city in its existing form, opponents of the new subway
could cite Jacobs.[9] But readers elsewhere rarely noticed what was missing.
For several years now, complaints that automobiles were strangling cities and
pleas for new rail lines had flooded newspapers. Outside Manhattan and San
Francisco, lovers of cities knew all too well the insufficiencies of their transit
networks. The New York subway itself had been starved of investment, and
when the book came out it was beginning to fall apart. People who took Jane
Jacobs seriously understood the need for more subways.[10]

Another weakness of *Death and Life* is the defensive nature of its prescriptions. We read much about *unslumming* but little about how to build places
that will never be slums. A chapter about how to make more lively neighborhoods is titled "Forces of Decline and Regeneration"—regeneration but
not creation. Here Jacobs, elsewhere so far ahead of her time, is very much a
thinker of her own day.

Nothing in the book is more prophetic than its warning of the curse of success. So many want to live in a diverse locality that the wealthy, and especially the wealthy and childless, crowd in and destroy what attracted them. "The demand for lively and diversified city areas," Jacobs realized, "is too great for the supply."[11] When these words were written, the pace of change was slow. The bohemian invasion of Greenwich Village was then sixty years old, yet part of the neighborhood had recently been condemned as a slum and more was threatened with the same. Today things move far more quickly. By now nearly every neighborhood Jacobs praised in 1961 has lost or is on the way to losing its diversity of income.

The needed supply of diverse neighborhoods, clearly, has not been forthcoming, but why? This is a question Jacobs does not answer. Her critique of zoning is thorough and pertinent, but she does not explain why the theories she refutes are so attractive. Here Herbert Gans was more perceptive. A major force preserving slums, he pointed out, is that "no one who has any say in the matter wants people of lower income or status in his neighborhood."[12]

As the end of *Death and Life* approaches, oversights accumulate and start to obscure the achievements of the early pages. But then Jacobs leaves us with a parting reminder of her brilliance, a stunning tour de force of intuition.

Her final chapter, about "the kind of problem a city is," leans heavily on an essay by the mathematician Warren Weaver, a founder of information theory. Weaver's paper on science and complexity is now a scientific classic, a groundbreaking effort that prefigured whole fields of research.[13] Jacobs had a research grant and an office at the Rockefeller Foundation, where Weaver was a vice president, and surely she learned directly from him. For someone with no scientific training, merely to recognize the significance of Weaver's concepts was an accomplishment. But she went further.

In an extended discussion of these ideas, Jacobs identifies cities as problems in *organized complexity*. Their behavior cannot be understood by mere addition of component parts or from statistical averages. She then goes forward on her own and lists some habits of mind useful for understanding cities. "Think about processes," she advises, and "seek for unaverage clues." A failed city is a place of low energy where nothing departs from the average; the unaverage, the interesting, what she has been calling the diverse, arises only in high-energy systems.[14]

Here Jacobs anticipates developments in the physics of complexity that were yet to come. She was no student of science. Fractal mathematics and nonequilibrium thermodynamics were surely not things she thought about or even would have understood if she had. She was a writer and thinker of genius.

Death and Life was an instant classic, and it still draws readers after half a century. Yet its message has been very incompletely heeded. Roads are still laid out in superblocks, streets deadened by empty plazas, new buildings kept apart from old. Mixed use and urban density now win the favor of architects and planners, but the public often still resists.

The illnesses that afflicted America's cities were more than the consequence of wrong ideas. The forces of sprawl were deeply embedded in the country's culture and economy. Jane Jacobs' intellectual achievement was only a starting point for change.

6

Saving the City

Ears were open to hear Jane Jacobs' message. The racial and economic illnesses of old urban neighborhoods were growing more acute, and the malady had begun to spread beyond their borders. Chronic psychological and circulatory disorders afflicted even seemingly healthy areas of recent construction.

Burgeoning suburbs offered no worthy substitute for declining cities. The spiritual emptiness of consumerism and conformism was matched by the physical ugliness of public places. A drive down a suburban commercial strip showed that empty space between buildings is no guarantee of architectural beauty.

The relentless spread of subdivisions destroyed time-honored landscapes of farm and forest. Pundits foresaw the growth of a single vast metropolitan area stretching from Virginia to Maine, annihilating vast stretches of countryside.

As the fear of human congestion receded, a new plague of automotive overcrowding took its place. The *New York Times* in 1959 highlighted a commuter crisis of traffic jams and failing railroads in three days of front-page articles. Headlines laid the blame on what was by then well-known as *urban sprawl*. The experts, other than what the *Times* called "a few radical advocates of the automobile," held it impossible to meet the transportation needs of the modern city without vast improvements in mass transit. New York, with its subways and railroads, was far better off than Los Angeles, "a jelly-like glob of humanity, oozing through a sea of smog on creaking wheels."[1]

The champions of suburbanization and road-building were now on the defensive, intellectually if not politically. As early as 1958, a National Health Forum could be told to look past "the well-advertised cracks in the picture windows of the suburbs." In 1960, a Brookings Institution economist felt compelled to stand up for the automobile against critics who said it was "polluting the atmosphere, clogging the highways, and destroying the city." The best case he could make was that it was better than the horse.[2]

Even Richard Nixon, sticking with the suburban status quo in his run for president that year, thought it wise to dress up inaction as a call for change. "We can deal with this so-called 'urban sprawl,'" he declared, "only by steady support of effective and farsighted zoning powers in states and counties."[3]

The well-entrenched sprawl machine, backed by powerful real estate and construction interests, could easily shrug off the complaints of intellectuals. Only the power of an organized political force might slow the juggernaut. But that force was gathering on the horizon. As the pace of highway-building and urban renewal accelerated, the destruction of urban neighborhoods brought forth a massive grass-roots opposition.

The first years of slum clearance, in the late 1940s and early 1950s, had not been without controversy. But the focus of early complaints was on what was built—and on the skin color of the new residents—rather than on what was destroyed. Where most voters were homeowners, as in Detroit and Chicago, opponents of public housing won quick victories. This left a legacy: urban renewal, in these cities, would keep away from white neighborhoods.[4] Only the black sections of town would be "renewed," and before long critics were saying that urban renewal might better be called "Negro removal."

The 1949 housing law, by bringing private developers into the rebuilding process, reinforced the destructive impetus. Land selected to be cleared now had to be capable of being rebuilt profitably. Where New Deal public housing programs had targeted the worst slums, developers wanted to go where new housing would be easiest to sell. Almost any older section of a city could be diagnosed with the vaguely defined malady of blight, so renewal agencies sent their wrecking balls to relatively healthy neighborhoods near downtown.[5]

As the pace of demolition accelerated in the late 1950s, a growing opposition could no longer be dismissed as racially motivated. The Achilles heel of urban renewal was relocation. A federal law that required equivalent replacement housing for the displaced was widely ignored. Renewal projects sent the poor flooding into surrounding areas, sometimes creating more slums than were removed. Blacks suffered doubly: they were the favored targets

South Margin Street in Boston's old West End awaits demolition as suburban-style towers rise behind it in Charles River Park.
(Courtesy of the West End Museum.)

for removal, and the prevailing pattern of segregated housing confined their search for new homes to a few already overcrowded neighborhoods.[6]

The turning point came for urban renewal with the destruction of Boston's West End, an area on the edge of downtown that was almost all white. This working-class neighborhood was designated as blighted based on studies that greatly overstated the amount of substandard housing. In 1954 the city chose as the developer a newly created company that had only $1000 in equity. At the head of this corporation was a twenty-seven-year-old Harvard-educated lawyer. He had gone to work for Mayor John Hines after organizing a "good government" group that delivered key political backing to the mayor's election campaign.

Residents opposed the plan, but they were slow to organize and made no headway in the face of united support for rebuilding from Boston's business, political, social, and religious leadership. In April 1958, eviction notices went out to 2700 households, and a year and a half later all were gone. Forty-eight acres of land were condemned for $7.40 a square foot, revalued at $1.40, and leased to the developer for around 9¢ a year. A singularly sterile assortment of luxury housing towers and institutional buildings replaced the West End; the dispersed residents mourned their loss for decades afterward.[7]

Other sections of the city observed the fate of the West End with horror. In South Boston and Charlestown, redevelopment faced fierce opposition from homogeneous Irish neighborhoods that wielded great influence in local politics. They saw urban renewal as an attack on the city's ethnic communities by the old Protestant elite. The South Boston project was stopped cold; in Charlestown, after a long struggle, rebuilding went forward on a much-reduced scale. Meanwhile, the renewal agency extended the emptiness of the rebuilt West End into the heart of downtown with Government Center, a vast bare plaza flanked by parking garages and a forbidding concrete City Hall.[8]

Urban renewal was already under attack from the grass roots in other cities, and then a series of books made it controversial at the national level. *The Death and Life of Great American Cities* in 1961 was followed a year later by Herbert Gans' description of life in the West End before its demolition, *The Urban Villagers*. The liberal authors of these critiques were joined by a conservative, Martin Anderson, whose *The Federal Bulldozer* pointed to many of the same defects in the program. He argued that renewal should be left to the workings of the marketplace.

The market for luxury high-rise apartments was quickly sated, and developers lost interest in buying large tracts of empty city land. By the early sixties, wholesale demolition became rare. Urban renewal programs then tried to reconstitute themselves by launching initiatives to rehabilitate neighborhoods. The federal program, enmeshed in controversy, finally expired in the Nixon administration. The precedent of using eminent domain to assemble land for private development lives on, used more selectively in the absence of federal subsidy but still a matter of controversy.

Resistance was gathering as well against the march of highway building. The first major victory came in Greenwich Village, won in large part by Jane Jacobs herself. Robert Moses had been trying for years to punch a four-lane extension of Fifth Avenue through Washington Square, which served the Village as its neighborhood park. Jacobs joined the opposition in 1955 and quickly rose to leadership. Thousands signed petitions, and such notables as Eleanor Roosevelt, Margaret Mead, and Lewis Mumford were drawn in. The campaign steadily gained momentum and in 1958 New York's political leadership was won over. The city scrapped the road plan and removed an existing bus turnaround from the park.[9]

But Moses had much bigger ideas. Back in 1929, planners had mapped out no fewer than seven east–west highways through the city. Moses first tackled the Cross-Bronx Expressway. Bulldozing over local opponents, he punched the roadway through seven miles of crowded city blocks. Healthy South Bronx neighborhoods turned into a legendary slum. Next on his agenda were

Malvina Reynolds sings to a rally against freeway building in San Francisco, May 17, 1964.
(Courtesy of The Bancroft Library, University of California, Berkeley.)

two elevated interstates across Manhattan. One, at 30th Street, hit obstacles in the 1940s and never made headway. But after his defeat in Washington Square, Moses moved ahead to build the Lower Manhattan Expressway, a mammoth ten-lane elevated highway through what is now SoHo. An epic ten-year battle ensued, with Jacobs again a leader of the opposition. Only in 1969 was the project finally killed.[10]

In San Francisco, too, resistance surfaced early. The sight of the first downtown elevated interstate, the Embarcadero Freeway along the waterfront, horrified the city. A petition drive led the board of supervisors to cancel seven of ten proposed interstates in 1959. Still on the books was the Panhandle Freeway, intended to create a through route for motorists across the heart of the city to the Golden Gate Bridge. It was a road that would not die, despised by the populace but resurrected again and again under state pressure. Even the election of an anti-freeway mayor in 1963 was not enough to kill it. The following May, thousands rallied on threatened parkland; Malvina Reynolds performed a new song written for the occasion, "The Cement Octopus." Two years later San Francisco's freeway-building era finally came to an end when the board of supervisors, by a narrow majority, issued a definitive rejection.[11]

In Washington, DC, the highway builders in 1959 put forward a grandiose plan for a spider's web of four concentric beltways linked by radial highways. Opposition sprang up immediately along the northwestern arm; the well-connected residents of upscale neighborhoods reached into the White House and managed to slow down the entire program. The radial that headed north traversed low-income black neighborhoods and the emerging bohemian enclave of Takoma Park; there a more radical opposition emerged. Leaflets called for "no more white highways through black bedrooms." In the end, only a piece of the downtown loop was built; nearly all remaining interstates within city limits were taken off the map in 1971.[12]

In Boston there were a dozen years of struggle before two interstates through the city's old streetcar suburbs were canceled in 1971. Here as elsewhere the movement was broadly based, but the order of assembly was the reverse of Washington's. Poor neighborhoods objected first; Harvard and MIT professors joined in later. Eventually the entire spectrum of political opinion from Samuel Huntington to Noam Chomsky could be found among the signers of a single protest letter.[13]

By the mid-sixties, highway battles raged in cities throughout the country, and activists were linking up. The 1966 Transportation Act restricted the destruction of parks and historic buildings by highways, and it downgraded the Bureau of Public Roads inside a new Transportation Department. President Lyndon Johnson appointed expressway skeptic Alan Boyd as secretary and put another reformer, Lowell Bridwell, in charge of its highway programs.[14]

The fight against urban expressways gained impetus when the Highway Act of 1973 allowed money designated for highways to be used for mass transit. Cities could cancel roads without losing federal aid and the jobs it brought. Interstate money saved the Washington Metro when budget shortfalls threatened the project's collapse and built new subway lines in Chicago, Boston, and New York. Still, the federal aid program remained heavily biased—transit projects required far more local matching funds than roads. And many states had their own rules, enacted years earlier at the urging of federal authorities and the highway lobby, that forbade transfer of highway money to transit.[15]

The highway revolts prevented vast destruction. Plans barely imaginable today, such as elevated interstates through lower Manhattan and New Orleans's French Quarter, had once seemed unstoppable. Still, the movement won only partial victories. The fundamental premise that expressways are a good way of moving people in cities was never overturned; highways were blocked by appeals to values that had nothing to do with transportation. And the juggernaut was not halted everywhere. The strength of broad-based movements, reaching across divisions of class and race, was required. Where these coalitions could not be assembled—and they were especially hard to bring together in conservative Southern cities, where black neighborhoods were often deliberately targeted for destruction—road-building went according to plan.[16] To this day, the centers of Houston, Miami, Los Angeles, Detroit, and other cities are choked by dense highway networks that rend their urban fabric into tatters.

Yet another front was opened in the sixties in the war to save cities. This was preservation of historic buildings.

The pivotal event was the destruction of New York's Pennsylvania Station. The great railroad terminal designed by Charles McKim was a masterpiece of the City Beautiful movement, with high-ceilinged waiting rooms surrounded by a grand colonnade modeled after the ancient Roman Baths of Caracalla. The railroad, at the height of its wealth and power when the station was built, came to parlous straits in the sixties. It sought to sell the air rights over its terminal, demolish the edifice, and move its operations to a low-ceilinged train station in the basement of the new structure.

New York's architects were horrified. The city's population, alerted by a protest committee that quickly won the backing of the *New York Times*, agreed. "The city's investors and planners have aesthetic as well as economic responsibilities," the *Times* said, but no law protected old buildings. Penn Station was torn down in 1963, replaced by a bland office building and an even blander sports arena.[17]

The legal gap was soon filled. In 1965 New York empowered its Landmarks Commission to designate historic buildings, which owners were forbidden to demolish. Federal legislation came a year later, establishing a National Register of Historic Places. Cities throughout the country were quick to follow New York's example.

These successes came at a price. The destruction of cities was halted with double-edged swords that protected the suburban status quo as well. Arguments against urban change dovetailed with the suburban insistence that what was built once should remain forever unaltered. Success in preserving city neighborhoods froze the existing pattern of development more firmly into place, driving new building outward into an ever-expanding sprawl.

For one thing, victories were largely defensive; activists struggled to keep what already existed. They brought to light the previously unrecognized merits of old neighborhoods and slowed the pace of their destruction, but what replaced what could not be saved was as bad as ever. This was a failing whose consequences seemed small at first but would bulk larger as time passed. Robert Moses was no more ruthless a destroyer of working-class housing than the nineteenth-century rebuilder of Paris, Georges-Eugène Haussmann—but Haussmann left his city the Boulevard Saint Germain while Moses' legacy is the Brooklyn-Queens Expressway.

With the issue framed as destruction versus preservation, rather than city versus sprawl, the cry of "stop the bulldozers" could be used to protect the exclusivity of upscale suburbs and newly gentrified sections of cities. Battles against highways and urban renewal were succeeded by fights against non-profit housing on empty lots. The striving to keep out people of lower status could be portrayed as a revolt of the oppressed people against rapacious capitalists, status-seeking disguised in a cloak of self-righteous egalitarianism.[18]

Another legacy of the battle to preserve the cities was excessive trust in the remedy of citizen participation. This was an idea in the air in the sixties, much like planning in the twenties. The rising student New Left organized around the slogan of "participatory democracy," and the centerpiece of President Johnson's War on Poverty was a Community Action Program that required the "maximum feasible participation" of the poor. The urban renewal program had explicit community participation requirements as early as 1961, and Secretary of Transportation Boyd, upon taking office in 1967, called for more community participation in highway decision-making.

The pitched battles of the sixties were succeeded by more mundane local skirmishes. The new rules were, for those with skills and time to deploy them, handy tools to use against public action of almost any kind. Few but the nearest neighbors of routine construction projects care enough to devote much time, and the skills to make involvement meaningful are held disproportionately by the affluent and well educated. The new rules thus empowered nearby property owners more than anyone else. The suburban system of land tenure, the right of landowners to control what neighbors build, was now at home in the city.

Citizen participation was conceived as a means of granting influence to the excluded, but in practice it advantaged those with the time and skills to participate. Affluent communities, urban and suburban alike, had a new way to stake an old claim—and they, unlike the urban poor, had wealth and power behind *their* assertions.[19]

Finally, the means used to halt highway-building were mostly procedural. On top of citizen participation, a 1969 law required Environmental Impact Statements for federally supported construction projects. The statute placed no limit on the damage a project did, but opponents could search for defects in the document. If they found any, and they often did, they could sue to delay the project until the paperwork was fixed. In the short run this helped highway opponents greatly; court-ordered delays legitimated their complaints, and they could use the time to build political support for full cancellation. But at the same time these procedural complexities created a new bias toward sprawl. The fewer the neighbors who might object, the easier it was to build. Highways through empty land on the fringes of cities moved ahead while urban projects, trains and roads alike, bogged down in studies and lawsuits.

The defenders of urban life paid a high price for their accomplishments, but it was a price that had to be paid. The victories of the sixties and seventies, however partial, were essential to the health of cities. Fighting uphill battles against entrenched bureaucratic and economic power, the organizers of the freeway revolt could hardly let the perfect be the enemy of the good.

Reformers of the sixties had another remedy for sprawl, one more forward-looking and endowed with more staying power. This was the revival of rail transit. Here again, success required allies, and in this case coalition-building was especially tricky. New rail lines needed the backing of the same urban business interests that were enemies in battles over highways and urban renewal.

Even at the peak of highway-building and streetcar abandonment, some rail transit was built. Chicago used New Deal public works funds to build a downtown subway tunnel in the thirties and forties. In the fifties, Cleveland built its first subway, and Boston added an off-street trolley line. By 1960, downtown business groups were promoting subway plans in Baltimore, Los Angeles, and Seattle as well, but two, three, and even five decades would have to pass before these efforts bore fruit.[20]

The real return of rail began in San Francisco. The city's geography ruled out freeway-building as the remedy for a declining downtown—there was no good place to put a second highway bridge over San Francisco Bay. By the early 1950s everyone outside the state highway bureaucracy dropped the idea of a new bridge, and downtown developers began to push for a rail tunnel to Oakland. A few years later the freeway revolt gained traction, making it clear that a new rail line was the only possible way to bring more people into downtown.

Progress was slow; there was no hope of funding from either Washington or the state. But in 1962 voters approved a bond issue and local sales tax increase to build a new rail network. Bay Area Rapid Transit, or BART, ran through a tunnel beneath the bay and fanned out in three directions across the East Bay. On the San Francisco side, BART went under Market Street in the bottom half of a two-tiered tunnel. Streetcar tracks were relocated from the street into the upper level of the tunnel, where they now bypassed traffic backups. After lengthy delays caused by the use of unproven new technology, the first passengers arrived downtown in 1973.[21]

Next behind San Francisco was Washington, DC. Here the initiative came from highway opponents, and business tagged along later. The city did not yet have home rule and the federal government ran it as a colony, so political connections were crucial. Road opponents had the ear of the John F. Kennedy administration and managed to win appointments to key planning positions. They put together a modest rail plan for the city and got it approved by Congress in 1965. Bigger things were in the works as Maryland and Virginia suburbs joined the city to establish a regional transit authority. In 1968 this body approved a plan for 98 miles of tracks, with three tunnels through downtown and nine arms reaching far into the suburbs, and it broke ground the next year. Enthusiastically supported by the populace, Metro overcame political perils, construction delays, arguments about routes, and almost endless financial tribulations. Trains began to run in 1974, and in January 2001, after thirty-one years of work, the last of the planned stations opened.[22]

Meanwhile, the Urban Mass Transportation Act of 1964 at last made federal money available for transit. By the seventies cities across the country were building "heavy rail" lines that ran in tunnels, elevated, or on fenced-off surface rights of way. Atlanta, Miami, and Baltimore joined San Francisco and Washington in building entirely new subways, and there were substantial expansions in Philadelphia, Boston, and Chicago. Even New York shook off the stagnation of the Moses years, digging a new tunnel under the East River.

As much as the subways of the seventies were a reaction against urban expressways, their designers shared a premise with the highway builders. The goal was to save the city by bringing suburbanites downtown. New rail networks bypassed dense neighborhoods in the urban core and stretched long tentacles out to distant parking lots. Commuters moved swiftly to downtown offices, but city dwellers' travel needs were less well served. Washington broke the pattern—civil rights leaders insisted on service for the urban poor, and its three rail tunnels span the city's inner residential neighborhoods as well as its downtown office core—and its new rail system is by far the most successful. Today the Washington Metro is the nation's second busiest subway, carrying more riders than older systems in Chicago, Boston, and Philadelphia.

When Malvina Reynolds recorded "The Cement Octopus," she put "Little Boxes" on the flip side. Sterile, conformist suburbs and the destruction of cities were two symptoms of a single disease. The suburbs demanded a solution too.

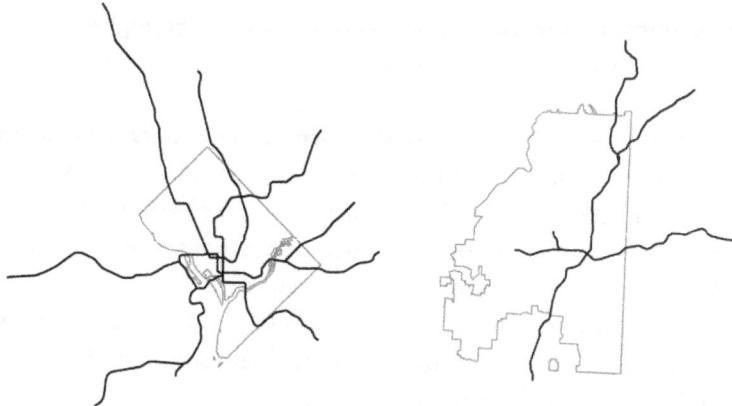

The Washington (left) and Atlanta (right) subway networks, drawn to identical scale. Both systems were designed principally for suburb-to-city commutes; Washington's is far more useful for trips within the city limits (outlined in gray).

The most visible of the suburbs' problems was ugliness, assaulting the eyes on highways lined with billboards and strip malls. This was something the reformist spirit of the sixties would not ignore. President Johnson's wife, Lady Bird, chose highway beautification as her signature issue. After a fierce legislative battle—the billboard industry did not lack for clout in congress—the Highway Beautification Act was passed, removing billboards from rural stretches of interstate highways.

Others sought less superficial remedies for suburban ills. The Garden City was not dead. Lewis Mumford, then renowned as a social critic, ended his 1961 bestseller *The City in History* with a plea for the revival of Ebenezer Howard's ideal. Mumford called for new cities, planned rather than built for profit, to restore the organic relationship of man to nature.

More practical people had similar ideas. By 1964 two idealistic real estate developers were building new towns outside Washington, DC. Reston, Virginia was the brainchild of Robert Simon. Columbia, Maryland, was developed by James Rouse. Both "planned communities" eventually flourished—they now have nearly 150,000 inhabitants between them—but as antidotes to suburban failure they fell far short of their founders' hopes.

What Reston and Columbia show today is how much better the sixties were at identifying problems than at solving them. Simon condemned suburbs in words that that make him sound like one of today's New Urbanists:

> Our present zoning ordinances are largely responsible for the diffusion of our communities into separate, unrelated hunks without focus, identity, or

community life. They have helped produce chaos on our highways, monotony in our subdivisions, and ugliness in our shopping centers. [23]

As a cure for these diseases, the two new towns offered a purer version of suburbia—a return to the vision of Radburn, where Simon's father had been a major investor. Homes were built for a range of income levels, but townhouses and apartments were separated from single-family houses and set amid seas of parking lots. Covenants enforced by homeowners' associations separated stores and workplaces from living quarters. Wide roads, built with no sidewalks, surrounded superblocks filled with dead-end streets. Pedestrians had paths of their own, hidden behind the houses.

The idealism of the founders lives on among current residents; liberal Democrats win far more votes than in newer developments nearby. And a city-style ethnic succession has begun, with minorities edging toward dominance on the east side of Columbia and in the southern half of Reston. Yet the labor expended in planning these communities yielded little fruit. Trees hide shopping areas from the road—but the view from the parking lot is the usual strip mall. Footpaths bring a few to workplaces and commuter buses; everything else enforces the usual suburban dependence on the car. Far out in the country when conceived, the two new towns have since been engulfed by exurbia. Little different today from their surroundings, they stand as monuments to a mistaken theory.

As more planned communities followed Reston and Columbia, developers dropped the vision and kept the sprawl. The goal of mixing incomes was forgotten. Roads still lacked sidewalks, and pedestrians got nothing in their place.

Still, suburbs were changing. No longer would they be pure expanses of single-family homes feeding commuters into the city. Powerful economic and political forces were bringing jobs to the suburbs, and with them came a demand for less expensive places to live. Land-use rules changed to fit the new market conditions, and dwellings of inferior social rank—row houses and apartments—were allowed into the suburbs. But politicians could not ignore the wishes of their constituents. Profit-seeking builders contended with status-conscious homeowners, reaching accommodations that left both only partially satisfied and led to consequences intended by neither.

Factories and offices were already springing up at the exits of the new interstates. The outward migration began in Massachusetts along Route 128, an expressway opened in 1951 as a bypass around Boston. At the highway's exits a new landform was created when real estate developer Gerald Blakeley set

An early industrial park on Route 128. Reservoir Place, Waltham, Massachusetts (to the left), which opened in 1955, is entered by a single road next to the cloverleaf.
(U.S. Geological Survey photo.)

out to build "garden type industrial parks." These complexes, their buildings surrounded by parking lots and arranged in vast superblocks, were reachable only by car. By 1957, 140 companies had moved out to Route 128; 96% of them came from Boston's old downtown and streetcar suburbs.

Soon the interstate highway program was ringing cities all over the country with beltways, and jobs followed outward as they had in Boston. Federal policy encouraged the new high-tech defense contractors to avoid downtown locations, presumed to be targets in the event of atomic war. Local governments, especially in the new, less expensive suburbs where children thronged the schools, often welcomed industry for its contribution to the property tax rolls.[24]

The rising price of suburban land meant that single-family houses could no longer be sold at the low prices of a Levittown. For residential builders who aimed at the lower end of the market, the only way to produce an affordable product was to put up row houses. At the same time, high-end developers wanted more flexibility in laying out their subdivisions. Both kinds of developers needed to put houses on smaller lots than zoning laws allowed.

Such clustering had to be sold to the existing residents, who controlled zoning boards. In 1960 the developers' Urban Land Institute floated the concept of the *planned unit development*. A buffer zone controlled by a homeowners association would surround new buildings, keeping overall densities low. Prestigious features such as landscaping, tennis courts, or golf courses could be placed on the unbuilt land. Extra protection against loss of status came from covenants that governed the appearance and use of houses in minute detail. The Federal Housing Administration agreed in 1963 to approve loans in such developments—it insisted on highly restrictive covenants that would unalterably fix the character of the future neighborhood—and the idea took off.[25]

Apartments were coming to the suburbs too. In the forties and fifties, more than 80% of new dwelling units were one-family homes, but multifamily construction rose sharply in the early sixties. Most of the new apartments were in the suburbs. The trend was accelerated by the introduction of condominium ownership, a concept previously unknown in American law. By 1967 all fifty states had legalized condos.[26]

Tax law changes and federal subsidies accelerated construction of rentals in the late sixties, and a full-scale apartment bubble followed. In the peak year of 1972, more than a million multifamily housing units were built, almost matching the number of new single-family houses. In 1974 the bubble burst. It left behind a heritage of cheaply built housing, a breeding ground for the suburban slums of the future.[27]

These apartments were built to satisfy zoning rules their single-family neighbors insisted on. Levittown had imitated the separated uses, setbacks, and superblocks of the Country Club District, and now the same features dropped another notch downmarket. The law required them even when they no longer served their original purpose. Budget-conscious developers squeezed in off-street parking as cheaply as possible, building "garden apartments" surrounded by parking lots. Row houses, too, were moved away from the street so that parking could go out front.

The placement of the new housing reinforced the suburbs' dependence on the automobile. With the best land already zoned for single-family houses, apartments were often pushed out to the fringes of existing towns and onto empty land beyond. Far from rail stations and stores, walled off in superblocks where even the bus stop was far away, only the poorest residents would do without a car.[28]

A dingbat in west Los Angeles.
(Courtesy of Eric M. Pietras.)

The dingbat, a California invention, carried automobile-centered design to an extreme. It gave cars the entire surface of the ground. In 1935, Los Angeles adopted a rule that required one covered parking space for each house or apartment. Builders responded by making the housing the roof. Thin-walled apartments were raised on sticks above the tenants' parking spaces. This was a cheap way to build parking anywhere that land was scarce, and by the 1960s dingbats were popping up throughout California's less expensive older suburbs.

Created in direct response to government rule-making, the dingbat served no one's purposes. It increased density while destroying walkable streetscapes. It was more expensive to build than traditional apartments, yet it did nothing—to say the least—to elevate the prestige of its surroundings. Dingbats were a sign of a regulatory apparatus escaping the control of its sponsors. Planners and realtors, like the Sorcerer's Apprentice, could only watch helplessly as their creation took on a life of its own.[29]

The rules that governed land use were still called zoning, but a look at the zoning map was now only the first step in learning what could be built. Through a variety of legal devices, each new construction project received individual scrutiny. The planned unit development allowed the owner of a large tract of land to build things that a zone did not ordinarily allow—not just row houses but also factories or even mixed uses. But this required individual permission, granted only after detailed plans were submitted for public scrutiny. Then there were the *special exception*, the *floating zone*, and the simple expedient of zoning all land for single-family houses and rezoning whenever someone wanted to build something else. By these techniques local government exercised an intrusive and sometimes arbitrary control over what could be built. The result could be systematic exclusion based on race and income. Public hearings were the norm, and the audience—inevitably dominated by neighbors of the proposed project—would be asked on occasion to give its verdict by a show of hands.[30]

Underlying this legal evolution was an implicit bargain between suburban homeowners and developers. The homeowners allowed in something of lower status than their own homes. In exchange, the developers subjected themselves to the suburban mode of land tenure in a particularly stringent form. When anything but classically suburban buildings like strip malls and single-family houses was built, adjoining property owners were empowered to negotiate every detail—down to the specifics of the covenants that would tell future homeowners what colors they could paint their doors and what plants could grow in their gardens.[31]

Even as the long decline of the cities culminated in the race riots of the late sixties, forces were gathering that would turn them around. New urban bohemias emerged from the countercultural explosion of the decade's last years. Small-scale imitations of the drug culture of San Francisco's Haight-Ashbury and New York's East Village sprang up in low-rent sections of cities large and small, attracting young migrants fed up with the boredom of suburbia. The faded walls of former streetcar suburbs erupted with psychedelic coloring; staid university towns like Boulder and Eugene were suddenly on the front lines of cultural revolution.

The hippies faded quickly, their outer markings absorbed into mass culture. As a movement they had only a brief moment in history, but the social consequences of their meteoric passage endured. Most important for our story here, the counterculture upended the ranking of social status. Cool outranked square; authenticity displaced wealth; old houses and old clothes were better than new.

Sex roles were changing rapidly. Young women flooded into the professions and postponed childbearing; gay men emerged from the closet. These singles and childless couples might be ready to settle down, but they had lived the tumult of the sixties. For many, a move back to their parents' suburbs would have been a defeat.

The places hippies had lived were by definition cool, so young people with steady jobs moved in. Elsewhere—around downtown Brooklyn, for example—working-class districts filled with nineteenth-century homes drew professionals in search of authenticity. By the late seventies whole neighborhoods were turning over, their long-time residents displaced by more affluent buyers who carefully renovated the old houses.[32]

Soon a pattern could be discerned. Artists, students, and intellectuals kick things off, arriving in search of low rents and escape from conformity. Once these pioneers gather, bookstores and cafes open—businesses that, like their customers, rank higher in social prestige than on the scale of wealth. As a bohemian enclave emerges, the neighborhood starts to gain status. Plucky homebuyers chance the renovation of old houses. Eventually profit-seeking builders arrive, the ground cleared in front of them by residents and small shopkeepers.

Change came fastest in the citadels of counterculture. Emblematic was the rapid evolution of San Francisco's Haight-Ashbury, hippie ground zero in 1967 and barely a decade later a fancy residential district. Today the commercial strip along Haight Street is a relic of the Summer of Love, a psychedelically painted homage to the sixties. The area around it has morphed into an upscale neighborhood, with the traces of its moment in the sun nearly gone. Visiting in 2011, I walked two blocks up Ashbury Street from Haight and counted four Mercedes and a BMW among the fifty-odd cars parked at the curb.

This trend imported a name from England—gentrification—and its authors, the young urban professionals, became known as yuppies. They were not the first to fix up run-down neighborhoods. Philadelphia's Society Hill, Washington's Georgetown, and the historic centers of some southern cities had preceded them. But for earlier renovators of old houses, bohemian enclaves had no special attraction. In New York after the Second World War, the German working-class neighborhood of Yorkville was rapidly transformed into the elite Upper East Side, while change came slowly to Greenwich Village.[33] The gentrification wave of the seventies was different. The manifestation in wood and brick of a new status hierarchy, it dwarfed what had come before. It washed into nearly every sizable city that possessed old neighborhoods and into some that didn't.

Still confined to select neighborhoods, this return to the city was less than a full-scale urban revival. Its greatest significance was as a sign of what was to come, a harbinger of changing values. Suburbanites might still think they stood at the top of the social ladder, but that ranking was now under challenge.

7

The Age of the Nimby

nto the real estate scene of the 1970s came a new social phenomenon. Neighborhoods across the country sent a message of "Not in my backyard" to, it sometimes seemed, anyone who wanted to build anything anywhere. The behavior was so common that the acronym of NIMBY, coined at the end of the decade, soon lost its capital letters.

Exclusion in itself was nothing new. Suburbanites had long labored to keep less prestigious people and activities out of their neighborhoods. Minimum house price covenants went back to the 1890s, single-family zoning to the 1920s. On occasion the urge to exclude had found potent political expression, as when Detroit voted Republican in the 1949 mayoral election. The sociologist Herbert Gans, writing in 1965, could observe as a matter of course that "middle-class homeowners use zoning as a way of keeping out cheaper or less prestigious housing, while working-class communities employ less subtle forms of exclusion."[1]

But this earlier exclusionism had a narrow focus. It aimed only to protect residential neighborhoods and had no animus against builders per se. In the 1920s, homeowners were commonly on the same side as development interests. Real estate dealers often organized the homeowners, mobilizing them to pass zoning laws and stop racial mixing.[2] Civic associations flourished in the new suburbs after the Second World War, but here they were less political. As late as 1966, an experienced zoning lawyer could write that "the average suburban community believes commercial and industrial developers are desirable suitors while residential developers are not."[3]

Just a few years later, this distinction had vanished. Now any building, of any type, had to be kept out, and nimby homeowners were the scourges of the real estate industry. Where homeowner associations existed under covenants, they took the lead. Elsewhere voluntary civic associations sprang to life. A full-fledged antigrowth movement emerged, equipped with ideology and political leaders. Horizons broadened as development was fought not just nearby but also throughout the town or even the county. City neighborhoods resisted as passionately as suburbs.[4]

Soon "slow-growth" activists were winning control of some suburban governments and gaining influence in many more. Incumbent politicians who managed to fend off the insurgencies found themselves adopting their opponents' agenda. The tide slackened briefly during the recession of the early eighties—the usual trigger for homeowner mobilization was an unwanted development project in the vicinity. The pause came to an end in 1985 when Florida adopted a statewide system of growth control, and the next year a wave of antigrowth activism washed over California from north to south. Growth limits continued to gain in popularity over the remainder of the decade.[5]

New tactics and old were employed in the fight against change. Zoning rules tightened. Whole neighborhoods became historic landmarks. A battery of new tools, advertised as *growth control* or *growth management*, were devised. Only rarely did the growth controls succeed in curbing growth—and, far more often, they gave further impetus to the spread of sprawl.

The slow-growth movement could often accomplish its purposes with the tried-and-true technique of rezoning. As suburbs sprawled outward, they engulfed former farming towns with zoning codes tailored for local landowners eager to cash in on development. The new residents, like suburbanites elsewhere, wanted a more exclusionary zoning.

Built-up places were rezoned too. Often, in neighborhoods built before the onset of zoning in the 1920s, small commercial landowners had dominated the zoning process. Caring more for profit than for status, they left themselves free to build to higher density.[6]

During the years of depression, war, and the single-family housing boom, residents of these less expensive areas paid little attention to zoning. Few apartments were going up anyway. In the most run-down districts, rentals dominated, and homeowners were too few and too impoverished to have much influence. But as city neighborhoods began to revive in the seventies, householders new and old mobilized against development. In southern California, longtime residents led the push to reduce the allowable building size. In Washington and Chicago, gentrifiers were first to call for "downzoning."[7]

Downzoning had its limits, though. Some states required time-consuming studies before land could be rezoned. If property owners objected—and the landowners most likely to build were the ones most inclined to object—they could throw up additional obstacles. On the suburban fringe vacant land was being developed faster than rezoning could stop it, and local governments devised faster-acting techniques that became known as growth controls. Meanwhile, in established suburbs and rebounding city neighborhoods, the new historic preservation rules were seized on to stop change.

Growth controls took many forms.[8] The most straightforward was a cap on building permits. Petaluma, California, and Boca Raton, Florida, pioneered this approach in the early seventies. Petaluma limited the number of permits per year; Boca Raton added a permanent ceiling on the city's population. Both cities' rules were challenged in court. Petaluma's approach was upheld, but the Florida courts struck down Boca Raton's limit (while letting stand a rezoning that banned apartment buildings outright).

Another commonly used technique is the Adequate Public Facilities Ordinance, or APFO. First introduced by Ramapo, New York, in 1969, these laws block new development that could overwhelm local infrastructure. If roads, schools, or sewers are overcrowded, builders must either wait for government to expand them or pay for the expansion themselves. The aim, ostensibly at least, is not so much to limit growth as to get infrastructure built by incentivizing developers. Sometimes the developers pay; more often they use their political power to get the taxpayer to pay. While these ordinances have linked development to many types of public facilities, their main use is for roads.[9]

Although promoted as a means to limit sprawl, the APFO turned out to make it worse. How fast cars move is the measure of whether transportation is adequate. If the nearest supermarket is 10 miles away and can be reached in 15 minutes, developers can build. If the supermarket is 1 mile away and it takes 5 minutes to drive there, they can't. The ordinance pushes new construction outward to where traffic is still light. Destinations spread farther apart require longer drives, and rules designed to limit traffic wind up making more of it.[10]

A common variant of the APFO, known as staging, has similar effects. Permits to build are released in waves, their timing often tied to the completion of new highways.

Among the strongest forms of control was the growth boundary, or greenbelt, which permanently preserves the land beyond a fixed line as farm or forest. Here it was the suburbs around San Francisco that took the lead. Slow-growth forces won control of Marin County in 1968; a general plan adopted in 1973 reserved more than half the county's land for agriculture and recreation. Development came to a near-halt, and the county's population, growing rapidly to that point, stabilized.[11]

Other California counties followed, usually with weaker laws, and the idea spread. Oregon in 1973 required all its counties to establish growth boundaries, and Maryland came close to passing a similar law a year later. Some of Maryland's large suburban counties acted in the absence of state law and reserved substantial portions of their area for agriculture. Toward the end of the decade, a referendum put California's entire coastline under control of a state commission, and New Jersey halted development in the state's Pine Barrens region.[12]

Only rarely did these boundaries succeed in containing growth. States had real power to direct growth, but only Oregon ever really tried. When small municipalities imposed controls, builders easily jumped past the city limits. County growth boundaries had more effect, but eventually the development tide ran past their borders.[13]

As regulation tightened, opportunities to build grew scarce, and grants of permission made property instantly more valuable. Local governments tried to capture this value for themselves by making developers pay for the right to build. Sometimes there was a straightforward tax. More often, an *amenity* or *proffer*—a public benefit built at the developer's expense—was negotiated case by case.

Politicians, caught between developers and homeowners, typically sought compromise. The new regulatory tools slowed the rate of growth; they rarely stopped it altogether. Absolute ceilings were further discouraged by the Boca Raton court decision, although its language did not definitively rule them out. Even the most ardent opponents of development sought to display moderation; they billed their program as slow growth rather than no growth, and growth controls acquired the less threatening name of growth management.

Wealthy city dwellers liked development no more than suburbanites, but calls to limit growth rang hollow in cities that weren't growing. Urban nimbys needed other tools, and they found one close at hand—another of the achievements of the sixties, the landmark preservation laws enacted after the destruction of Pennsylvania Station.

Historic preservation from landmark to parking lot: Pennsylvania Station, New York (top), and Sam's Park and Shop, Washington (bottom), soon after each was built.

(Courtesy of the Library of Congress, Detroit Publishing Company and Matson collections.)

The lost railroad terminal had been valued as a landmark, the monumental gateway to the city. Its defenders fought on aesthetic grounds; the opponents of demolition called themselves the Action Group for Better Architecture in New York. The building was beautiful, and everyone knew that what replaced it would be ugly.

Years before, a different group of activists had begun to struggle in obscurity for legal protection of old buildings. These preservationists, who reaped the fruits of victory after Penn Station, had an agenda much broader than better architecture. They refused to make aesthetic distinctions; for the head of New York's landmarks commission a few years later, the buildings to be preserved were "not merely the best of them, mind you, but the most charac-teristic." The idea of landmarks—particularly notable structures—faded into the vague concept of historical significance. The purpose of preservation was, as a widely cited 1985 paper put it, the pursuit of "stability, identity, and envi-ronmental control" by "retaining diverse elements of the past" and "perpetuat-ing the diverse identities of places." Within these cloudy categories, almost any resistance to change could be justified.[14]

It fell to a suburb-like section of Washington, DC, to test the limits of historic preservation. In 1981, the new Metro reached Cleveland Park. Riders entered down a stairway alongside the parking lot of a fifty-year-old strip mall. The owners of Sam's Park and Shop wanted to replace it with a larger, more urban structure. But the wealthy and influential homeowners who lived nearby liked things as they were—the neighborhood had led the successful fight against freeways two decades earlier—and they didn't want any new con-struction. Tersh Boasberg, the local leader, told the *Washington Post* that "the central question is, 'Can an urban neighborhood control what happens to it, or is development inevitable?'"[15]

Historic preservation was the community's chosen tool. In the unique political structure of the nation's capital, this offered better prospects of suc-cess than zoning. Two federal appointees, unlikely to bend to local pressure, sit on the five-person zoning board. Preservation, on the other hand, is within the full purview of the elected city government.

Sam's Park and Shop, its neighbors thus proclaimed, deserved protection as a pioneering example of strip-mall architecture. But for the historic designa-tion to succeed in blocking new construction, it wasn't enough for the store building to remain intact. The parking lot had to be saved as well.

The residents' case was not an easy one to make. In front of the original Park and Shop were a gas station and a car wash (an "automotive laundry" in the preservationists' inflated prose), later torn down to make room for more parked cars. Nearby stores were built in a hodgepodge of styles, without park-ing of their own. But no matter:

It is the integrity of the entire complex which is important...the rhythm created by tall and short, projecting and receding, and the general overall appearance and feel of the streetscape combine to make this a very human and appealing place in which to do one's shopping.

It was a long way from landmarks to human and appealing places to shop, but in 1986 the fight for the parking lot ended in victory. "They paved paradise and put up a parking lot" had been Joni Mitchell's lament in the 1970 hit folk song "Big Yellow Taxi." Now, a few years later in Cleveland Park, a parking lot *was* paradise.[16]

By 2007, twenty-seven historic districts ringed downtown Washington. They contain more than twenty-five thousand structures, all subject to strict control of new construction. The rules have an uncanny resemblance to the architectural review that Frederick Olmsted's sons devised for "high-class" subdivisions. Construction in today's historic districts must match the "massing, size, scale, and architectural features" of its surroundings while being "differentiated from the old"; ninety years ago John Charles Olmsted advised clients to allow only "a single style of architecture and a limited choice of exterior building materials" while avoiding "tiresome monotony." Decisions are made by a board of specialists, but residents have heavy input. Homeowners in these districts now possess the control over their neighbors' land that Tersh Boasberg sought. A third pillar of suburban land tenure stands alongside covenants and zoning.[17]

Unwilling to admit—and often unable to recognize—the status-seeking motivations that lurk behind their agenda, opponents of development search for any convenient excuse to oppose something that might be built nearby. Traffic is a perennial objection, blessed by the Supreme Court in *Euclid v. Ambler* and never since out of favor. Another common tactic is to go after the builder rather than the building. Homeowners appeal to the sympathies of the uninvolved, presenting themselves as innocent victims of oppressive developers.

If roads are empty and the builder is an uninviting target, other arguments are at hand. There's too much parking or too little. If houses are proposed, offices are what the neighborhod needs; if offices, houses would be better. Property values will go down; we will be priced out of our homes.

When all the usual arguments fail, new excuses must be cooked up. In this endeavor the drafters of 1920s zoning rules set a high standard of creative thinking—the ostensible reason to ban billboards in residential zones was to deprive fornicators of opportunities for concealment—but more recent generations have not lacked in imagination. One French bistro in Beverly Hills, wanting to open a second restaurant nearby, found neighbors worried that its patrons would urinate in the street while waiting for their foie gras.[18]

Ever since the 1970s, large-lot suburbs have played the environmental card. When growth controls first blossomed in Marin County, there was an unspoiled ecosystem to protect and such arguments had a real point. But in Los Angeles, complaints of "Eden in jeopardy" came from wealthy retirees who built mansions in the fire-prone desert canyons of the Santa Monica Mountains. Political influence here overcame the deficit of plausibility, and the National Park Service began to buy up land in the vicinity.

Development then spilled over into the next county, and the Santa Monica Mountains homeowners fought back by putting into office an insurgent county supervisor named Maria VanderKolk. The novice lawmaker misperceived the priorities of these suburban environmentalists. Elected on a promise to preserve a mountain tract called Jordan Ranch, she succeeded in making the entire ranch a park, along with two adjacent canyons. This achievement, in her sponsors' eyes, was a betrayal—the deal that saved the ranch authorized urban-style building on nearby flatlands. VanderKolk, when her term expired, became a private citizen again.[19]

When antigrowth homeowners ventured onto the wider political stage, they tended to adopt the political coloration of their surroundings. In most suburbs, that put them on the right. The California civic associations that led the downzoning drive of 1972 were soon the shock troops of tax revolt. Los Angeles homeowners boasted of being the fathers of Proposition 13, a tax-cutting amendment to the state constitution that a statewide referendum approved in 1978.[20]

Elsewhere, fear of housing integration fed lower-middle-class nimbyism. After the Fair Housing Act of 1968 banned outright racial discrimination by homesellers, the civil rights movement turned its attention to the more subtle barriers that still blocked integration. Exclusion by income often amounted to exclusion by race, and even when the victims had the same skin color as the perpetrators it had similarly pernicious effects. With integration of schools and lunch counters fresh in everyone's memory, it was easy to see how talk of "neighborhood character" or "compatibility" could be code words for something else. Massachusetts in 1969 empowered a state agency to overturn "snob zoning" rules that kept subsidized housing out of suburban towns. Similar laws were passed by the Connecticut and New York legislatures, but they fell victim to the governor's veto in one case and repeal in the other.[21]

In New Jersey, lawsuits demanding construction of subsidized housing in all-white suburbs triggered a right-wing insurgency. To fend off court pressure, the state's Republican governor, William Cahill, proposed a law in 1972 to override local ordinances that excluded apartments from municipalities. Fevered opposition arose in the state's white ethnic suburbs. Joining with more affluent areas, they organized as the United Citizens for Home Rule.

Loathing of the bill was so intense that Cahill was defeated in the next year's Republican primary by a defender of local autonomy.

In the general election Republicans were defeated across the board, but new suburban Democrats in the legislature shared their predecessors' devotion to local zoning. A twelve-year tug-of-war followed among courts, local governments, builders, and fair housing advocates. In the end, New Jersey enacted a relatively mild law. It brought apartments to towns that excluded them entirely but delivered little affordable housing.[22]

Racial fears have surely not vanished as a nimby motivation, but they have greatly weakened since the 1970s. Dislike of apartments has not abated with the fading of racial prejudice; instead, the battle to preserve status has broadened. As the years have passed and the civil rights movement faded from memory, the political atmosphere shifted rightward and exclusion could be defended more openly. A second wave of growth control, even bigger than the first, arrived in the late eighties. Townhouse residents now fight apartments while single-family householders battle townhouses. Almost anything at all that might be built near someone's house is a potential target; schools, ball-fields, and even nature paths can come under attack.

Closer to downtown, the nimby wave got started on the Left. Its strongholds were the bohemian enclaves, where suburbia was rejected by activists and ordinary residents alike.

Activists had the wind at their back in neighborhoods that had defeated urban renewal and highway-building. But it took time for a full-fledged antigrowth politics to emerge. Early gentrifiers had moved to the city to live among a mixture of races and income levels. Once renewal agencies stopped building the towers of the 1950s, they were willing and sometimes even eager to live with new low-income housing. Jane Jacobs led a campaign for subsidized rental apartments in Greenwich Village.[23]

Attitudes subtly shifted with the rise of the student New Left at the end of the 1960s. Hostile to all large institutions, and to technology in general, every instinct of this movement made it suspicious of official proposals. More specifically, it counted the universities among the main pillars of an oppressive system. For a student movement, the schools were the nearest at hand of those pillars, and thus the first target of attack. Students for a Democratic Society, the main New Left organization, launched a national campaign against expansion of universities into surrounding communities.

SDS burst onto the national scene when Columbia University students went on strike in 1968. The main demand of the strikers was a halt to construction of a gym in nearby Morningside Park, a crime-ridden and decrepit strip of land at the bottom of the slope that led down from the heights where the university stood.

The gym was to be used by the community as well as the students, and neighbors welcomed the idea when first proposed in the early sixties. The area around the university was then anything but upscale, and across the park stood Harlem, one of the city's worst slums. The gym would redeem land that was at best useless, and in many eyes an active danger to its surroundings. Jane Jacobs enthused over the project in *The Death and Life of Great American Cities*. "Columbia University," she wrote, "is taking a constructive step by planning sports facilities—for both the university and the neighborhood—in Morningside Park."

But critics gathered on two sides. Guardians of the city's parks, drawn from New York's old elites, questioned the propriety of selling off grounds designed by Olmsted and Vaux, however much the masters' work had gone to seed. In mid-decade they were joined by the new Black Power movement, which saw the gym as an intrusion of the white power structure into a quintessential urban black turf. Even worse, black youth would go in through a door at the bottom of the hill, while students would use a separate entrance at the level of the heights. In early 1967, with construction near on the horizon, the militant leader Rap Brown threatened to burn the gym down if it were built—not an idle menace in those years of urban unrest. When digging began the following winter, students joined Harlem residents in a series of demonstrations.

On April 23, 1968, SDS gathered to confront the university authorities. Kept out of the school library, they marched down to the park to tear down the fence around the gym foundation. Then they returned to campus and seized university buildings. After a week, the New York police stormed the campus with tear gas and ended the protest. In the aftermath, the gym project was canceled. In 1990 the gym excavation was turned into a pool and waterfall, and today Morningside Park is a pleasant urban refuge, flanked on both sides by gentrified neighborhoods.[24]

The New Left imploded at the end of the sixties. A few of its adherents tried to live out revolutionary fantasies; many more settled down in newly gentrifying urban neighborhoods and strove for a better society by more prosaic means. There they made common cause with moderate leftists and liberals, groups they had not long before derided as sellouts.

Among these former New Leftists, a residue of hostility remained toward anything big and anything industrial. Their new allies joined in the skepticism of giant building schemes. The freeway revolt was on the upswing, and the bitter aftertaste of urban renewal was still on the tongue.

The new urbanites, their numbers greatly reinforced by the changes of the sixties, forged a political program with wide appeal. They brought together tenants, labor unions, left-wing activists, gentrifiers, and homeowners of all income levels in established single-family neighborhoods. This movement, dubbed the "new urban populism," aimed to preserve cities as they were, protecting homeowners with downzoning and tenants with rent control. It made war against highway-building, and even public transit could come under suspicion—in San Francisco, the local "alternative" weekly newspaper warred against BART as a developer plot to "manhattanize" the city. Mayors elected on platforms of this sort (minus, usually, the hostility to downtown office development) included Boston's Ray Flynn, Chicago's Harold Washington, and a host of others in cities large and small.[25]

The program of freezing the urban landscape with rent control and downzoning protected residents when cities were in decline, and it gained political punch by mobilizing renters. But when the pace of gentrification picked up in the late seventies, the homeowner–tenant coalition became harder to sustain. By now the federal urban renewal program was gone, and the battle against urban highways had run its course. Gentrification of existing buildings, rather than wholesale demolition, was the main threat to affordable housing. Tenants and their left-wing allies wanted poorer residents to stay in improving neighborhoods; they sought to build subsidized apartments as stand-alone projects or as "sweeteners" in larger private developments. More conservative homeowners, in newly gentrified districts as in long-affluent neighborhoods, were hostile to any new building and disliked subsidized housing most of all.

It did not take long for fissures to open among the gentrifiers. The first wave of New York brownstoners, drawn to the city in search of a racially and economically mixed environment, were challenged in the late seventies by more recent arrivals who did not share their egalitarian politics. Within a few years, the latecomers were organizing their own political clubs and community groups. A similar breach opened in San Francisco after a 40-foot ceiling height was imposed on residential districts in 1978 and downtown office development was capped in 1986. Soon wealthy neighborhoods battled their erstwhile allies over stores and subsidized housing.[26]

In cities with a more conservative political culture, gentrifiers allied with real estate interests from the outset. Dallas preservationists joined in the ruthless expulsion of low-income black residents from a redevelopment area north of downtown and stood by when the city razed nearby public housing. Phoenix, attempting to fabricate an upscale downtown by means of wholesale demolitions, echoed the urban renewal of the 1950s.[27]

The rightward-trending politics of the gentrifying inner city provided an electoral base for the emergence of centrist "new Democrats" in the 1980s and 1990s. This was a group notable for lack of principle, even by the lax standards of American politics. Dick Morris, who rose from Manhattan's West Side to be Bill Clinton's chief triangulator in the White House, is an extreme case, but keeping closer to home was no bar to opportunism. Mayors like San Francisco's Gavin Newsom and representatives of downtown council districts like Washington's Jack Evans forged de facto alliances between upscale nimbys and real estate interests. New building was kept out of wealthy neighborhoods while the developers, denied the most profitable building sites, were compensated with subsidies for development elsewhere. The city as a whole, its coffers drained of revenue, paid the price when this coalition of the comfortable arranged truces in the development wars.

Left-wing opposition to development did not, to be sure, vanish from the scene. As hippie enclaves aged, sharply etched branding brought slow-growth politics to places like Berkeley, Boulder, and the Washington suburb of Takoma Park. The image here was small-scale funk rather than the grit of Greenwich Village or the glitz of Beverly Hills, but it was protected with no less ardor. For not a few residents, their distinctive neighborhoods were not examples for emulation so much as signs of grace, distinguishing the elect from the ordinary suburbanites around them.[28] As gentrification progressed, development came under stringent control. New apartments were forbidden and commercial building strictly regulated. Today one sees retail strips that look like cryogenically preserved remnants of the 1970s.

In recent years, the rise of the antisprawl movement has put resistance to change in conflict with left-of-center social and environmental goals. The antidevelopment consensus has broken down, and battles now rage over redesign of streets and plans for new apartment buildings in old downtowns. Opponents of urban infill are fewer in number, but they have not abandoned the fight. The rhetoric of the environmentalist Left remains on their lips, but the substance of their agenda has begun to converge with the familiar exclusion of old-line suburbs.

The evolution of left nimbyism is exemplified by Zelda Bronstein, a socialist feminist historian who chaired the Berkeley Planning Commission from 2002 to 2004. Among the numerous construction projects she has fought is

The west parking lot at the Ashby BART station, a valuable open space according to some neighbors.
(Courtesy of BART.)

a plan to replace a parking lot at the Ashby BART station with housing and stores. She and other opponents contend that the area around the station—occupied by less than eight dwelling units per acre—is too dense and needs more open space and recreational facilities. "The Ashby BART west parking lot," their manifesto argues, "is, in its funky way, the largest open space in the area."[29]

When Left nimbyism first emerged in San Francisco, the opponents of BART suggested that satellite cities should be built so that downtown would not have to grow. Neither mass transit nor freeways would be needed, they argued, because jobs would be so close to housing that "many people can even walk or ride a bicycle to work." Forty years later, Zelda Bronstein has emerged as Berkeley's leading opponent of bike lanes.[30]

What set off the slow-growth explosion of the early seventies? Some frequently cited explanations don't hold water. Economists frequently think of nimbyism as a means of protecting property values,[31] but homeowners resist commercial rezonings that would raise the value of their land manyfold.[32] Nor are traffic jams the underlying issue; opponents of development projects who complain about overcrowded roads often ask as well for more free parking—hardly a means to discourage driving. And neither congestion nor property values explains why the slow growth movement emerged in the 1970s and not earlier or later.

Neighbors who opposed this hotly contested development in Chevy Chase, Maryland, surely did not fear that their property values would decline.
(Photo by author.)

Other suggested causes have more plausibility. To some degree, the rise of growth control was a reaction to the suburban apartment boom. In southern California, for example, the proliferation of dingbats provoked a wave of opposition. In 1972, slow-growth forces there won control of many towns and put a halt to apartment construction. Parsippany, New Jersey, saw its population double between 1962 and 1967 as five thousand low-end garden apartments were built; it then banned all new apartments.[33]

Another factor was the growth of environmentalism, which emerged as a mass movement in the fifties out of struggles to protect wilderness from dams. Rachel Carson's 1962 bestseller *Silent Spring* raised the stakes. Pesticides, pollution, and overdevelopment were not mere nuisances but a threat to the planet, and preservation of undeveloped land now seemed far more urgent. Upscale San Francisco suburbs, where the slow-growth movement built on earlier campaigns for parks, pioneered growth controls in the early seventies.[34]

The new ecological consciousness gathered influence through the sixties, reaching a peak in 1970 when millions turned out for Earth Day protests across the nation. Joni Mitchell, lamenting parking lots in "Big Yellow Taxi," reached back to Rachel Carson: "Hey farmer farmer, Put away that DDT." Poisons, parks, and parking were all tied together.

Other social forces were at work too, and in retrospect they seem more influential. The sixties upended the hierarchy of social status, giving authenticity a prestige to rival wealth. This reversal outlasted the counterculture that gave birth to it; the new rankings had an economic function to fulfill. In *The Conquest of Cool*, Thomas Frank describes how American capitalism in this period shifted away from mass marketing and tailored its products to distinct market segments. Advertisers aimed to make their brand somehow different from what the conformist masses bought. Customers looked for the designer label; the clothing was an afterthought.[35]

With housing such a large part of the economy and so closely tied to its consumers' self-image, this transition was inevitably reflected in the real estate market. Homeowners sought psychological differentiation in neighborhoods as in soft drinks, clothing, and automobiles. Large suburban houses and their carefully groomed lawns were no longer unambiguous badges of success; the owners risked being classed with the reviled conformists. In one wealthy Silicon Valley suburb, the "semi-rural Los Altos streetscape image" became so important that the city now requires new houses to have plain fronts and look smaller than they really are.[36]

Social status was more precarious than before, threatened from every side. Upscale suburbs already had images worthy of protection; elsewhere new brands were brought to life. By means of house tours, block parties, and civic associations, gentrifiers undertook mental renovations that carved out distinct neighborhoods from featureless stretches of urban decay. Brownstoners resurrected long-forgotten local history to turn pieces of South Brooklyn into Cobble Hill and Carroll Gardens. Districts with polyglot populations gained narrow ethnic identities—the more exotic the ethnic group, the more authentic and the more desirable the new brand. In Chicago's Argyle, a once-thriving Jewish center that now has an Asian flavor, a rabbi promotes Vietnamese shopping and wants kosher delis to go somewhere else.[37]

Run-down suburban subdivisions, too, could assert their unique character. Anything that might carry lower status had to be excluded, and even a big new house, something that formerly only added prestige, might threaten the brand image. The only safe course was to resist all change.

The neighborhoods with the strongest brands were most opposed to growth. The nature of the brand mattered little; expensive old-line suburbs and gentrifying bohemian enclaves were swept up alike in anti-development fervor. In 1970s California, growth control was embraced in both liberal San Francisco and conservative San Diego, but rejected by the characterless Central Valley. Oakland, the place of which Gertrude Stein said "there is no there there," bucked the nimby tide that swept over the rest of the Bay Area.[38]

The apartment boom surely was a trigger, and environmentalism was a genuine force; however, the shift in status hierarchies is the fundamental reason that nimbys flowered in the seventies. Wealth was still something to flaunt in 1967, when a Connecticut town defended its four-acre zoning by saying

"Greenwich is like Tiffany." Three decades later, the similarly upscale suburb of Chevy Chase, Maryland, was fighting against a commercial development that Tiffany would anchor.[39]

Another fifteen years have now passed, and the battle for suburban prestige is waged as tenaciously as ever. Apartment houses are no more welcome than in the 1920s, but authenticity has replaced exclusivity as the rationale for keeping them out.

"How many more generic, developerville town centers do we need?" This, according to the leading opponent of development in the affluent suburb of Kensington, Maryland, is why six-story buildings should not replace gas stations and run-down strip malls. Brand name, for the post-sixties nimby, is better than generic, no matter how shabby the brand might be. "We," our Kensington friend explains, "are just battling for the soul of a place that *already* is different from the surrounding area."[40]

The new nimbyism, essential to stopping downtown highways and urban renewal, proved a very mixed blessing for city life once those battles abated. Opposition to development on the suburban fringe helped limit sprawl; when similar movements gained strength near city centers, they only pushed building outward. And the form of what was built was altered too. While growth boundaries did encourage clustering, other controls made suburbs even more dependent on the automobile.

Quite aside from the specifics of individual disputes, the politics of not-in-my-backyard work against urban vitality. Nimbys are strongest in the most distinctive and unconventional places. Bland, boring suburbs with no brand image let builders in. What gets reproduced is what no one cares about enough to want to keep the same.

8

Spreading like Cancer

Despite the struggles of the 1970s, or perhaps because of them, sprawl moved on. It spread over wider territories. It mutated into new forms. The eye was assaulted by landscapes never seen before. Fields of McMansions sprang up in the countryside, gated communities cowered behind stucco walls, office towers were sprinkled among parking lots.

The outward wave was now propelled by its own momentum. New homes and workplaces, reachable only in a car, dumped traffic back into older neighborhoods. There the fight against change was fought even more fiercely, as the urge to wall out the automotive flood reinforced the sentiment of status-seeking. Development was driven out onto the fringe; highways, widened to carry ever more traffic, became unwalkable; sprawl begot more sprawl.

Planners had come to reject the old orthodoxies. But the new theories, when they made their way into rules at all, were heavily watered down, and what got built seemed little better than what came before. Advertised cures like growth controls and cluster zoning all too often made things worse. Sprawl seemed immune to all attack. It grew like a cancer, ever changing, leaping over whatever obstacles were set in its path, swelling even as the city that gave birth to it shriveled.

By the 1980s the interstate highway system planned in 1956 was nearly finished, aside from canceled urban segments. Yet this gargantuan feat of engineering had hardly banished traffic jams. Housing tracts spread outward along the new interstates, their inhabitants compelled to drive farther and more often. Cars sat interminably on crowded downtown expressways, and backups spread to once-empty suburban streets. More roads, it could be seen, only brought more traffic.

Congestion worsened, but highway construction went on. Interstates got wider and new expressways appeared on maps. Road builders, closely allied with the oil, automobile, and trucking industries and powerful suburban real estate interests, had enormous clout. New roads brought new sprawl and even more driving. The average American drove two-and-a-half times as far in 2000 as in 1960.[1]

The highway lobby did face resistance. The urban freeway revolt had faded, but environmentalists remained on the attack. The Clean Air Act of 1970 empowered the Environmental Protection Agency to block new highways that threatened to pollute the air. Still, even after the law was strengthened, state highway agencies found ways to get around the rules. They claimed, for example, that road widenings would purify the air by getting rid of stop-and-go traffic. They built carpool lanes as a way to clean up. These arguments, however dubious, won acceptance from public agencies reluctant to confront the well-connected road interests.

The new roads had to be paid for, and gasoline taxes rose steadily. The highway lobby, initially opposed to the gas tax, reversed course and went along with a jump to 3 cents a gallon in 1956 to pay for the interstates. After President John F. Kennedy hiked the tax another penny in 1961, increases were avoided for years. But the inflation of the late seventies drove up the cost of new highways, and repair bills mounted as the interstates aged. States were raising their tax rates, and in December 1982 Congress approved an increase to 9 cents in a federal transportation bill proposed by President Ronald Reagan.[2]

The federal gas tax was raised twice more in the early 1990s, but it has not gone up since. In the states, too, increases have lost popularity. Between 1998 and 2008, more than half the states did not raise their gas tax at all, and only five states increased it faster than the rate of inflation.[3] Other trends squeezed revenues as well. As cars got better gasoline mileage, drivers paid less tax per mile. And the spread of suburban superblocks forced traffic onto major arteries and off the local streets built by city and county governments. The indirect subsidy of state highways by real estate taxes shrank, because state highway departments derived a smaller portion of their tax revenue from gasoline consumed on roadways they did not pay to maintain.

As suburbs spread and highways could no longer punch through open countryside, the cost of new roads exploded. Price tags now reach two or three billion dollars for roads that serve just one sector of a metropolis. By the 2000s, highway budgets were in a tight pinch.

The highway lobby was no more deterred by lack of money than by air pollution or its failure to reduce congestion. Money went into new roads, while old ones were allowed to fall apart. States issued bonds to be paid back with future federal aid. New toll roads, rare in the years when federal funds were pouring in, once again made their appearance.

The road builders had largely given up on the centers of big cities, but they still wanted to lay asphalt in built-up suburbs. Here they faced a thorny problem when they tried to justify their plans. When traffic backs up, people drive less than they would if the roads were clear. New lanes added to the highways quickly fill up with trips that no longer have to be forgone, and cars move no faster than before. Spending money on highway construction seems a waste if it doesn't make traffic move faster.

To maintain the promise of congestion relief, highway backers came up with the idea of adding toll lanes next to toll-free expressways. Tolls in these lanes vary from hour to hour. As traffic thickens, the rate goes up so that more drivers will be unable to pay. If you can still meet the price, you get to drive the speed limit.

These toll lanes were quickly dubbed Lexus lanes, and they deserve the name. A study showed that drivers with incomes above $100,000 were four times more likely than those who earn less than $40,000 to have used the toll lanes on their last trip. Tolls can reach levels that seem astronomical to drivers accustomed to free interstates, yet they rarely bring in enough money to pay back the cost of construction. Most Lexus lanes need heavy subsidies.

Highways are thus segregated by economic class, much like suburban neighborhoods. Lexus lanes, by design, serve a minority—if most of the cars were in the pay lanes, the free lanes would move at the speed limit and there would be no reason to pay. The tolls are primarily an allocation mechanism, and only incidentally a source of revenue. Their purpose is to deter those less able to pay from using the new lanes. Those wealthy enough to afford the tolls bypass the traffic jams, while everyone backed up on the free lanes gets to pay the bills.[4]

Not only did the interstates and their clones proliferate, but lesser roadways were dedicated ever more exclusively to automotive use. Those who still tried to walk found little welcome. Children's games were no longer tolerated, even where dead ends and closed loops ensured that traffic would not be blocked. Some states banned street play by law, and there are suburbs where even play on sidewalks is forbidden. In 2000, the Federal Highway Administration announced that "children at play" signs would no longer be allowed—because they might encourage play.[5]

For a new suburban generation, the only way to get around was in a car. In 1969, 49% of elementary school pupils still walked or biked to school; by 2009 the figure was 13%. Instead of walking to friends' houses, children were chauffeured to prearranged play dates. A Rockville, Maryland, mother who allowed her ten-year-old to take the public bus to school risked an investigation for child abuse. Other parents complained to the principal that her behavior was dangerous—in a place where car keys are routinely handed over to seventeen-year-olds.[6]

The layout of new suburbs and redeveloped downtowns reinforced the primacy of the automobile. Wide lanes encourage cars to speed. Pedestrians, forbidden to cross on one side of an intersection, need three green lights to get to the other side. If they reach a corner when the light is green, they face "don't walk" signals timed to pen them in so cars can turn faster. At one suburban intersection—in an area designated for transit-oriented development—crossing the street is a journey of 8½ minutes across twenty-eight traffic lanes.

The curved roadways that Lewis Mumford and George F. Babbitt had so insisted on were now ubiquitous. Even residential streets that carried little traffic widened—room is needed, it is argued, for fire engines to turn around.[7]

There was a subtle but profound alteration in the way street corners are built. Curbs no longer meet at right angles; they swing around in broad curves. It became standard even in cities for the curb to start bending back 25 feet from the cross street. On busy suburban roads, the bend begins even farther from the corner. Those on foot must choose between dangerous crossings of broad asphalt expanses and annoying zigzags to where the road narrows. Cars round the turn at highway speed. The simple act of walking down the street is so perilous that pedestrians are sometimes warned to wear reflective clothing, as if they were in the woods during hunting season.[8]

These changes were no mere whim of car-loving traffic engineers. Behind them stood the lobbying might of the trucking industry.

The truckers had fought for decades to put bigger vehicles on the roads, but they were long stymied by the railroads. A major battleground was Pennsylvania, where the Pennsylvania Railroad held sway over the legislature and limits on trucks were especially strict. A few weeks before the 1950 election, the Pennsylvania Motor Truck Association divided $76,000 between the chairpersons of the state Democratic and Republican parties. It was, the association's treasurer later conceded under oath, like betting on both teams at

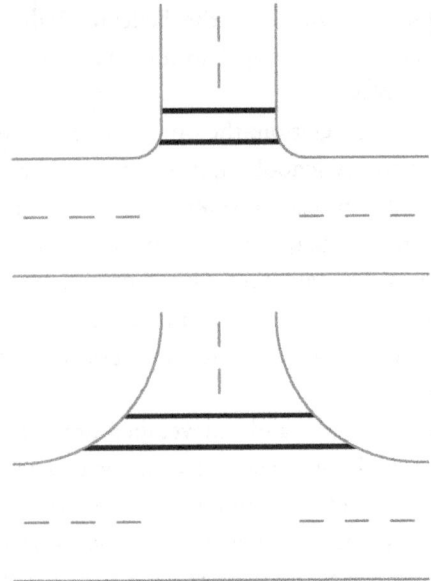

Pedestrian crossings on streets with sharp (top) and broadly curving (bottom) corners.

a baseball game, but he countered that "nothing was hidden, it was all out in the open."[9]

The truckers gained ground in the 1970s as their old antagonists weakened. But they still faced strenuous opposition from local governments and the American Automobile Association. Even highway engineers objected; they worried that bridges weren't built to carry the weight of big trucks. Just before the 1974 election, the Truck Operators Nonpartisan Committee made last-minute campaign contributions to 117 congressional candidates from both parties. Six weeks later, the House of Representatives reversed an earlier vote, and weight limits were raised on interstate highways.[10]

In December 1982, the truckers won full victory. The Reagan administration agreed to their demands in exchange for the industry's acceptance of a tax increase that hit trucks harder than autos. Weight limits were raised again, and state limits on the length and width of trucks were overruled. Tractor-trailers could have trailers up to 48 feet long; soon the limit in most places was 53 feet.[11]

A key provision, not fully understood by critics when the law was rushed through a lame-duck Congress, legalized the big trucks on many local roads as well as on the interstates. Road-builders had a new justification for designs that encourage cars to speed; pedestrians, ignored when the issue was under

debate, were the victims. Lanes grew wider; curbs were pushed back at intersections so that extra-long vehicles could make the turn. And, because it was
written into the statute, the neighbors had no way to object.[12]

As the years went by, builders put up fewer apartments. From 1969 to 1973,
apartments were 38% of all new housing. The ratio dropped sharply when the
bubble burst in 1974, and it never recovered. A smaller multifamily housing
boom came in the mid-eighties, but even at its peak apartments did not exceed
32% of new homes, and in the post-2000 housing bubble they were only one
out of every six units. In 1972 900,000 apartments went up; in the best years
after 2000 the number barely reached one-third of that.

Why did builders switch from apartments back to one-family houses
after moving so eagerly the other way in the sixties? There was no lack of
demand. Economic trends, demographics, and shifting tastes all favor apartments. Single-family houses are less affordable; since 1973 real income has
gone down for people in the bottom half of the income distribution, who
make up the majority of apartment dwellers. There is no greater demand for
yards for children's play; nearly half of all households had children in 1960
but only a third in 2000. And gentrifying neighborhoods, with their row
houses and apartment renovations, show that multifamily living is hardly
losing popularity.

Only the tightening of land use regulation in the nimby era can explain the
falloff in construction of apartment houses. Their builders face stricter zoning,
growth controls, and aroused neighbors.

A telltale sign that regulation is at work is the near-disappearance of the
two-to-four–family house. If dislike of urban living were causing the drop in
apartment construction, two-family houses would stay in fashion—they are
much more like single-family homes than high-rises are. But when rules are
tightened, small rental properties cannot bear the cost of lawyers and paperwork. Census data show that the construction of two-to-four–unit dwellings has fallen off even more than that of larger buildings. In 1972 more than
140,000 new dwelling units of this kind came onto the market; in the best year
after 2000, the number is 43,000.

The latest housing market collapse has hit small multifamily buildings especially hard. In 2010, just 11,400 apartment units of this type were built—only
5000 or so new two-to-four–family structures in the entire United States. Yet
there are willing buyers and able builders for such homes. Even after the bust,
gentrifiers snap up this kind of house in dilapidated neighborhoods. The small
construction firms that did mansionizations during the boom would have no

trouble building two-family houses. The demand is there; only the law stops them.[13]

Homeowner associations, once rare outside the wealthy neighborhoods that could bear their operating costs, moved downscale after the FHA issued its endorsement in 1963. Some localities forced developers to set up associations that would maintain streets, sewers, and parks. The current residents wanted more tax revenue without the cost of maintaining new infrastructure. Only five hundred subdivisions had homeowner associations in 1962; in 1975 the figure rose to twenty thousand; and by 1994 80% of all new housing was subject to these private governments. Architectural review, imposed only by a few high-end developers in the early part of the century, became a routine feature of suburban life. Covenants, never expiring and nearly impossible to change, embalmed neighborhoods with a permanence that the developers and zoners of the 1920s could only aspire to. Constitutional protections of free speech and free assembly vanished when streets and parks were privately owned.[14]

The privatization of the suburban public realm advanced another step with the gated community. By the end of the century, fenced-off subdivisions were ubiquitous in suburbs of the south and west, their walls sometimes lining both sides of a highway. The design impulse behind the superblock was taken to an extreme, with entry limited to a few openings where uninvited visitors could be turned away. Inside the fence, the homeowners association was more powerful than ever, controlling physical access as well as land use and design. And the automobile held residents in a tight grip; with so few gates open, travel by any other means was a near impossibility.

The sales pitch for these subdivisions appealed to emotions of fear and snobbery. The biggest market was retirees. They had lived the suburban migration of the 1950s and watched, usually at a distance, the urban troubles of the 1960s. Retirement communities let no one under fifty-five reside within the gates; those compelled by the vicissitudes of life to raise their grandchildren must move out. Another target group was parents of young children, who had grown up in a tightly controlled world of tract houses and play dates. Observers of gated communities noted the unusual homogeneity of their population, not just economically but racially as well.

Walls and fences provided little real protection against lawbreakers—the crime rate in ungated neighborhoods of similar nature was already low, and barriers did little to lower it. But a vague dread of the different and unfamiliar took hold. Such fear was behind the much-debated death of seventeen-year-old Trayvon Martin in 2012. Martin's killer, George Zimmerman, patrolling an

The central portion of Tysons Corner, the country's largest edge city, in 1980.
(Photo by Scott Boatwright, courtesy of Fairfax County Library, Virginia Room.)

economically hard-pressed gated subdivision in Sanford, Florida, may or may not have been guided by racial animus. But there is no dispute about Zimmerman's first explanation of what made him call the police: "This guy looks like he's up to no good or he's on drugs or something. It's raining and he's just walking around looking about." The gated community was so thoroughly suburban that "just walking around looking about" could be seen as a criminal act.[15]

Workplaces moved steadily out from the city center. Factories had been leaving the cities since the 1940s, eager to avoid city-based unions and in search of more room for spread-out assembly lines. Offices now followed, with corporate headquarters joining high-tech businesses in the flight to suburban office parks. By 1998, only 23% of the jobs in the country's hundred largest metropolitan areas were within 3 miles of the center.[16]

What was happening here? Jobs began moving into the suburbs somewhat later than the spread of residences; it is tempting to think that the purpose of the exodus was to shorten commutes. But the jobs did not go to the same

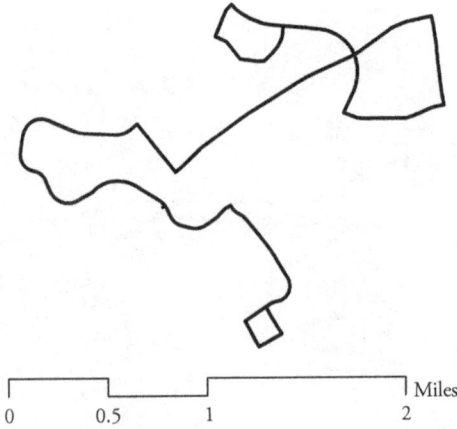

0   0.5   1   2 Miles

A slow bus in and out of suburban superblocks. Montgomery County Ride-On route 83 takes 21 minutes (more in traffic) to travel 2 miles of straight-line distance.

places as the homes. Population spread out fairly evenly around the cities; employment clustered where the housing was highest-priced, in what real estate experts call the "favored quarter." Big shopping malls moved in the same direction; department stores were attracted to people who had spending power.[17]

The most important factor determining where a corporate office moved was proximity to the chief executive's home and golf club.[18] Jobs concentrated near the fanciest houses. In places like Stamford, Connecticut, Mountain View, California, and Bethesda, Maryland, old town centers near rail stations blossomed into urban downtowns. More often, "edge cities" grew up on left-over land near freeways, vast agglomerations of office towers and shopping malls set among parking lots. Tysons Corner, the biggest edge city, borders the expensive Virginia suburbs of McLean and Great Falls; Houston's Post Oak is next to River Oaks; Los Angeles' Century City is across the road from Beverly Hills.

Edge cities forced nearly everyone into cars. They were so dense that cars were unavoidably stuck in traffic, but nearly impossible to reach by any other means. Buses ran, at best, once or twice an hour. They took long detours in and out of superblocks, following routes so twisted that they sometimes looked like they needed tomato sauce. Few but those too poor to own an automobile would put up with the delays.

Even within the superblocks, six- and eight-lane roads ran between the parking lots, nearly impassible on foot. To cross the street to buy lunch, you got in your car. The CEO had a short drive home on back roads and an assistant who ran errands during the day. The lower ranks sat in traffic jams.[19]

It was the market that jammed jobs into a favored quarter, but the consumer was not sovereign in this market. The consumers of office space are the people who work there—and they had no say. Their bosses forced them into long commutes on overcrowded highways. Indeed, when jobs moved to the suburbs to escape unions, the employers' very purpose was to *deprive* workers of a voice in decisions.

As these trends came together, house-building accelerated. Restrictions drove up the price of land, and a self-reinforcing dynamic set in. Houses came to be seen as a financial investment as much as an object of consumption. Rising prices no longer curbed purchasers' demand for dwelling space, as conventional economic theory holds, but stimulated more of it. Financial bubbles emerged in the housing market as prices in many cities soared in the late 1970s and again a decade later. Both booms were cut short by economic recession, but by the late 1990s prices were shooting upward even faster than before.[20]

By now suburbs were no escape from urban ills. Tract housing aged and did not always age well. Traffic often was worse than downtown. Poverty and crime plagued run-down garden apartments.

With unions largely banished, suburbs abounded in low-wage service and construction jobs, and immigrants flocked to them. The working poor, hardly able to afford a car even when they qualified for a driver's license, led a precarious life amid the landscape of strip malls and subdivisions. From a rented room, a dangerous walk along the side of the highway led to a long wait for the bus.[21]

Affordable rentals were scarce, and homeowners struggled to pay their mortgages. Yet it was illegal to divide houses into apartments. In earlier generations, idle construction workers could make up for lost wages by adding rental apartments onto small houses. Now this escape route was shut off. Declining neighborhoods, still zoned single-family long after their veneer of prestige had worn off, were unable to upgrade by the residents' own efforts. They were dragged down by rules meant to uphold their social standing.

Elsewhere, the old formula for escape was still in use. Workplaces leapfrogged to the outer edge of the favored quarter; real estate was cheap, and the boss's drive to work would be against traffic. People moved outward too; the population was whiter, the houses newer, the roads not yet filled up. Exurban subdivisions sought to stand out from the Levittowns, and the average size of a newly built house ballooned from 1785 square feet in 1974 to 2582 in

2008. Large lots and thick foliage created an illusion of rural isolation. Homes were harder to walk to, they were farther from the city, and they were more restricted than ever.

Middle-income buyers, their incomes stagnant, needed generous financing to pay for the big houses, and the pace of building went up and down with changes in the lending market. Savings and loan associations, earlier the main source of private mortgage loans, could no longer meet the demand; they had sought quick profits in commercial real estate after a 1980 deregulation allowed them to diversify and were crushed by the bursting of the speculative bubble that followed. Fannie Mae and Freddie Mac, federal agencies that had been privatized in the sixties, wanted to keep growing, and they filled the gap. They bought up mortgages with money borrowed cheaply thanks to taxpayer backup. The mortgages, in a process called securitization, were packaged into bonds and sold.[22]

Fannie and Freddie could push things only so far. Still somewhat tied to the government, they had rules that deterred overly risky lending. To really blow up the housing market, private enterprise had to work its magic. Wall Street did not shy from this challenge. It took securitization a step further, slicing and dicing loans and sorting the pieces into bonds that were said to be much safer, thanks to the magic of statistics, than the original mortgages.

Repeal of the Glass-Steagall Act in 1999 deregulated banks, allowing mortgage lenders to merge with stockbrokers. New financial giants arose, seeking growth at all costs. The faking of paperwork became routine; lenders and homebuilders had sales targets to meet. Bonuses were paid on what you did this quarter, and, when disaster struck, banks that were too big to fail would be bailed out anyway. The flood of new capital fueled a vast construction boom. By the time it peaked, unscrupulous bankers were encouraging bad loans so they could place bets against them.[23]

Before the bubble ended in disaster, it gave one more push to suburban sprawl. There were few bankers left with the local knowledge to judge the value of a small parcel in a city neighborhood. Wall Street had squeezed them out. A big downtown office tower could still borrow on its own merits, but lesser mortgages had to be assembled into packages and sent out into the financial marketplace.

The rationale for this process rested on large numbers—whether an individual mortgage will be paid is unpredictable, but if bond buyers took the average of enough loans and compared them to similar loans that have already paid off, they could know what to expect. So the securitizers needed mass-produced mortgages, resembling as much as possible the mortgages of years past. To write mortgages that all looked just the same, the big banks wanted little boxes—and not-so-little ones—that all looked just the same. Developers were happy to supply the copycat buildings that eager lenders demanded. Strip malls and office parks lined the highways, all built in the same pattern. South Carolina, seen from the road, could have been California. Stores, offices, and houses were financed by Wall Street number-crunchers who cared only for cookie-cutter buildings that fit the established car-centered mold. The bankers' bonuses rose and fell with their deal-making, so how easily a loan could be packaged mattered more than the value of the property behind it.[24]

Fueled by speculation and financial fraud, the wave of building gathered force and grew to a mighty crest. In the twelve months of 2005, 1.7 million one-family houses were built, a quarter-million more than any year before or since. The houses of the new outer suburbs were bigger and more spread out, and their inhabitants had no choice but to drive more.

In 2008 the flood began to retract. The real estate bubble, already letting out air for three years, collapsed so suddenly that the world's financial system nearly went down with it. Barely a quarter as many houses were built in 2009 as four years before. Prices tumbled, falling most in the new subdivisions farthest from downtown. Some developments were abandoned, half-finished, when builders went bankrupt. Others were awash in foreclosures and empty houses.

The ever-bigger houses of the boom years had been matched with ever-stricter covenants and ever-tighter zoning. Architecture and governance alike were designed for perpetual affluence, and the aftermath of a popped bubble brought troubles no one had prepared for. Soon vigilante patrols were mounted to keep squatters out of empty McMansions. Mosquito control officers sprayed abandoned swimming pools; Lee County, Florida, had so many foreclosures that it used helicopters to find the pools. A gated community outside Atlanta, in the habit of fining residents $250 for planting unauthorized flowers, discovered that it lacked means to shut down a bordello operating in one of its houses.[25]

The great migration was over. A half-decade after the crash, suburban building has resumed, but it will never again be the same inexorable outward surge. The landscape created by the migration remains, embodied in houses, stores, roads, habits, and laws. What we do with that landscape will determine what kind of country we make in the century to come.

9

The War of Greed against Snobbery

At the edge of the metropolis, where tract housing intrudes into farm and forest, local politics falls easily into a time-honored pattern of consensus. Once the houses go up, neither homeowner nor developer wants anything to change. Builders have room to do their work and little need to disturb their neighbors. Keeping past customers happy brings buyers to new subdivisions. Planners do their work in peace, laying out house lots and strip malls.

But the land fills up, the development frontier moves on, and this happy state of affairs comes to an end. The interests that had thrived in harmony now conflict. Zoning constrains the builders who earlier profited from it. Homeowners come to think that new construction injures them: even when there is no physical intrusion, it takes a psychic toll.

Soon one side or the other upsets the political equilibrium, and the pendulum swings sharply back and forth. There are midnight rezonings by lame-duck pro-growthers after election defeats, "temporary" building moratoriums that never reach an end, and the contentious lawsuits that such maneuvers trigger.[1] Builders jump to take advantage of sudden reversals while they can, spraying structures across the landscape in a patchwork that adds to sprawl.

Eventually the balance of forces reaches a stable equilibrium, and the wild oscillations settle down into a steady orbit. New systems of control emerge to reconcile the quest for profit with the striving for social status. Neither free market nor central planning, these arrangements blend law, politics, and economics. Five patterns of governance will be sketched out in this chapter: snob zoning, industrial cities, tollbooth regulation, fiscal zoning, and bureaucratic "paralysis by analysis."

These are pure models, only approximations to a fluid reality. Mixtures are common, and as communities evolve their regulatory systems change with them. Greed and snobbery, moreover, are hardly the only human motivations. Unselfish civic activism, omitted here for clarity, can have great influence. Still, these pure cases are well worth study. Stripping off complexity makes it easier to see underlying mechanisms.

The simplest stable pattern of land use governance is snob zoning. A small locality excludes almost everything other than single-family homes on large lots. Here snobbery trumps greed; the residents' overriding concern is the elevated status of their neighborhood. They do desire higher property values, of course, but not if it detracts from the prestige of the locality.

This works best when the territory is small enough to make internal conflict rare. Elections are rarely contested, and the administrative burden is so light that there is little need for a bureaucracy that might develop interests of its own. The governing body—a town council, zoning board, homeowner association, or historic commission—faithfully executes the wishes of its constituents.

Close approximations to this ideal type are easy to find. They are common in upscale suburbs and in suburban-style neighborhoods within city limits. Locally controlled snob zoning is the dominant form of governance in the wealthy areas around older cities like Boston, New York, Philadelphia, St. Louis, and Chicago. It has proved a reliable tool for resisting change, enabling elite subdivisions to preserve their original appearance for a century and more.[2]

The affinity of small municipalities for snob zoning is on display in the suburbs of New York. In the first years of the twentieth century, the robber barons whose heirs would later frustrate Robert Moses built opulent estates on the North Shore of Long Island. They pushed a law allowing municipalities to incorporate with as few as fifty residents through the obedient New York legislature in 1911, and tiny villages sprang up whose only inhabitants were the estate owners and their house servants. The initial purpose of the maneuver was to keep taxes low and repel outsiders—the villages forbade parking on the few public roads allowed to penetrate their territory.

The children of the nouveau riche mansion-builders had neither the bank-rolls of their forebears nor their passion for ostentatious social climbing, and as the properties were passed on the North Shore began a slow decline. By the late 1930s, the land was worth more as house lots than as estates. The little municipalities then enacted zoning ordinances that forbade construction on lots smaller than 1, 2, or even 5 acres. Today the estates are gone but the villages survive, preserved by zoning rules as heavily wooded enclaves of upper-middle-class privilege.[3]

Other affluent suburbs rushed to incorporate, in states where the law allowed it, as soon as the new zoning powers became available in the 1920s. By the late 1930s, middle-class subdivisions near New York and St. Louis were imitating them. The postwar years saw neighboring communities fighting "border wars" over control of land use and tax revenues, using incorporation and annexation as weapons of battle.[4]

This technique of restricting land use took another step down the social ladder in mid-century California. What was called the Lakewood Plan let owners of the new assembly-line houses run skeletal governments on a tight budget. Lakewood, when established in 1954, was a city of 17,500 newly built houses on small lots next to a Douglas Aircraft plant. The motive for incorporation was to avoid annexation by the adjoining city of Long Beach. Inspired in part by study of Long Island, Lakewood's leaders escaped the burden of paying for a separate administration by contracting with Los Angeles County for fire, police, and other services. Zoning powers they kept for themselves. The device proved effective and was copied across the state.[5]

Houston, often hailed as an outpost of the free market because it lacks a zoning ordinance, is understood more realistically as an extreme instance of snob zoning. Under the Texas statute passed in 1965, covenants may be imposed by majority vote, and they are enforced by the city government. This law makes an unparalleled transfer of power to small districts. Elsewhere only neighborhoods outside the boundaries of the central city can incorporate to gain control of land use; Houston grants this prerogative, clothed in another legal form, even to subdivisions within its borders. The city's affluent districts have not been shy in making use of it.[6]

Long Island's robber barons were not the first to incorporate tiny municipalities and run them as private fiefs. A few clever entrepreneurs preceded them, profiting by the creation of low-tax havens for factories. Some of these cities, like Teterboro in New Jersey and industrial cities around Los Angeles, persist to this day.

Here the profit motive governs, and zoning laws reinforce its rule. Nearly all human habitation is forbidden; only a select few are granted admittance. The residents are carefully chosen, reliable voters picked to ensure reelection of the incumbent officeholders.

Operating like private businesses, these entities market their advantageous legal status to industrial companies. Manufacturers who buy in escape taxation for schools, social programs, and other inconvenient costs of human existence. Factories also avoid the bother of satisfying sometimes exacting neighbors, and they can try to bypass even minimal obligations to public health and safety. When smog first struck the Los Angeles basin in the 1940s, the industrial cities refused to join the remainder of the region's governments in imposing air pollution controls. Only an act of the state legislature that created a county-wide air pollution control district could overcome their recalcitrance.[7]

Vernon, the largest of the California cities that resisted smog control, bears the words "exclusively industrial" on its city seal. Established in 1905, it now contains 1800 businesses and has a budget of $300 million. The founder's grandson, mayor from 1974 to 2009, resigned shortly before being convicted of election fraud. Other top officials, paid salaries running from $800,000 to well over a million dollars, were charged with various diversions of public money and forced out.

Nearly all of the city's fewer than one hundred residents live in city-owned housing, an arrangement that allows the city administration to handpick the voters who keep it in office. The entrenched incumbents take no chances with the composition of the electorate. To ensure that security guards who work the night shift will not claim residence, the city zoning ordinance bans the possession by these workers of even a cot to recline on.[8]

Greed and snobbery, more commonly, are both contenders on the political battlefield. Local politicians are then most comfortable maintaining a steady balance. They can operate the apparatus of land use regulation as if it were a tollbooth where payment, in cash or in kind, is exacted from developers as the price of passage through the barrier of neighborhood objections.

Landowners have a theoretical right to use their land, so payment is not explicitly required. But in zoning as on the highways, routes that bypass the toll plaza are arduous and unpleasant by design. The most common technique for forcing developers through the tollbooth is to zone for much less density than anyone really wants—on land intended for high-rises, single-family houses or strip malls might be prescribed. When someone wants to build, they either apply for rezoning or seek approval of an "alternate" use of the land.

These requests are voluntary in legal form, so the governing body has discretion in granting them. But for the landowner, gaining approval is a practical necessity, because the buildings that the property is zoned for are too small to repay the purchase price of the land.

The amount collected at the tollbooth depends on the wealth and influence of the objecting neighbors; the manner of payment and the identity of the beneficiary vary with the local political culture. Benefits may flow to the public at large, to the objectors, or to the gatekeepers themselves. Concessions to demands issued by the neighbors are normal. A donation, in cash or in kind, is often made toward the expense of local government. Campaign contributions are almost always in the mix, and flat-out graft is hardly unknown. Developers make sure to hire a well-connected lawyer—even when there is no influence involved, an experienced guide is needed to emerge unscathed from the maze of local governance.

The neighbors can be propitiated by a multitude of means. Structures shrink—property owners, knowing that concessions will have to be made, frequently begin by seeking approval for something bigger than what they really want to build. There can be an added measure of prestige: rentals become condos; Safeway gives way to Whole Foods; fine dining displaces drive-throughs. The developer may pay for playgrounds or otherwise improve nearby subdivisions. A zoning lawyer in Philadelphia reports that civic associations sometimes come to him and say, "We like the project, but we don't know what to ask for."[9]

The mechanics of tollbooth regulation vary with the structure of government and the relative strength of the contending forces. Where builders have the political upper hand, the entire process can be scripted. A political consultant's how-to manual for developers offers practical advice along those lines:

> It usually also makes sense in proposing a controversial project to let the mayor appear to wring concessions from the developer, thereby creating political cover for officials to grant project approval. This involves a preexisting *sotto voce* agreement on what the developer will provide, followed by a public demand in the newspaper from the mayor that the developer provide it. After an orchestrated closed-door meeting at which the mayor ostensibly lectures the developer on the project's shortcomings, the developer sheepishly emerges and reluctantly agrees to the mayor's demands, to the applause of the citizenry and local news media.[10]

When greed and snobbery are more evenly matched, government officials find it easier to stand aloof. They handle disputes in much the way Britain once managed wars on the European continent. The zoning board and city council, burdened by heavy workloads and wary of public criticism, hold back while the battle rages fiercely. They keep their powder dry and intervene only when one side is about to collapse. On those rare occasions, they step in to restore the balance of power. This ensures that both parties are tied down in the struggle and neither has enough freedom of action to disturb the overseers' peace. Otherwise they wait until the warring armies reach exhaustion and ratify whatever settlement the adversaries negotiate among themselves.[11]

Yet another variant of tollbooth regulation grows out of the practice of *district courtesy*, common since the earliest years of zoning. Where local legislators are elected by districts, they agree to vote on land-use matters according to the wishes of the member who represents the property in question. This habit, once entrenched, is nearly impossible to eradicate; someone who refuses to go along loses control of what happens in his own district without gaining any influence over decisions elsewhere.

Inherent in district courtesy is a grant of arbitrary power, a temptation even for those of unblemished character. Prince George's County, Maryland, where the practice has a long tradition, illustrates the consequences. In 2010 the FBI raided the home of the outgoing county executive and found $79,000 in cash stuffed in his wife's bra. This might have happened anywhere, but the county's next scandal was peculiar to the district courtesy system. A council member of unquestioned personal honesty went regularly to developers and demanded contributions to community organizations. "You have these people making millions, and all this density and all the traffic [we'd] absorb on Route 1. You mean to tell me you have nothing to help out our schools?" he explained when the practice was exposed.[12]

For many local politicians, continued strife serves self-interest. When every future development approval is at risk in the next election, the continued flow of campaign contributions is assured. Pro-development members of city councils will appoint a resolute slow-growther to the zoning board. This shows impartiality to the electorate, and at the same time it keeps a fire lit under campaign contributors. Less scrupulous legislators have been known to maintain captive civic organizations that spring suddenly to life as indignant nimbys if a builder resists the usual shakedown.

It might seem that tollbooth zoning would not favor any particular kind of development, but this political arrangement tends in practice to promote sprawl. For one thing, district courtesy empowers local interests, and especially nimby homeowners, at the expense of outsiders who want houses or jobs. Beyond that, the magnitude of the toll exacted often depends on the strength of homeowner objections. The fewer the neighbors, the less the expense—a substantial incentive to build near empty land.

The slant toward sprawl affects the nature of new buildings as well as their location. Concessions are negotiated not with the entire community but with the portion that objects most actively. Not only is this group usually composed of near neighbors, but it is also almost always the segment of opinion most hostile to density and most attached to traditional suburban life.

A developer's first priority is to get the project approved; maximizing the saleable square feet comes second; design is where it is easiest to yield. When the negotiation is concluded, the shape of new urban areas has been dictated by the most anti-urban section of the population. Housing becomes less affordable, front doors face away from streets, buildings sit behind a moat of empty parking lots. In the declining industrial suburb of Dundalk, Maryland, for instance, neighborhood activists blocked a street-front mixed-use, mixed-income redevelopment project as they welcomed a plan for a gated enclave of luxury apartments and a marina.[13] The outcome, here as elsewhere, was a de facto collusion of builders and neighbors against the wishes of the larger community.

Avarice is not, of course, a trait peculiar to real estate developers and public servants. Homeowner politics seeks pecuniary advantage along with higher status, and low real estate taxes are a recurrent theme. From California's Proposition 13 in the 1970s to today's Tea Party, tax revolts have found a mass following among the defenders of snob zoning.

The desire for low taxes manifests itself in land-use regulation as *fiscal zoning*.[14] Towns approve only those new buildings that will yield more in real estate taxes than the cost of the public services they demand. This logic favors one-bedroom apartments, unlikely to send children to public schools, over larger apartments, and high-price McMansions over affordable housing. Where local governments depend on sales tax revenues, they subsidize high-volume retail operations. Planners put strip malls and office buildings next to boundary lines, dumping the cost of access roads onto the adjoining town.

Fiscal zoning is a particular temptation for medium-sized localities, with populations of a few tens of thousands. Large enough to have their own schools and services, and thus bear the financial costs of the choices they make, they are still sufficiently small that unwanted uses can be pushed off into the next town.

Recent years have seen an upsurge of fiscal zoning. Inner-ring suburbs, their budgets stretched by economic decline and loss of state and federal aid, are hungry for revenue. Towns compete for cash cows like department stores and factories, offering financial incentives on top of favorable zoning. Bidding wars can grow so intense that the eventual winner gains little new revenue, merely shifting the burden of its taxes from business to residences.[15]

Zoning is now approaching a century in age. As time passes, the rules accumulate detail, and the effort needed to administer them grows unceasingly. Beyond a certain point, the very complexity of the system begins to determine outcomes. Big bureaucracies have tendencies that are independent of the purpose of the apparatus. The most extreme example of central planning, the former Soviet Union, developed characteristic pathologies, and American zoning bureaucracies, when they grow large, exhibit many of the same traits.[16]

Montgomery County, Maryland, although by no means a purebred specimen, vividly displays the behaviors of bureaucratic land use regulation. The county first adopted zoning in the 1920s, closely tracking Herbert Hoover's model legislation. Beginning in the 1960s, an expanding consensus of the county's residents recognized the need for a different pattern of growth, and the county moved gradually away from the suburban model of single-use zones and automobile dependence. Mixed-use downtowns around Metro stations in Bethesda and Silver Spring are outstanding examples of successful transit-oriented development.

To legalize this evolution, the county had to make substantial changes in its land use rules. But single-use zoning was never abandoned. It remains on the books, encumbered with a maze of added rules for approval of large buildings. The system thus created has strong elements of the tollbooth model. What the county wants to see built is specified not in the zoning ordinance but in master plans drafted by a planning board and approved by the county council. When a landowner wants to build, she must return to the planning board for approval of the size and design of each building and the nature and amount of amenities she will provide. Studies, reports, neighborhood meetings, and public hearings multiply—the county's characteristic style is called *paralysis by analysis*.

As the county introduced more urban design concepts, new categories emerged alongside the old ones and an ever-increasing number of exceptions made their way into the rules. When developers and neighbors reached compromises not envisaged in the regulations, still more exceptions and categories appeared. Each step along the way added new complexity. A half-century of this evolution has brought forth a confusing tangle of rules, fully understood by none but a few insiders.

A county of a million inhabitants keeps a large staff of planners busy reviewing new buildings. There is not enough time to keep all the plans up to date, and major revisions occur only when developers' eagerness to build overwhelms the system's inertia.

The saga of a shuttered Dodge dealership shows paralysis by analysis in full inaction. The property is in a mixed-use zone next to the Shady Grove Metro station. But when the area's master plan was adopted, the car dealer was happily selling vehicles and housing was assigned to other parcels. A few years later, Dodge went bankrupt and put the dealer out of business. The land found a buyer who was eager to put up a 417-unit apartment building. This proposal won the support of the neighbors, and it clearly conformed to the county's smart growth policy. But the planning board, its staff reduced by budget cuts, didn't have time for the studies and hearings required for master plan amendments. Even hundreds of new apartments near a subway station were not enough to justify the effort.[17]

The county's steady flow of construction generates so much paperwork that the planning board and county council cannot possibly absorb all the detail. As in Soviet central planning, power inevitably flows downward to the people directly concerned, the only ones with enough information to make intelligent judgments. Overworked low-level staff are happy to accept decisions negotiated between the developer and the neighbors, and no one higher up knows enough to overrule them. Paralysis by analysis empowers the directly interested parties to collude against the wider public, and the same deleterious effects emerge as in the tollbooth model.

Soviet planning is mirrored as well in a bias toward large-scale investments. Buildings on small lots rarely yield enough revenue to repay the cost of studies and hearings needed for approval, and small parcels can't be chopped up into enough pieces to meet all the requirements. Large developments are preferred by regulators, too, because it takes more time to review and approve many little projects than one big one.

As Jane Jacobs emphasized, diversity of ownership helps create lively urban centers. By making urban-style building impossible on small lots, the county forces small landowners to sell out to large developers. New developments arrive in a corporate style, and the public—often the same people who insisted on the lot-size restrictions—complains about their sterility.

The defects of this system come together in Montgomery County's parking rules. The ordinance announces that every housing unit must have two off-street parking spaces and follows with a long list of ways to have fewer. Some reductions are voluntary and some mandatory; all involve expensive paperwork. A builder of apartments above a supermarket near the White Flint Metro station ran into rules that directly contradict each other. Traffic has to be controlled by limiting the number of arriving cars. Yet off-street parking is still required. The owners wind up counting cars entering the garage to prove that no one parks in spaces the county made them build.

In recent years, financial pressures and changing public attitudes have challenged this way of doing things. A rewrite of the zoning code is under way. And an ambitious plan for the White Flint area, adopted in 2010, sweeps away many older rules to replace superblocks and strip malls with high-rises fronting on a grid of streets.

Suburban construction is not the only sector of the economy where status sells. Nightclubs, like neighborhoods, thrive on exclusivity, and both employ gatekeepers to maintain the desired aura. These functionaries—bouncers, doormen, and planners—bring diverse credentials to their work, but they all have the same task. Their job is to keep the riffraff out while carefully trading off revenue against cachet. The balding hedge fund manager with a taste for champagne gets seated in the VIP section for the same reason the office building is allowed to go up along the interstate.

Restricting access to nightspots does little substantial harm. No one is compelled to visit them, and getting shut out brings no physical detriment beyond the loss of time. Clubs, moreover, fill only a small part of the demand for alcohol. If all you want is a beer, there is no need to wait behind a velvet rope.

Housing and jobs, on the other hand, are necessities of life. Land-use controls crop up everywhere, and no one who needs to earn a living or find a place to sleep can escape their grasp. At the zoning board as in the nightclub, the coupling of snobbery and greed fosters wasteful extravagance and unnecessary humiliation. But to be put out on the sidewalk by the sheriff is a very different matter from being detained there by the doorman.

10

A New Thirst for City Life

merica, at the end of the millenium, could seem like one big subdivision. The suburban status-seeking impulse had acquired a life of its own. As it marched down the social totem pole, each layer of society in turn imitated those above. Fed by a vast complex of vested interests, it had swatted away the scorn of intellectuals and the lawsuits of integrationists. It overpowered even the political muscle of the real estate developers who first set it in motion. In city and town alike, single-family houses and automobiles were the unquestioned normal; any other mode of life seemed somehow deviant.

A formidable apparatus of covenants, zoning ordinances, and historic districts protected the residential pecking order. These devices preserved more than neighborhoods; they maintained status distinctions inherited from long-past eras. The 1890s, when city folk looked down on the agricultural masses, lived on in rules against farm animals. The 1920s motorist's disdain for streetcar suburbs imposed off-street parking minimums. Preservation boards continued the 1960s search for authenticity.

But status symbols lose their power when everyone has them. The prestige of suburbia failed to impress those who grew up knowing no other life, and the values of a new generation clashed with inherited institutions. The first challenges to the suburb's superiority over the city came in the sixties with the apartment boom[1] and the beginnings of gentrification. By the end of the millenium, suburban living was clearly losing cachet. Highway builders still poured concrete and zoning boards chased away apartments, but the emotional foundation of the entire structure was rotting away.

Shifting status rankings were reflected in popular culture. The late fifties and sixties were the years of TV sitcoms like *Leave It to Beaver* and *Ozzie and Harriet*. Suburban families lived the only life that was truly normal. A partial return to the city accompanied the gentrification wave of the seventies and similarly petered out in the Reagan years. Then in the late nineties, following the success of *Seinfeld*, Manhattan was glamorized in *Sex and the City* and a flood of other shows.[2] The suburbs were hardly forgotten, but they had a new image; it was a long way from the family in *Father Knows Best* to the one in *The Sopranos*. By 2010 the return to the city could be taken for granted; Manhattan was almost passé as Brooklyn turned trendy.

Status symbols were eroding right in front of the house. On midcentury lawns, homeowners labored to keep lawns carefully mowed and to exclude broad-leafed crabgrass from their precious turf. The intrusive species was such a symbol of suburban living that Kenneth Jackson's history of the suburbs, published in 1985, was titled *Crabgrass Frontier*.

Once sod grew in front of rich and poor alike, it lost prestige. Manicured lawns have hardly disappeared; many homeowners like the look. But they are no longer a national obsession. The war against crabgrass has ended in surrender; people under thirty barely know what Kenneth Jackson's title means. Google in 2009 rented a herd of goats to nibble down the turf around its headquarters, and this once-forbidden practice[3] has become a fad. Cities are changing their laws to allow grazing in residential zones.[4]

Even the quintessentially suburban game of golf is losing its allure. In 2011 in the United States 11% fewer rounds were played than in 2000. The number of golf courses peaked in 2005 and began to decline.[5]

Yet the norms of suburbia remain deeply ingrained. Homeowners still wedded to the old values—among them most civic association leaders and many government officials—find it inconceivable that others might want to live differently. Affluent city dwellers, when too numerous to be ignored, are dismissed as hipsters acting out a soon-to-be-outgrown stage of immaturity.[6]

Suburban nonconformity still meets stiff resistance, with concessions made only grudgingly. Nature lovers let their lawns go to seed, and neighbors demand strict enforcement of grass-cutting ordinances. A Michigan woman, in 2011, was threatened with three months in jail for growing vegetables in front of her house.[7]

Bitter battles erupt between adherents of the now-fashionable "locavore" movement and defenders of the long-standing exclusion of farm animals from residential zones. When Montgomery County moved to legalize backyard henhouses, sharp criticism came from both wealthy Chevy Chase and more modest neighborhoods. At a public hearing, one witness called the proposal "a cultural slap in the face" at African Americans who had grown up poor. With success, she said, "they left behind the poverty and the stigma of racism associated with the chickens. For many that achievement included a suburban single-family home and neighborhood."[8]

Elsewhere zoning boards debate at length the fine distinctions between unproductive pets, which homeowners may harbor, and useful livestock that are proscribed. This last issue came to a head in Belmont, California, which advanced the cause of scientific land use planning by pioneering the separation of pet goats from farm animals. The city's lawmakers adopted a 1600-word ordinance laying down conditions under which pygmy goats of the species *Capra hircus* may be raised in residential zones.[9]

The growing popularity of cities was felt most of all in real estate markets. After a pause of a decade or so, gentrification resumed in force in the mid-nineties. It was now the rule rather than the exception in cities that enjoyed prosperity and good transit. A decade into the new millenium, waves of upscale newcomers had washed across the entire island of Manhattan; reached through San Francisco, Boston, Chicago, and Portland, Oregon; and touched nearly every corner of Washington, DC. In places like Denver and Salt Lake City, a skimpy light rail network was enough to spark a new flowering of downtown, and a few smaller cities like Portland, Maine, managed vigorous revivals with no rail at all. Even in Detroit, where the local economy was worst, residential districts near downtown began to revive.[10]

Once the return of the affluent was a mass phenomenon, city living lost its subversive overtones. Upscale neighborhoods now attract families along with the childless. Lower Manhattan is awash with children; turf battles in Brooklyn bars pit singles against stroller-pushing parents.[11]

Gentrification, as the public sees it, is still the progression from starving artists to granite countertops that urban bohemias experienced between the mid-fifties and the nineties. But that image is out of date; today real estate interests often take the lead. Speculators may jump in first, buying up property even before the neighborhood begins to improve. New apartment buildings can precede renovation of the existing housing stock. The developer, in a gesture to tradition, may kick things off by renting loft-like apartments to

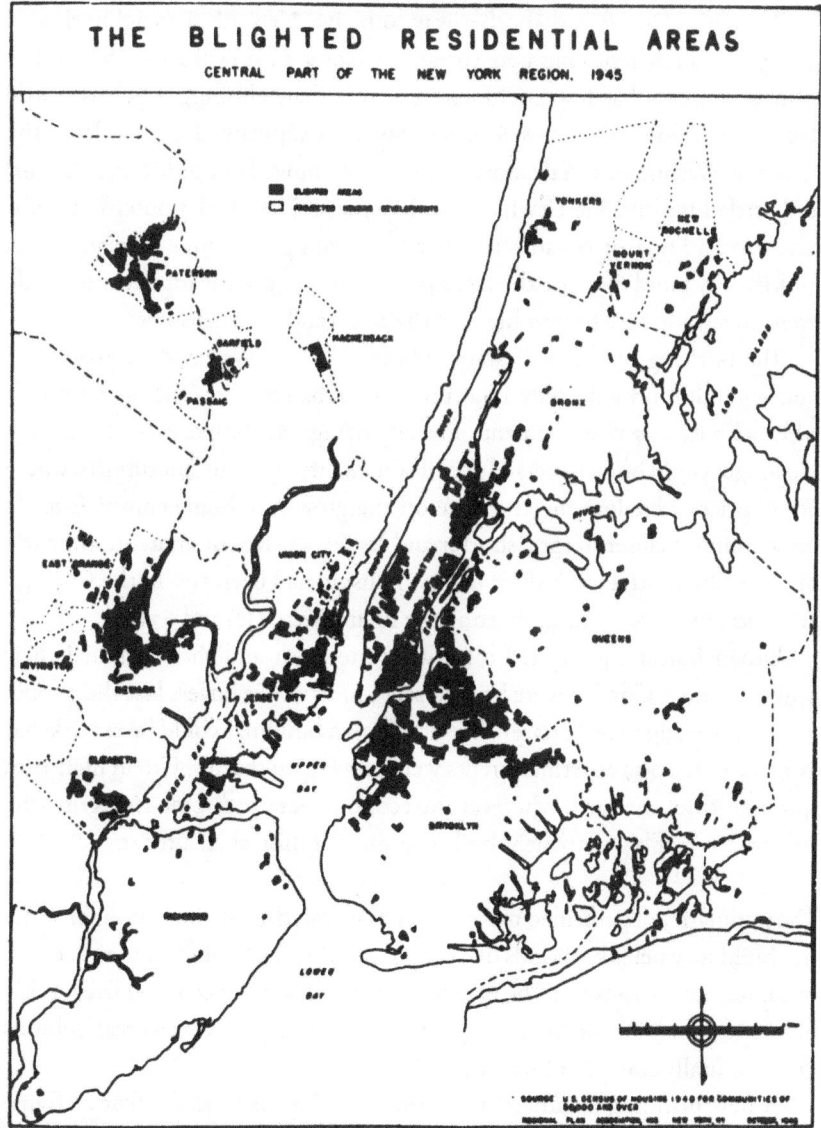

THE BLIGHTED RESIDENTIAL AREAS

CENTRAL PART OF THE NEW YORK REGION, 1945

What are today the expensive sections of New York, Jersey City, and Hoboken were the cities' blighted areas in 1945.

(National Housing Agency map reproduced in Scott, American City Planning.)

artists at a loss. Or the bohemian phase can be skipped entirely—an omission concealed by real estate promoters' habit of decorating their merchandise with status markers that have lost their original function. One comes across "arts districts" whose residents are no more likely to earn their living with paintbrush and easel than a McMansion with a carriage driveway is to have a coach-and-four stabled in the back.[12]

And cities have found another way to revive. New ethnic neighborhoods spring up, often replacing concentrations closer to downtown. New York's Chinatown now has fewer Chinese residents than Flushing, Queens; Little Tokyo, near downtown Los Angeles, has been supplanted by Gardena; the center of Washington's Salvadoran community moved out of Mount Pleasant and settled beyond the city limits in Maryland. New York's outer boroughs have seen a burst of construction activity; immigrants built so many small multifamily buildings that the city's population, in decline for decades, made up its losses and rose to new highs in the 2000 and 2010 censuses.

The bursting of the real estate bubble in 2005 devastated exurban tract housing, but it brought only a hiccup to the urban market. The time was past when a house was an investment; now city living was cheaper as well as cooler. No longer could homebuyers "drive til you qualify" into distant suburbs where house prices were low and then live off the growth in home equity. It made sense to move closer in for a shorter and less expensive commute. In the early nineties, the central city's share of new housing had been 11% in the Chicago area and 18% in New York. By 2008 the figures were 51% and 67%.

Urban housing prices fell a bit after the crash and then resumed their upward course. Condos were hard to sell—prospective buyers lost their appetite for investing in real estate—but downtown buildings could be remarketed as rentals. By 2009 apartment rents were moving up sharply. Urban high-rises sprouted from the earth wherever the economy retained some strength—the construction of big apartment buildings did not drop at all after 2005.[13]

The popularity of gentrified urban districts inspired an obvious thought. Why not build new neighborhoods like the old ones? It was a simple question to ask but not so easy to answer. The nature of the city had been changed irrevocably by the automobile and by zoning; the conditions that let streetcar suburbs grow naturally could not be replicated.

A new planning paradigm was needed; architects were the first to frame one. Andres Duany and his wife, Elizabeth Plater-Zyberk, won a commission in the 1980s to design a resort from scratch on the Florida panhandle, with the freedom to write their own zoning code. Kentlands, a suburban community outside Washington, soon followed. The success of these projects led to meetings with like-minded architects around the country. In 1993 they founded the Congress for the New Urbanism and issued a twenty-seven-point manifesto.[14]

At the heart of the New Urbanism was a root-and-branch rejection of the doctrines that created suburbia. Planning is art, not engineering. Districts of varying density and style, purposefully arranged along a "transect," replace

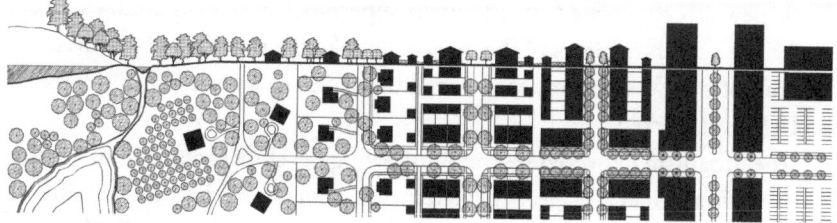

New urbanist transect.
(Courtesy of Duany Plater-Zyberk and Company.)

sprawl. The struggle against "human congestion" is no more; houses are built on small lots close to sidewalks. Walking and transit are preferred to the automobile. Workplaces, stores, and homes stand side by side; all ages, races, and incomes live together.

The creators of the first New Urbanist communities were in no position to take on nimby neighbors and zoning codes. They located in outer suburbs or even in rural areas, giving up the chance to build near transit. But the success of these pioneers showed that money could be made. Other developers followed, men and women with the patience, the political savvy, and the financial strength that it took to redevelop built-up areas.

The capital markets were still set up to finance cookie-cutter buildings, and it did not take long for a standardized, dumbed-down New Urbanism to emerge. By the late nineties, lenders and investors had bought into two conventional varieties of urban-style development.

One was the downtown apartment building with, perhaps, a shop or two on the first floor. In big cities with expensive land, it would be ten to twenty stories high with underground parking. In suburbs and smaller cities, a parking structure would hide behind four or five floors of wood-frame apartments. Where the surroundings were right, such buildings contributed to a genuinely urban setting, and if near a railroad station they added riders.

The other new standard was an odd hybrid, the "lifestyle" shopping center. Its stores were arranged along a pseudo–Main Street with wide sidewalks. The shopping area was surrounded by parking, and buses, if allowed onto the property at all, were kept out of the shopping area and made to stop on the far side of the garage. Still, the owners had at least begun to recognize what the market was looking for.[15]

Developers and architects were learning as they went, and after 2000 their work came closer to the goals of the New Urbanists. Apartment houses filled out the ground floor with stores; lifestyle shopping malls added offices or housing upstairs; infill was built near rail lines instead of subdividing empty land; new streets opened up suburban superblocks; excess parking was cut back. The new showpieces of the movement, like the Bethesda and Clarendon stations of the Washington Metro, had the access to transit that a Kentlands and a Seaside lacked.

The urbanism delivered by trend-following developers was still of varying quality. West Broad Village, launched in 2009 outside Richmond, Virginia, is more than two miles from the nearest bus stop. The row houses that builders advertise as "urban brownstones" are made of wood and plasterboard. A little patch of grid streets is marooned inside a superblock, with houses and stores fronting roadways that dead-end in grass and parking lots. West Broad Village may be no more than a life raft adrift in a sea of sprawl, but it delivers something the subdivisions around it lack. The condos are selling briskly.[16]

Far more successful was the transformation of older suburban downtowns. Market trends brought mixed uses to what had been mostly commercial centers. During the housing bubble, condo prices rose much faster than office rents. Apartment houses were put up on empty lots between the office towers. Here was the diversity of uses that, as Jane Jacobs observed years earlier, somehow works better when it comes spontaneously than when it's planned.

The builders of the new mixed-use areas were carried forward on a current of popular demand, but they swam with weights tied to their ankles. Only after a safe passage through the treacherous waters of negotiations and approvals could they put a shovel in the ground. Along the way they invariably had to compromise urbanist visions to meet the demands of traffic engineers, zoning boards, and suburban neighbors.

So great was the risk and expense of this journey that few embarked on it without the promise of large profits. New Urbanist projects went up, for the most part, in the wealthiest sectors of the metropolis. In less affluent areas— where prospective residents had far more need for the lower cost of living that jettisoning one's automobile brings—developers still adhered to the tired suburban formulas of setbacks and parking lots.

The automobile, once a luxury and now a necessity, suffered the same loss of status as the lawn. Pleasure driving gave way to the killer commute. Carhops were a memory preserved in films like *American Graffiti*; drive-throughs were everywhere. Drive-in movies were nearly extinct. The magic carpet to glamor and prestige had become a ticket to drudgery.

In time, the altered values led to changes in behavior. The miles Americans drive, after rising steadily for a half-century with only brief interruptions for recessions and gasoline price spikes, leveled off in the prosperous years after

2004. Ridership on transit, which stagnated in the eighties and fell during the recession of the early nineties, took off in 1995. The biggest increases were on subways and light rail lines.

Economic factors, especially rising gas prices, helped these trends along, but the underlying causes were cultural and generational. Carpooling continued a long-term decline, the opposite of what would happen if cost were the main reason people drove less. The drop in automobile use, moreover, was almost entirely among drivers under forty.[17]

For a sizable minority of young adults in the new millenium, living without an automobile ceased to carry shame. With fear of global warming growing, it could even be a badge of environmental honor. It was easier, too; car-sharing services offered the convenience of driving a car now and then without the cost and bother of owning one. Some now boasted of being "car-free."

The most dramatic transit revival took place in Washington. In 2000, barely a quarter-century after the city's first Metro line opened, the number of rail passengers surpassed the sum of Boston's subway, light rail, and commuter trains. The city was now second only to New York in total rail ridership. Auto registrations in the District of Columbia dropped 6% between 2005 and 2008, although the population grew 2% and gentrification was driving income levels upward. The downtown commercial office district, confined before the Metro opened to the seven or eight blocks west of 15th Street, spread eastward as far as the Capitol and then leapfrogged south. In-town residential neighborhoods, where auto use had been the norm, evolved into a walking city, and new apartment districts sprang up on the edges of downtown.[18]

The biggest growth in transit use was not for traditional commuting into downtown but for nonwork travel. This reflected a shift in lifestyle as people no longer organized their lives around the automobile. Between 1999 and 2010, the number of people boarding the Washington Metro during the morning rush hour—a good measure of commuting travel—increased 34%. Over the same period, ridership increased 64% on Saturdays and Sundays.[19]

Train travel from city homes to suburban jobs spiked upward. Reverse commuting on New York's commuter rail lines doubled within ten years, while the number of such trips taken by car barely budged. This was cultural change, not demographics. Affluent new residents of downtown neighborhoods could easily have afforded cars and suburban houses, but they chose city life and trains instead. By 2011, the international banking firm UBS was thinking of relocating its offices from Connecticut back into Manhattan. In the suburbs, explained a city landlord, "they just can't hire the bankers and traders they need."[20]

By the end of the 1970s the destruction of old trolley lines was nearly complete. Less than 200 miles of track in seven cities remained. Most survivors were routes that ran in tunnels beneath downtown streets; this was the case in Boston, Philadelphia, Newark, and—after the 1973 completion of the BART subway—San Francisco. Cleveland's trolley ran through downtown in a trench; Pittsburgh's passed through a tunnel south of town. Only in New Orleans did streetcars still run entirely at ground level.

Northern Europe had not abandoned its streetcars, and its cities, like San Francisco, were upgrading old networks by moving them off the street. American transportation planners, troubled by the high price tags of the subway systems then under construction, saw these hybrid systems as a less expensive alternative. They coined a new term, *light rail*, to describe them. Powered like streetcars by overhead wires, light rail would be separated from car traffic as much as possible, but costs would be held down by running, most of the time, at ground level with traffic lights at street crossings.[21]

The first new light rail line in the United States was in San Diego. This rapidly growing city had studied transit options for years, but in a heavily Republican region that was still building freeways there wasn't enough money for anything like San Francisco's BART. An opportunity to do something more affordable arrived suddenly in 1976. A tropical storm destroyed a freight rail line that ran from near downtown to the Mexican border, and the local transit agency quickly bought the right of way. It rebuilt the single track and opened service in 1981. The "Tijuana trolley" was an immediate success, and within three years a second track was needed. Extensions to the east and north followed.

The San Diego model—trains moved slowly on downtown streets but sped up in the suburbs where they had their own right of way—was an attractive compromise between cost and speed. It found many imitators, especially in western cities with little tradition of transit use and few of the dense old streetcar suburbs that could generate walk-on riders in large numbers. A succession of cities opened lines that expanded into networks: Portland in 1986; Sacramento and San Jose in 1987; Los Angeles in 1990; and Denver, Dallas, and Salt Lake City later in the nineties. By 2010 there were twenty-six cities with light rail systems; route mileage had nearly quadrupled in three decades.

Congress gave transit a victory in 1991 by allowing the transfer of highway money to rail projects virtually without limit. But almost nowhere did states use this new authority. Denver, Dallas, San Diego, and Salt Lake City still built freeways; they paid for light rail with sales tax increases pushed through by alliances between downtown business interests and environmentalists.[22] The new rail lines revived these cities' fading downtowns and stimulated New Urbanist development around outer stations, and they were immensely popular. Yet they only modestly deflected the overall direction of growth. The bulk of new jobs and housing still went to the car-dependent suburban fringe.

In Portland and Sacramento, light rail lines took the place of canceled freeways. The greatest change in urban form occurred in Portland, where the growth boundary constrained sprawl. Los Angeles, too, turned in a more urban direction as the force of demographic change and the public's craving for rail overcame the frictional resistance of endlessly squabbling politicians. Immigrants remade former automotive suburbs, and riders poured onto trains and buses.[23] But California lacked Oregon's state-level land-use controls, and the real estate boom brought an explosion of exurban sprawl alongside the downtown revival. Los Angeles and Sacramento are now cleaning up after burst bubbles of McMansion-building in their outer reaches.

New light rail lines were built in older eastern cities too. In Jersey City and Hoboken, where light rail connected to older rail tunnels under the Hudson to New York, a high-rise boom town rose on a decrepit old waterfront. In St. Louis and Buffalo, with much weaker economies, new rail access supported a modest gentrification in neighborhoods near downtown.

Transit would not remake a city if you couldn't walk to the station. But the traffic engineers' premise that roadways were for cars was by now a widely held belief. The idea that streets should be designed for other purposes was slow to take hold.

The earliest corrections of past mistakes were removals of urban expressways. The first highways to go actually collapsed on their own—New York's corroded West Side Highway in 1973 and San Francisco's Embarcadero Freeway, trigger of the revolt against the interstates, in a 1989 earthquake. Voters saw that the absence of the highway did not bring traffic gridlock, and after pitched political battles the elevated expressways were replaced with surface boulevards. These examples were contagious—highway demolition led to neighborhood rebirth—and after 2000 cities began to experiment gingerly with the removal of highways that still functioned.[24]

But lesser streets were slow to change. Outside the densest cities, those who walked had little voice. In old automotive suburbs with rapidly changing populations, immigrant pedestrians risked life and limb on roads engineered for the rapid movement of native-born drivers. New suburban transit stations were often ringed by parking lots and high-speed roadways, discouraging all but the poorest or most committed from reaching them on foot.

Bicyclists were far better organized than pedestrians, and they had worked for decades to have their needs recognized. They succeeded, at first, mostly in getting off-road bike trails that were designed for recreation and served few commuters. John Forester in the 1970s had introduced the concept of vehicular cycling—the idea that bicycles could often move faster and more safely by sharing traffic lanes with cars rather than on separate pathways where they were vulnerable to collisions with turning cars. Cyclist organizations pursued this idea, but they made little headway in getting traffic engineers to accept the idea of designing streets for nonmotorized users.

In 2003, bicycle advocates broadened the idea of bicycles in traffic lanes into the "complete street," a roadway designed for all of its users, pedestrians as well as cyclists. The slogan took hold far faster than the reality. By 2010, more than a hundred places had written policies endorsing complete streets.[25]

These ideas were put only slowly into practice. It took two high-profile city transportation commissioners to shake things up. Janette Sadik-Khan took charge of New York's streets in 2007, and Gabe Klein followed a year later in Washington. Soon cars were giving up space downtown to make room for wide sidewalks, and new bicycle lanes were fenced off from moving cars. Klein trumpeted the new approach with a high-profile bike lane down the middle of Pennsylvania Avenue from the Capitol to the White House.

Even more visible was Sadik-Khan's remaking of Broadway, for the previous century a four-lane avenue where the car was king. Through most of midtown, cars were now limited to one through lane. One lane was reserved for bikes, and pedestrians got space to walk and sit. Times Square, long renowned for its jammed sidewalks, became a vast pedestrian plaza that cars could enter only when passing through on cross streets.[26]

Elsewhere change rarely went as far. Palm Beach County, Florida, which did more than most suburbs, shows how far there is to go. The county calmed traffic in a few of its scattered downtowns, but these are small corners of a sprawling suburban domain. Elsewhere it continues to build six-lane highways with no on-street parking, 50-mile speed limits, and turn lanes at nearly every corner. Sidewalks jut up against the roadway, separated from stores, homes, and hospitals by walls and ditches. Narrow bike lanes painted next to high-speed traffic are little more than a futile gesture.

In the nineties these trends—the return to the city, New Urbanism, the transit revival—converged with long-standing worries about sprawl.

Broadway at 41st Street, with former traffic lanes now used by pedestrians and bicycles.
(Photo by Jim Henderson.)

Bicycle lanes are a futile gesture when placed amid forty-five lanes of motor vehicle traffic. Forest Hill Boulevard and State Route 7 in Palm Beach County, Florida.
(U.S. Geological Survey photo.)

Environmentalists, facing the menace of global warming, desired more than ever to curb the use of cars. To escape from the political trap created by the failure of growth controls, they sought a new synthesis.

They dropped the slogans of "no growth" or "slow growth" in favor of a new theme of "smart growth"—the idea of accepting new building and directing it into compact, ecologically sustainable nodes where people can get around without driving. The smart growth advocates reached out in two directions, building coalitions with rural preservationists and urban real estate interests. Seeing how sprawl had leapfrogged over local growth controls, they made their push at the state level.

The idea, but not the name, was pioneered in Oregon. State planners, given a veto over local zoning rules by the 1973 growth boundary law, insisted that cities allow at least half of new housing to be apartments and townhouses. In the Portland area, home to half the state's population, rules promoting multi-family housing were further strengthened in 1990 and 2000.[27]

Maryland put smart growth on the national agenda. In 1997, Governor Parris Glendening proposed an initiatiye of that name, aimed at controlling sprawl by concentrating growth in older neighborhoods. Growth boundaries and state review of land use rules were out of the question politically—local zoning was defended by rural development interests and suburban home-owners alike—but Glendening managed to push a weaker concept of "priority funding areas" through the legislature. As in Oregon, each county would draw a line around the areas designated for development, and the state would pay for roads, schools, and other infrastructure only within the boundary. Glendening held office for another five years, and state funds were redirected toward urban centers.[28]

The smart growth movement has spread around the nation, winning support from both left and right. But its legislative achievements have been modest. Advocates have secured the passage of growth management laws in many states. But in Maryland and elsewhere, politicians hesitate to challenge local control of zoning. It is now three decades since any legislature empowered state planners to overturn snob zoning rules.

The political climate is not hospitable to new directions. The public openness to social reform of the 1960s and 1970s is long gone. With growth controls under constant assault from the right, environmentalists hesitate to grant power to unelected state officials; they fear it will be used not to promote urban revival but to override protections of rural land. Conservative office-holders fear to pit their business backers against homeowning constituents. Change in laws comes far more slowly than in the marketplace.

11

Backlash from the Right

By the end of the millenium planners and downtown developers had embraced smart growth. People in their twenties and thirties flocked to cities. But urbanism did not lack for enemies.

A long-established principle, the social superiority of single-family houses, was in question. Neighborhood activists, wedded to the status quo, were numerous and vocal; the nimby worldview had deep roots in the branded neighborhoods of the postindustrial economy. In a world of growing income inequality, the wealthy strove to separate themselves from the merely well-off, and the marginally affluent struggled to stand apart from the poor.

New Urbanists tried to mollify their critics by pointing out that no one wanted to get rid of traditional suburbs. They insisted that they sought only to open up additional choices for those who wanted them. But this missed the point. A world of smart growth might let owners of single-family houses keep their structures, but it deprived them of their privileged place in the residential pecking order.

Economic interests that profited from sprawl were at risk as well. They had money, and they knew how to use it in politics. The highway lobby, always dependent on government contracts, was adept at keeping those contracts coming. The developers of tract subdivisions lived by their ability to influence local governments and their land-use rules.

These two forces—homeowners and politically connected businesses—could be stronger joined together than either could on its own. Neither grass-roots protest alone nor backroom influence-peddling could turn back the smart growth tide; lobbying needed electoral backing. Protecting the status quo of sprawl required an alliance, and the alliance would need a political program to mobilize the homeowner masses.

Experienced partisans were at the ready, prepared to fill this demand. Beginning in the 1970s, foundations and research institutes funded by the Mellons, the Kochs, and other wealthy conservatives had nurtured a cadre of far-right public policy experts.[1] For these ideologues for hire, smart growth was a business opportunity. The real estate industry had already turned to them for arguments against growth control. They now jumped at the chance to target public transit too.

A separate group of anti-transit consultants was already in the field—they had entered the market niche opened up by referendum battles over light rail. Once the Smart Growth movement took off in the late nineties, the right-wing network invited the rail critics in. Sam Staley became deputy director of the Reason Foundation; Wendell Cox received part-time appointments with both the Heartland Institute, a center of global warming denial, and the Heritage Foundation; Randal O'Toole wound up on the staff of the Cato Institute.[2]

How would these advocates frame the issue? Development battles, up to then, had been fought largely on local issues. Without any general principles to call on, opponents of smart growth had no good way to explain what they disliked. Open avowals of status-seeking had always been rare, and other rationales had problems of their own. The ecological argument for growth controls in particular had to go; environmentalists were now on the other side.

Defenders of suburbia could still say that a "way of life" was under attack. But the argument had to be made carefully—the way of life must be something loftier than keeping people with less money out of the neighborhood. The right-wing think tanks, specialists in protecting wealth and privilege by waging culture war, knew what to do. They drew up a case for sprawl that rests overtly on population statistics and economic theories but conveys an underlying cultural and emotional message. The single-family suburb embodies true Americanism, under attack by an alien cultural elite.

There was nothing new in this maneuver; appeals to conformism and nativism have long buttressed the single-family neighborhood. Already in 1922 George F. Babbitt, Sinclair Lewis' fictional realtor, denounced long-haired professors and invoked American supremacy. After World War II, Senator Joseph McCarthy held lengthy hearings where builders denounced public housing as un-American and contended that rental apartments breed communists. For Governor Thomas Kean of New Jersey in 1983, a court decision that allowed lower-income housing in exclusive towns was moving toward "a socialistic country, a communistic country, a dictatorship."[3]

Now that the prestige of suburbia is past its peak, the same themes play to anxieties of declining status. Cox, trained as a demographer who calculates numbers, calls his book on sprawl *War on the Dream*. Robert Bruegmann, himself a professor of art history, disparages the smart growth movement as an elitist revolt against the healthy masses. Joel Kotkin tells us that California is waging "war against single-family homes" on behalf of "aging hippies who made their bundle during the state's glory days and settled into places like Mill Valley."[4]

The conservative defenders of sprawl were adept at pushing these emotional buttons, but they had a logic problem to deal with. The fundamental tenet of their libertarian think tanks is that government may not tell property owners what to do with their property. But suburbia has little to do with the free markets that libertarians claim to believe in. Covenants, zoning, subsidies, and exclusions created it and kept it alive.

It wasn't just principles that libertarians had to ignore when they made the case for sprawl—there were facts, too. In gentrifying downtown neighborhoods, and at transit stations in upscale suburbs, property values have spiked upward and apartment construction has surged. This puts the critics of smart growth in a bind. In the market worldview, it is an article of faith that prices reflect consumer preferences. The rising price of urban real estate irrefutably contradicts the claim that suburban sprawl is where people want to live. It's hard to argue that the market's wrong when you start from the premise that it's always right.

The core of the problem is suburban land tenure—the homeowner's power to control what happens on a neighbor's land. The entire edifice of free-market economic theory rests on the supremacy of consumer choice. But in the single-family suburb a collectivized status-seeking apparatus overrides the preferences of individual property owners.

To be accepted in the conservative network, writers must defend suburban land tenure yet appear to uphold the doctrine of the sovereign consumer. It isn't easy. Robert Bruegmann tries to justify zoning as an exercise of consumer sovereignty, empowering people to choose how and where they live. Liberal critics of suburbia, as he sees things, fail to appreciate how much ordinary people value choice.

This point is illustrated with the example of a woman who takes three buses from a trailer park in central New Jersey to a low-paid job at Newark Airport. Sprawl, Professor Bruegmann argues, gives her the benefit of choosing to live in the trailer park. The reader can only guess what he would think if the woman's hometown outlawed mobile homes. The professor has no grounds for objecting to the change of rules—the rezoning would be an exercise of consumer sovereignty, just like the snob zoning that first made the bus odyssey necessary. Now that the airport worker is homeless, his logic would suggest, she has more choice, and so she's better off than before. Before there was only one trailer park—now she can choose among so many trees to sleep under![5]

Bruegmann at least makes an effort to reconcile land-use controls with consumer sovereignty; many of his cothinkers simply ignore the contradiction. Randal O'Toole tells us that he first turned against smart growth out of outrage that his neighbors might be allowed to build multifamily housing on land they owned—when government failed to impose a ban, he contends, it was impermissibly telling people how they should live. Wendell Cox denounces nimbyism and exclusionary zoning when they stop suburbs from being built and lets them pass unnnoticed when they keep suburbs from changing into something else.[6]

Joel Kotkin, as he looks fifty years ahead, takes more pains to cover his tracks. "In the 21st century," he assures us, "families and businesses will have ever more freedom to locate where they wish." Kotkin goes on to denounce urbanists who want Americans to be "crammed into high-density communities." The good news, he reports, is that the future will be Phoenix and not Boston; "resistance from largely lower-density communities close to the core" will save the cities from cramming. Kotkin carefully navigates around the means by which this resistance makes itself felt. In a 243-page book about land use, the word *zoning* never appears.[7]

Prosprawl theorists could get only so far by ignoring zoning. Their mass constituency, the preservers of the single-family neighborhood, expected an active endorsement of their most powerful weapon. Yet the thinkers could not abandon the deregulatory agenda of their funders. They needed a supple doctrine, one that condemns antisprawl land-use rules as intolerable interference with the free market yet explicitly endorses exclusionary zoning.

It was no mean feat to devise a coherent argument in support of two propositions that so manifestly contradict each other, but the right-wing think tanks specialized in this sort of intellectual gymnastics. A 2001 manifesto called the Lone Mountain Compact laid out the orthodox defense of sprawl. The leading transit opponents joined academics and a scattering of right-wing luminaries as signers.

The manifesto starts out, as expected, with ringing affirmations of the free-market faith. "The most fundamental principle is that…people should be allowed to live and work where and how they like," and "Densities and land uses should be market driven, not plan driven." Such principles might logically have led into a defense of property owners' right to build as many apartments near transit stations as tenants want to rent.

But here it takes a detour. The Lone Mountain Compact does not reject all constraints on landowners' right to develop their property—it condemns only those that are "centrally directed." It's just fine for small wealthy enclaves to infringe on property rights by zoning out apartment buildings. Even better if renters are denied the right to vote on these rules: "Local neighborhood associations and private covenants are superior to centralized or regional government planning agencies."[8]

This was a deft maneuver. As libertarians, the compact signers could distinguish deed covenants, agreements entered into voluntarily, from growth controls imposed by law. But after carefully drawing a sharp line between private contract and government fiat, they immediately rubbed it out. Zoning, they decided, is acceptable when imposed by small townships where everyone owns property, because there it works in practice like a covenant. There was no need to spell out what it is the two have in common—the denial of voting rights to the people who are kept out. Land-use regulation, Lone Mountain doctrine holds, is not evil per se. It's wrong only when it's enacted democratically for the benefit of the whole community.

Peter Gordon, a more systematic thinker than other Lone Mountain signers, makes the exclusionary logic explicit. Gordon concedes that individual landowners cannot always be free to use their property as they want; some form of collective governance is unavoidable. What he objects to, as a matter of principle, is democracy; dollars, not people, deserve to vote. "The very features that may give political institutions strength at the same time create severe problems," he complains. "Voters are often not landowners (e.g., the 80 percent renter population in the politically active city of Santa Monica, California). Many zoning decisions negatively affect landowners."[9]

In any case, the libertarian distinction between laws and covenants hardly stands up to scrutiny. Consider the buyer of a house in the planned community of Columbia, Maryland. The deed she signs binds her to rules James Rouse established in 1963. That is a free consumer choice, the doctrine holds, while growth controls elsewhere in that state are an assault on liberty. But this is a difference in form alone. The Columbia homeowner association can be escaped only by leaving town, and the same remedy is open to those who dislike the land use rules of local governments.

For that matter, Maryland itself was established as a private enterprise. Lord Proprietor Cecil Calvert and his heirs ruled the colony, granted to them by the king of England. Settlers who bought their land became subject to their government. These purchases, for white residents at least, were as voluntary as any other real estate transaction; the colonial government rested on the same basis of consent as today's Columbia Association. Today Cecil Calvert and James Rouse are equally dead. After Calvert's passing, however, the events of 1776 intervened, and only Rouse's government still operates under the law of real estate. That, if you follow the libertarian reasoning to its logical conclusion, is a misfortune; the people of Maryland would be freer if George III had won the war and the state was administered as a private corporation.

The arguments might be frail, but they serve their purpose. The political and legal campaign against growth controls under way since the 1980s has a rationale. The movement's slogan is property rights, and its central aim is to win compensation for landowners prevented from developing their land. But its targets were carefully marked off—single-family zoning was left alone.

The political ground zero of this campaign was Oregon. Landowners outside the state's growth boundaries organized as Oregonians in Action to overturn the rules. Large timber interests paid many of the bills, but the message was the populism of the right-wing think tanks. Growth control backers, the group's lawyer said, "are intellectual elitists, driving with their tops down in their Saabs, drinking Chardonnay." [10]

When Oregonians in Action went into action, the principle of property rights had only selective application. In 2001 the organization tried to overturn zoning rule changes that, by allowing more apartments to be built on vacant land within the growth boundary, enlarged the rights of landowners. Its 2004 property rights referendum, approved by the voters but overturned in court, explicitly exempted from its scope all zoning rules older than the state's 1973 growth boundary law. The right to property, in practice, was the right to build single-family houses and nothing else. [11]

The property rights movement's legal strategy yielded mostly losses, but the courtroom successes it did achieve had the same selective effect as its political action. One partial victory was the 1992 case of South Carolina developer David Lucas. The Supreme Court decided that while no compensation is due when government restricts the way land is used, owners must be paid if no use at all is permitted. This ruling left local governments free to promote sprawl with single-family zoning but limited their power to restrain it by stopping development altogether. The limitations were not severe—later cases narrowed the impact of this ruling—but they were one more obstacle in the way of sprawl control.[12]

The movement pressed on in the face of legal defeats, and it was able to score political wins. Some western states passed laws that required compensation for "partial takings"—regulations that limit the use of land. The Republican tide of 2010 brought further gains. In Florida, a new right-wing governor and conservative legislature repealed very mild growth controls that had been enacted in 1985.

The rise in 2009 of the Tea Party, which married dislike of cities to fervor against government, enlarged the grass-roots base of the campaign against growth control. A movement where calls were heard to keep government out of Medicare was hardly bothered by the inconsistency between deregulation and tight suburban zoning. Donna Holt, the leader of Ron Paul's Campaign for Liberty in Virginia, worried that rural landowners will not be able to sell their farms to developers if housing is built in cities. "Infill development and vertical sprawl are overtaxing urban environments," she warned. Holt urged fellow believers in the free market to oppose "restrictive zoning" that forbids tract housing. At the same time, she encouraged bans on the building of apartment houses—such zoning, somehow, is not restrictive.[13]

The Tea Party's attention soon turned to a 1992 United Nations resolution called Agenda 21. This lengthy document, little known until it drew the ire of Tea Party activists, exhorts member nations to conserve open space through denser growth. It suddenly came under attack as a nefarious plot. As one activist describes it, Agenda 21 is "the action plan implemented worldwide to inventory and control all land, all water … all information, and all human beings in the world."

Exposés spread through Tea Party networks and made their way onto Fox News. Glenn Beck wrote a novel titled *Agenda 21* that starts out, "They took Mother away today." Denunciations of apartment houses and bike lanes as elements of a worldwide conspiracy flooded into zoning boards and town councils.[14]

By 2012 the outcry became Republican Party dogma. In January the party's National Committee passed a resolution that denounced Agenda 21 as a threat to "the American way of life of private property ownership, single family homes, private car ownership and individual travel choices." Later in the year the party's election platform denounced the Barack Obama administration for "replacing civil engineering with social engineering as it pursues an exclusively urban vision of dense housing and government transit." Residents of apartments and townhouses were, by implication, un-American, especially if they went to work on a bus.

Here the cultural agenda of the Tea Party was manifest. As much as the campaign against Agenda 21 advertised itself as a property rights movement, what it really sought is enforced uniformity of living arrangements. Zoning rules are good when they force people to live in single-family houses by denying landowners the opportunity to build other kinds of homes. Only regulations that keep land undeveloped are evil.

Not all right-wingers place political convenience above intellectual rigor. In the last decade a school of libertarian urbanists has emerged, propounding a free-market case against sprawl. Harvard economist Edward Glaeser, a paragon of careful empirical research, sees density as almost a cure-all for urban problems. For others in this group, such as Michael Lewyn and Stephen Smith, deregulation allows a variety of living arrangements to emerge and frees consumers to pick whichever pleases them.[15]

These writers offer trenchant critiques of current land-use rules and useful suggestions for reform, but their version of libertarian theory shares an underlying flaw with the prosprawl variety. Both ignore status-seeking. The premise of free-market economics is that markets are efficient because they set people free to choose what they buy and how they use what they buy. But the market for land and buildings is full of people who choose to deny their neighbors choice by excluding buyers and preventing use. Such markets free some by fettering others.

The libertarian urbanist vision, in its pure form, is even less plausible than the left-wing dream of a world without acquisitiveness. To reach either utopia, human motivations must change. Socialists can make a moral argument for "share and share alike." What rationale can libertarians offer for "greed is good, snobbery bad"?

In any case, the market urbanists' independent thinking is of little interest to the conservative establishment. In the right-wing research-propaganda complex, nothing is more important than staying on message. Discipline is enforced so strictly that the Heritage Foundation shut out its own founder's point of view. Paul Weyrich, until his death in 2008, was a fervent advocate for railroads and especially for light rail. A cultural conservative rather than a libertarian, he argued that neighborhoods built around train stations would "foster a sense of community... to uphold morals and maintain standards of behavior." Weyrich had to advocate for light rail from his Free Congress Foundation, not much more than a one-man operation; Heritage promotes the views of Wendell Cox.[16]

Smart growth threatened road builders as much as subdividers. The highway lobby had long taken a decidedly nonideological approach to politics, relying on a shower of campaign contributions that fell generously on incumbents of both parties. But as circumstances changed, the pavement people began to find right-wing religion. As early as 1977, conservative writers had complained of a war against the car. "The war against automobiles is never-ending," the political scientist James Q. Wilson wrote in 1998, and from then on the slogan repeated in a steady drumbeat.[17]

Where the property rights movement was at first orchestrated from top down, the defense of the automobile was more spontaneous. After seven decades of suburbanization, the idea that motorists possessed an exclusive right to use streets was built into the landscape and inculcated in public consciousness. Everything in the suburban environment said that roads were made for motor vehicles alone. Drivers were quick to pick up the theme of "war on cars" and run with it whenever they felt inconvenienced.

The cultural subtext of the automotive backlash is easiest to discern in the vehemence of attacks against bicycles. It is hard to make a reasoned case against bikes; they waste no one's money and abridge no one's freedom. The most one can say is that cyclists violate traffic laws, but it would be hard to find a complaining driver who never exceeds a speed limit or rolls through a stop sign. Deprived of rational argument, the various strands of anti-urbanism erupt in an explosion of status anxiety. Each uses its own language to express the same disdain for the lower orders who want to share the public roads.

Urban cyclists are belittled as "hipsters"—low-income immigrants make up a large share of cycle commuters, but they pose no threat to social standing and thus are invisible to the critics. When bike riders fail to show motorists the expected deference, they are "smug" and "self-righteous." The only motorists so labeled are Prius owners, as if no one buys a Mercedes or Cadillac to show off.

According to a Tea Party Republican candidate for governor of Colorado, short-term bicycle rental in Denver is part of the Agenda 21 strategy to rein in American cities. From a more cosmopolitan starting point, a Jaguar-driving *New Yorker* business writer reached a similar conclusion. Admitting an "emotional reaction to the bike lobby's effort to poach on our territory," he justified his animus with the complaint that bike lanes were making it impossible for him to find free parking near Manhattan restaurants.[18]

Bicyclists were not the only intruders whose presence aroused the fury of motorists. Bus lanes, speed cameras, and even pedestrians legally crossing the street in crosswalks drew angry criticism.[19] In Seattle, charges of a war on cars rained down on environmentalist mayor Michael McGinn. It was an effective mobilizing device, appealing to drivers' unthinking certainty of their possession of the roadways.

This feeling of entitlement was on clear display in 2011 when a jury in Cobb County, Georgia, found Raquel Nelson guilty of vehicular homicide. A car struck her four-year-old son and killed him while the family was crossing a five-lane highway to get from the bus stop to their garden apartment. The mother was a criminal, according to prosecutors in the wealthy Atlanta suburb, because she did not walk, with two young children and an armful of packages, a quarter-mile to the nearest crosswalk and a quarter-mile back. None of the jurors who convicted her had ever ridden a local bus.[20]

Right-wing publicists might ignore a Raquel Nelson and leave their followers to think of her as an aggressor in the war against the automobile. But they still face a problem of inconsistency when they hitch a ride on motorists' belief in the divine right of cars. Their free-market theory has little in common with reality. Suburban roads, even more than suburban neighborhoods, are made by government.

And the devotion of the automobile culture to free roads and free parking poses another even greater problem for these writers. It clashes directly with the agenda of the people paying the bills.

In an era when the highway lobby's old funding formulas have stopped working, road builders hope that toll lanes will save the day. The Reason Foundation is a center of toll road promotion; Peter Samuel, the editor of a newsletter for the toll road industry, was a signer of the Lone Mountain Compact. These and other prohighway publicists marshal economic theory to justify tolls as user fees that simply make drivers pay for the roads they drive on.

But at the grass roots, the motorist's sense of entitlement says just the opposite. Paid parking and tolls are just as much a war on drivers as bike lanes and crosswalk signals. Careful steering is required to keep the heavy artillery of the culture war pointed away from the economic interests of the sponsors.

The congestion charge, a daily fee assessed on anyone who drives into a congested downtown, brings this contradiction into the open. The issue first flared up when London's left-of-center Mayor Ken Livingstone imposed a $15 per day charge. American rightists seconded the criticism levied by British conservatives, with Wendell Cox weighing in loudly if inconsistently.[21]

The Reason Foundation, as the main center of agitation for privately operated toll roads, has no choice but to endorse user fees in principle. But when a city actually tries to impose a congestion charge, the foundation joins Cox in finding reasons to say no. Excuses were not easy to find when New York Mayor Michael Bloomberg proposed a fee on drivers in Manhattan. The best Sam Staley could do was to complain, under the headline "Bloomberg vs. the Car," that enforcement by photographing license plates raised "legitimate and troubling questions about the surveillance systems needed to implement these programs." When toll road operators three years later sought to use the same surveillance system, Staley enthused that "video license plate reader technology eliminates most of the hassle for consumers and users."[22]

Caught between their doctrine and motorists' attachment to the subsidized status quo, the road warriors keep finding reasons to reject in practice what they support in principle. Randal O'Toole wants to get rid of rules that require off-street parking in new buildings—but not now, only after public parking rates go way up. Marc Scribner of the Competitive Enterprise Institute endorses the concept of deregulating land use in Virginia—but he opposes an attempt to actually do so. The reason he gives is that streets with narrower lanes, shorter blocks, and sharp corners will somehow "force inclusion." These writers are the St. Augustines of the free market—end government regulation and make me chaste some day, they pray, but don't take away my subsidy just yet.[23]

When all else fails, conservatives raise the issue to the level of philosophy. "The real reason for progressives' passion for trains is their goal of diminishing Americans' individualism in order to make them more amenable to collectivism," writes George Will. Randal O'Toole wants to "give people freedom to choose what they want" by turning city neighborhoods into gated communities. "The war against suburbia reflects a radical new vision of American life which, in the name of community and green values, would reverse the democratizing of the landscape that has characterized much of the past 50 years," adds Joel Kotkin.[24] The battle to preserve sprawl is a defense of freedom.

12
The Language of Land Use

reedom and democracy, George Orwell once wrote, are words that are "often used in a consciously dishonest way. That is, the person who uses them has his own private definition, but allows his hearer to think he means something quite different." Such, surely, is the freedom of the gated community and the democracy of snob zoning.

"Politics and the English Language" was Orwell's topic,[1] and politics has done much to debase the language of land use. The day is long past when the buyers and sellers of houses boasted openly of their restricted communities. Old-school homeowners, here and there, still speak frankly among themselves, but they do better to dissemble when they make their case to the electorate as a whole.

In more enlightened circles, status-seeking is frowned upon, and here self-deception is the rule. Pretenses are maintained in closed conversation and even private thought. Orwell understood this too—rote phrases, he wrote, "perform the important service of partially concealing your meaning even from yourself."

The law shares blame with politics for this corruption of language. Suburban land tenure, the right of a property owner to obstruct building on nearby land, is not a recognized legal doctrine. While commonly asserted and often successfully exercised, it invariably comes disguised as something it is not.

The Supreme Court ruled that zoning, the main enforcement mechanism of suburban land tenure, is constitutional. But it upheld it as an exercise of the "police power" and not a property right. Under this doctrine, the legitimate basis for restricting owners' use of their land is the protection of concrete, tangible interests of the larger community—there must be, in Alfred Bettman's words, "a motive related to safety or comfort or order or health." Reality, from the beginning, has been otherwise. Zoning mainly serves an intangible interest, the social status that accrues to the neighborhood through the intentionally wasteful nonuse of property.

A second chasm soon opened between fact and legal theory. The courts used the rationale of convenience to connect zoning to the police power. Dividing land into zones for designated uses, they said, gives property owners advance warning against building something that would interfere with neighboring properties. Landowners, knowing from the beginning what could and could not be built, would avoid wasting time and money on infeasible projects. Society would gain too by avoiding costly and disruptive disputes.

The promise of simplicity and certainty has, to say the least, not been fulfilled. As zoning has evolved, anything but a tract of single-family houses on large lots, or maybe a strip mall, is judged case by case. The outcome, hanging on the whims of neighbors or the push and pull of local politics, is often unforeseeable. Yet the law still conceives zoning as an exercise in systematic forethought to avoid identifiable hazards. To withstand judicial scrutiny, a city council or zoning board must justify its verdict before the courts as a rational application of fixed criteria.

Historic preservation brought yet more purposeful confusion. Nimbys who pose as preservationists speak of why they like the old building, when their real passion is dislike of the new one.

Social convention and legal fiction weigh down heavily on those engaged in land use matters, leaving them unable to speak frankly about basic concepts. If you don't want something built, an honest statement of objections invites defeat in court. Developers and their lawyers have equally compelling reasons to engage in self-censorship. When your aim is to get the project approved before the money runs out, it makes no sense to question the whole system. Straight talk is unlikely to convince the judge or the zoning board, and it risks offending neighbors who might otherwise agree to a compromise.

Now and then, in the aftermath of utter defeat, builders openly vent their feelings. Richard Babcock quotes a developer's letter to a wealthy New York suburb that did not let him put up an apartment house for the elderly. In Briarcliff, the spurned builder wrote, zoning aims to guarantee "that each newcomer must be wealthier than those who came before, but must be of a character to preserve the illusion that their poorer neighbors are as wealthy as they."

Babcock himself was an attorney of such eminence that he had license to unusual frankness. The paramount purpose of zoning, he wrote, was "the protection of the single-family house neighborhood....As might be expected, such a motive is rarely articulated as a rationale for this popular device, either by the supporters or critics of zoning."[2]

Such plain speaking is rare indeed. Developers and nimbys, although everyday antagonists, share a common interest in the prestige of the neighborhood, and both use words as tools to that end. One party directs its linguistic creativity into salesmanship. Row houses turn into *townhomes; garden apartments* grow parked cars in the gardens; dead ends are translated into French as *cul-de-sacs*. The other side, hiding its aims from the world at large and often from itself, has a weakness for phrases whose meaning slips away when carefully examined.

Land use disputes thus come before the public veiled in a thick fog of evasion, euphemism, and flat-out falsehood. From this miasma rises a plague of obscurity that infects the language itself. Terms devised to conceal reality become so familiar that they are uttered without thinking. Critics find themselves unable to question received dogmas for want of words to express their thoughts.

A tour of this vocabulary must begin with *compatibility*. The concept is at the heart of land-use regulation. In the narrow sense, incompatible uses are those that cannot coexist, like a smokehouse and a rest home for asthmatics. But the word has taken on a far broader meaning.

Compatibility, in the enlarged sense, is often thought of as a sort of similarity. But the nature of the required resemblance is hard to pin down. At times, the concept seems to disguise circular reasoning. Incompatible land uses are forbidden in the zone. What is compatible? Land uses of the kind that are allowed in the zone.

The key to deciphering this word lies in a crucial difference between compatibility and similarity. If two things are similar, they are both similar to each other, but with compatibility it is otherwise. A house on a half-acre lot is compatible with surrounding apartment buildings, but the inverse does not follow. An apartment building is incompatible with houses that sit on half-acre lots.

Compatibility, in this sense, is euphemism. A compatible land use upholds the status of the neighborhood. An incompatible one lowers it. Rental apartments can be incompatible with a neighborhood that would accept the same building sold as condos. An apartment house and a ten-room mansion are both incompatible with an older subdivision of small expensive homes: the one because apartments are inferior to houses; the other because its yard, overshadowed by the structure, fails to manifest the conspicuous waste of land that gives such areas their special cachet.

The euphemism is so well established that the narrow meaning has begun to fall into disuse. Neighbors who object to loud noises or unpleasant odors just lay out the specifics; incompatible has come to mean "I don't like it and I'm not explaining why." The word is notably unpopular with New Urbanists. Faced with such an obvious case of incompatibility, in the literal sense, as a parking lot in a walkable downtown, they call it a "disruption of the urban fabric" or a "wasteful use of land."

Compatibility may be the most pervasive linguistic deformation, but it is hardly the only one. Homeowners will complain about the *impact* on their neighborhood when basement apartments are rented out or high-rises are built nearby. This word conflates purely psychological desires, among them the wish to keep away from people with lower incomes, with physical detriments like smell and shade. Its value lies in its vagueness—objectors can make a case without saying concretely what their objection is.

The term *growth controls* refers in common usage only to rules enacted after the magic year of 1969. A law passed in 1972 that limits a 1000-acre village to 250 houses is a growth control. A zoning ordinance that went into effect five years earlier is not, even if it accomplishes the same thing by specifying that every house must sit on a 4-acre lot.

Another slippery phrase is *public use*. Here the word *use* conveys almost the exact opposite of its common meaning. Montgomery County has a definition: *public use space* is "space devoted to uses for public enjoyment, such as gardens, plazas, or walks." A common example is the plaza that sits empty between an office building and the street, elevating the status of its surroundings through the display of conspicuous waste.

The operative word in the definition is not *use* but *enjoyment*. In other words, no productive work can be done in the space. By this definitional sleight of hand, disuse becomes a kind of use, and indeed the only kind allowed. In one case in 2011, the planning board forbade the placement of a barbecue in a public use space when a neighbor complained that it would encourage the public to use the space.[3]

A similar shell game shifts the meaning of *exemplary*. In its ordinary dictionary definition, the exemplary is something fit to serve as an example for others—in other words, a thing of unusual value. This, surely, is how the public understood it when laws were passed to protect exemplary buildings. But once those laws were in effect, buildings and districts were called exemplary simply as examples of something old.[4] The intent of designating exemplary buildings as historic was to preserve the outstanding. The practice, with this linguistic trick, is to embalm the ordinary.

The word *plan* retains its original meaning, but it can conceal more than it reveals. In plain English, a plan represents an intention for the future. Plans often do express the intentions, or at least the hopes, of city leaders. But many master plans merely describe current land uses, providing a legal justification for zoning. Elsewhere plans remain on the books long after they become obsolete; no one takes the trouble to update them until a developer is ready to move. It is not rare that the intended future use of land is altogether different from what is written in the plans.

Our linguistic tour would hardly be complete without a visit to the *greedy developer*. The key to decoding this phrase is that the word *greedy* lacks semantic content. Antipathy to developers has no relation to their degree of avarice; if anything, nonprofit builders of low-income housing encounter more hostility than the truly greedy. The ostensible target is the wealthy entrepreneur who builds new houses; the real one is the people who will live in them.

The builder stands accused, often enough, of the sin of *manhattanization*. When first used in San Francisco in the late 1960s by opponents of downtown skyscrapers, this was a vivid and descriptive coinage. But just as the developer's first name lost its connection to avarice, manhattanization became unmoored from New York City. The term, in current usage, can refer to almost any structure that rises above its surroundings.

A campaign against manhattanizing Menlo Park, California, objects to a proposed master plan that would allow two-, three-, and four-story buildings around the train station. The movement's leader explains her goals by asking, "Are we going to remain a small town, with low-density development, or are we going to be more like Redwood City and Palo Alto?" Manhattanize might seem an odd choice of word to convey the meaning of "make it look like Palo Alto," but stale metaphor, as Orwell pointed out, does a service. It releases the speaker from the need to explain, or even figure out herself, exactly what she means to say. The premise of the argument against density is left unstated and thus immune from challenge.[5]

A somewhat different illness afflicts the terminology of transportation. Vocabulary again impedes critical thinking, but the problem here is not what words conceal as much what they unconsciously express. It is what is called

A rebuilt El Camino Real, the central artery of Menlo Park, California, as envisioned in a plan seen by detractors as manhattanizing the town.
(Courtesy of Perkins + Will.)

windshield perspective, the penchant of elected and unelected policymakers to see streets exclusively through the eyes of a driver.

Streetcorners, the places where Jane Jacobs found the life of the city lived, become *intersections* whose only function is to move you someplace else. When turn lanes are added it's called an *improvement* even though pedestrians find the street harder to cross. Walking, bicycling, and transit are *alternative* transportation.[6]

This windshield worldview is ingrained in the technical terminology of traffic engineers. An intersection is deemed to *fail* if cars need too much time to get through. It doesn't matter how long those on foot must wait to cross. If a car stops because a pedestrian is in the crosswalk, it is a *conflict*—something the engineers abhor. But no conflict occurs when heavy traffic keeps that same pedestrian from making a legal midblock crossing.[7]

Built into such language is the idea that nothing but cars belongs on the roads. Talk and write this way long enough, and it starts to be taken for granted that automobiles are the only normal way to get around. This becomes the unthinking assumption even when everyone knows the facts are otherwise. Thus, in Washington, DC, where only 41% of employed residents drive to work, the American Automobile Association complains that the city is being unfair to motorists because it wants to make cars optional.[8]

A brief interlude of frank discussion of zoning began around 1965. Twenty years had passed since the postwar building boom began, long enough to bring to light the weaknesses of the new suburban system. Meanwhile, the success of the civil rights movement in breaking down formal barriers of separation had turned attention to informal ones. Books appeared like Richard Babcock's *Zoning Game*, Seymour Toll's *Zoned American*, and Michael Danielson's *Politics of Exclusion*. Laws that challenged snob zoning were enacted in a few states and debated in many others.

The window closed after a decade and a half. The sixties were fading into the past, and the national mood swung rightward. On what remained of the left, moreover, egalitarianism gave way to relativism. Authenticity was now what mattered,[9] and whatever else one might think of nimbys, they certainly express an authentic strand of neighborhood opinion. Questioning the declared intentions of grass-roots groups, always a risky political maneuver, became intellectually suspect as well. Even critics of suburban land tenure found it easier to take the arguments of the system's defenders at face value. Few probed beneath the surface of words like incompatible and impact. With issues understood in such categories, the right to exclude again seemed a natural part of the background of life.

"If thought corrupts language, language can also corrupt thought," Orwell warned in his famous essay. For half a century and more, deformed language has made it hard to think clearly about the communities we live in. Our system of land use will be the easier to understand the more we use words that say plainly what we mean.

13
Breaking New Ground

Americans have long since lost their love for sprawl, yet they struggle to put something in its place. The urbanist movement has turned for inspiration to a few communities that succeeded in swimming against the current. Portland, Oregon and Arlington, Virginia, embraced smart growth before the name existed. In Maryland, grass-roots activists revived a light rail project that powerful nimbys had struck down and left for dead. Advocates and scholars have carefully studied the planning and architecture of these groundbreakers to see what worked and what did not. Their politics and governance deserve the same attention.

Portland leads the nation in smart growth policies. It has a booming downtown, an expanding light rail network, policies that promote infill development, and streets rebuilt for sharing by pedestrians, bicyclists, and drivers. Portland's success is often seen as a triumph of good planning, and it is; however, years of political organizing and coalition-building made the planning possible. Oregon voters laid the groundwork for the city's transformation with three choices they made in the 1970s.

First came the election of Neil Goldschmidt as mayor of Portland. In the sixties, the city was a magnet for the young and hip, and low-key versions of bohemian enclaves had emerged in old streetcar suburbs on its east side. Through these very neighborhoods, highway engineers planned to drive the 5½-mile-long Mt. Hood Freeway. In the politicized atmosphere of the times, residents new and old rose up against the threat. Goldschmidt, a twenty-nine-year-old antipoverty lawyer who had helped organize the Freedom Summer civil rights campaign in Mississippi, was elected city commissioner in 1970. He was among the first of the new urban populists to win office. Two years later he ran for the city's highest office and rode a wave of protest to victory over fierce opposition from the city's business elites.[1]

The young mayor proved adept in the exercise of political power. Taking the helm of a city in decline, he perceived the need for a program of economic revival that went beyond the concerns of the neighborhood activists who had elected him. To that end, he immediately set about building coalitions with the business interests that had opposed his election. Consensus emerged rapidly on a new land-use policy. Business got a vigorous promotion of downtown development, with the city's dense core encouraged to expand outward. For neighborhoods, there was a new emphasis on housing rehabilitation; money for parks; streets rebuilt to make room for pedestrians, buses, and bicycles; and a formal role for neighborhood associations in local governance.

The new direction in transportation was slower to emerge. Plans for more downtown parking were quickly axed, but the Mt. Hood Freeway kept moving ahead. Only in 1994 did the city and county vote to scrap the interstate. Even then there was no agreement on what to do with the money that decision freed up, and other road projects remained in dispute. The dominant power in state transportation planning was Glenn Jackson, the prohighway president of the local electric utility and chairman of the Oregon Transportation Commission. Goldschmidt forged a close personal relationship with the much older Jackson. In 1975 the two of them worked out a plan not fully revealed to the public for another two years. Jackson accepted the loss of the Mt. Hood Freeway and another planned expressway; Goldschmidt would allow a third contested interstate on the east side of the city to go forward. The freeway money was divided between the new multipurpose streets, the widening of yet another expressway, and a new transitway running east from downtown.

What kind of transit would go in the transitway was still up in the air. Goldschmidt's staff was taken with the new concept of light rail; their boss, whose downtown bus mall was then under construction, inclined toward rubber-tired vehicles. Grass-roots activists and county officials favored rail, but state highway bureaucrats were skeptical and their studies focused on busways. Then, as the mayor was fending off a profreeway challenger to his reelection, he reversed course behind the scenes. By the start of 1977, light rail was suddenly the favored option. Goldschmidt went to Washington in 1979 and served two years as federal secretary of transportation, construction of light rail began in 1983, and the line opened in 1986. The former mayor came back to

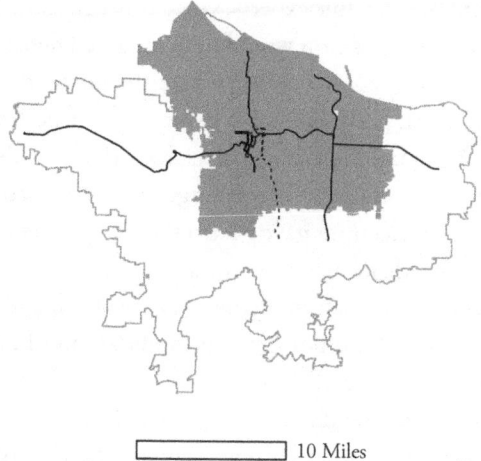

10 Miles

Portland, Oregon; city shaded, growth boundary shown as gray line. Light rail network in black, with line under construction dashed.

Oregon, served a term as governor in the late eighties, and remained the state's premier power broker until felled by a sex scandal in 2004.[2]

The second choice that shaped Portland came the summer after Goldschmidt became mayor. A moderate Republican governor, Tom McCall, pushed through the legislature a plan to draw growth boundaries around all metropolitan areas. The law established a new state agency with a veto over local land-use regulations. Its main aim was to preserve farmland in the rapidly urbanizing Willamette Valley, and its core backers were slow-growth environmentalists; McCall famously invited outsiders to "visit, but don't stay." Support came as well from farmers in the valley.[3]

In initial inspiration, Oregon's growth boundary plan differed little from the rural land reserves established elsewhere in the 1970s. But it had two key features that controls in other states lacked. Because the law applied statewide, development could not leapfrog past the boundaries into friendlier jurisdictions. Even more important, perhaps, was a rule that originated as a concession to opponents. Urban areas had to be enlarged to make room for twenty years of future population growth. This gave environmentalists, who wanted above all to keep the boundaries from moving outward, a strong stake in urban density. The more infill development was allowed, the less land would be gobbled up on the fringe.[4]

The third crucial vote came in 1978. The Portland area created an elected metropolitan government, known as Metro, with power over land use. Metro's structure, proposed by academic experts, sailed through a low-key referendum. In other states such a proposition would have triggered fierce resistance to the loss of local control over zoning. Here, where the power to oversee land use had already been centralized and suburbanites had little fear of a minority population that was small even in the city, the arrival of this new governing body seemed a mere administrative rearrangement. It turned out to be much more than that; direct elections gave Metro the independence and legitimacy it would need to override local zoning rules.[5]

The growth control law left many issues unresolved, and the new system emerged slowly; Portland did not draw its boundary until 1979. Yet the plan was hotly contested from the beginning. Three times in its first decade, opponents forced statewide referenda; the voters upheld it each time. McCall, when he left the governor's office, founded a new environmental organization called 1000 Friends of Oregon. The name went quickly out of date as the membership climbed past five times that number. Set up to protect the new growth boundaries against legal challenges, 1000 Friends broadened its horizons as time passed. By the end of the century it was defending growth control on many fronts—in referendum battles, in the courts, in the legislature and in county seats, and with its own research and planning studies.[6]

While the leadership of Neil Goldschmidt and Tom McCall launched Portland on its new course, the structure of the Oregon economy opened the way for them. For one thing, housing costs were low—this was one of the city's attractions for the bohemian influx of the 1960s. Portland rents were under the national average in 1970 and were far lower than in New York, Boston, and San Francisco. They went up little faster than inflation in the seventies and hardly at all in the eighties. Movements for rent control gained little traction, and an issue that could have gotten in the way of Goldschmidt's neighborhood-business alliance was never on the table.[7]

A second factor was the collapse of Oregon's lumber-dependent economy at the beginning of the 1980s and the political consequences that ensued. Bad times continued through most of the decade, and real estate prices plunged— adjusted for inflation, the average house in Portland lost more than 30% of its value between 1979 and 1989. Gentrification, which took hold in Portland's bohemian neighborhoods as elsewhere in the late seventies, halted when the turnover of population did not raise prices. The city's east side stayed affordable while its population changed. Portland had yet to see the dilution of its bohemian flavor that was already perceptible in Brooklyn and San Francisco, and newcomers to the city were slow to generate the sort of conservative nimby politics seen elsewhere. This political current emerged only a dozen or so years later, and in the interim linkages between infill development and growth boundaries were set in place.[8]

The local economy returned to health after 1990, propelled by a rapidly growing semiconductor industry in the affluent western suburbs. Older sections of the city shared in the prosperity, bringing the same social and economic pressures that afflicted other healthy urban areas. But the institutions that Portland had created over the previous two decades gave the city a unique ability to control its land use.

Metro's planners, required to look twenty years ahead, faced two challenges. One was the need to update the growth boundary to make room for future growth. The other was a new state rule aimed at curbing the use of cars, imposed under pressure from 1000 Friends. It mandated a 10% cut in miles driven per person and an equal reduction in parking spaces.

Planners of the early 1990s did not foresee the shifting preferences and soaring gas prices that curtailed automobile use after 2004. They judged the target of 10% less driving to be nearly unreachable. Businesses revolted against the loss of parking. The only way to cut car use, all sides agreed, was to concentrate future development at transit stations. But this would not satisfy the law unless someone could demonstrate that it would work.

The planners' computer models were capable of making the needed predictions, but only if a specific menu of land-use changes was plugged in. Local governments, fearing an eruption of public anger if they even thought about massive rezonings, were unwilling to draw up the needed menu. 1000 Friends stepped into the breach. It obtained a federal grant for its own study and hired the consulting firm doing Metro's modeling to carry out the work. The 1000 Friends report, known as LUTRAQ (for Land Use, Transportation, and Air Quality), concluded that if light rail expanded and dense urban areas were built at the stations the amount of driving would come down substantially. This combined strategy could accomplish much more than either land-use rules or new transit lines alone.

This planning process put big-picture decisions about the future of the region before the public. It left the details of what would happen on particular parcels of land to be worked out later. With the issues framed this way, LUTRAQ won wide support. Metro adopted plans that minimized expansion of the growth boundary by promoting dense transit-oriented development. Portland, in 1998, amended its zoning code to allow apartment additions on houses even in areas zoned for single-family homes.[9]

By now Oregon's growth control laws were under attack again. The concept of urban growth boundaries was too well accepted to be taken on directly.

The opponents, organized as Oregonians in Action, adopted a strategy that was the reverse of the other side's—they drew attention away from the overall policy choices and tried to undermine the structure of growth control by calling referendums on individual rules that were less popular. An appeal to Portland-area nimbys came up empty—a rollback of the zoning changes that allowed mixed-use development was beaten at the polls. But they had better luck when they stressed the rights of property owners and personalized the issue with stories of small landowners just outside the growth boundaries. Voters approved two statewide referendums that required local governments to compensate landowners when growth controls lowered property values. Courts overturned the first, in 2000; voters drastically trimmed back the second when they saw local governments hit with large compensation bills for popular rule changes—but smart growth advocates knew they were under political siege.[10]

Coalitions shifted back and forth as the two sides struggled to define the battleground. The homebuilding lobby was closely allied with 1000 Friends when infill was the issue, but it backed the Oregonians in Action property rights referendums. Homeowner groups in the Portland suburbs swung the other way.

Still, the basic contours of conflict were static. Loggers in southwest Oregon and ranchers in the east opposed growth control for economic reasons. Within the metropolis, election returns reflected clashing status hierarchies. Backing for urbanism was strongest in Portland's new downtown and the walkable neighborhoods around it. In built-up areas close to the growth boundary—where, economists found, controls exerted the most upward pressure on property values—calls went out to halt smart growth and "let the suburbs be suburbs." Oregonians in Action drew votes from expensive auto-oriented neighborhoods as it mocked the elitism of the newly fashionable district just north of downtown.[11]

If property rights were smart growth's greatest political vulnerability, light rail with its promise of jobs and real estate profits was its strength. The rail network, from its first days, aimed not just to carry people on trips they were already taking but also to create a new pattern of travel by changing land use. In 1998 a tunnel punched through to the city's prosperous western side, extending the line that already ran east from downtown. With tracks now reaching the city's favored quarter and neighborhood nimbys undercut by growth control rules, dense town centers rose around suburban stations. The light rail system added more suburban branches in 2001, 2004, and 2009, and the city built slower-moving streetcars to serve growing neighborhoods close to downtown.

Light rail was now Portland's point of pride. Its renown as the symbol of the city's renovation surpassed its role in the region's transportation network. (The Portland light rail trains carry six trips a day for every hundred residents; Washington's Metro, built just a few years earlier, carries seventeen.) In 2011 construction began on the most ambitious expansion since the tunnel to the west, a 7-mile line that will run south on the east side of the Willamette River after crossing on a new bridge.[12]

The Washington suburb of Arlington, Virginia, follows Portland on most lists of smart growth success stories. Along five stations of the Metro Orange Line between Rosslyn and Ballston, high-rise mixed-use development has remade a 3-mile-long commercial strip. The corridor has gained twenty thousand housing units and more than fifty thousand jobs, yet many roads carry less traffic now than forty years ago: 40% of the residents take transit to work, and fewer than half drive.[13]

Arlington's unique geography set the stage for this makeover. A city-sized county, it was created in 1846 when the section of the District of Columbia lying south of the Potomac River was returned to Virginia. Expansion of the federal government in the 1930s and 1940s brought rapid suburban growth, given an extra boost by the construction in Arlington of the world's largest office building, the Pentagon. By the mid-fifties single-family houses and garden apartments blanketed the county, and the tide of suburbanization swept outward past its borders.

As elsewhere, Arlington's initial infatuation with transit grew out of a fight against highways. Opposition to I-66, connecting Washington to western suburbs, was near-unanimous—the interstate cut through local neighborhoods and benefited only those who lived beyond the county's borders. In need of a substitute, Arlington gave enthusiastic backing to plans for Washington's new Metro. But Congressman William Natcher of Kentucky, who chaired the subcommittee that controlled Metro's funding, warned that he would kill the subway project if any interstates were canceled. Highway opponents in the District of Columbia overcame Natcher after a long struggle, but Arlington conceded and agreed to build both Metro and I-66. As a compromise, the road was narrowed to four lanes, with only carpools allowed during rush hour.[14]

At first Metro's planners wanted to run the Orange Line down I-66, the least expensive route. But the county insisted on putting the tracks underground beneath Wilson Boulevard, a downtown-style commercial strip that was losing business to newer shopping malls. And Arlington wanted as many stations in this corridor as possible; it wound up with five. Voters gave strong

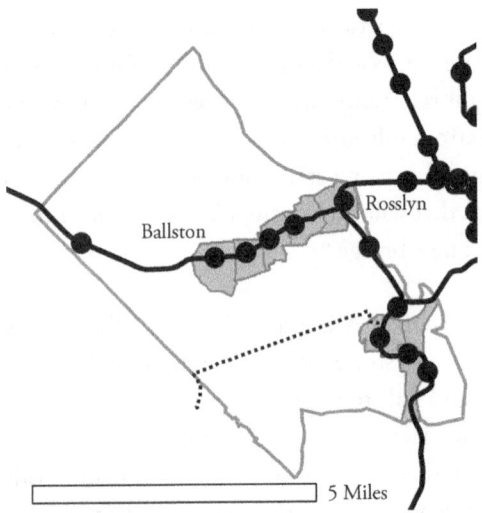

Arlington, Virginia, with areas zoned for transit-oriented development shown in gray. Metro is solid line; planned Columbia Pike streetcar route dashed.

support to these decisions. A referendum on a bond issue to pay for Metro won 70% of the votes.

Soon after the first spade went into the ground, Arlington began planning for its new subway. The nimby wave arrived on schedule here; a Committee on Optimum Growth, organized in 1971, argued that stations should be surrounded by parking lots instead of high-rises. But redevelopment around the new transit stations was a given—the county had chosen the Wilson Boulevard route for that purpose. Neighborhood associations reconciled themselves to the coming redevelopment as an unavoidable evil that could at best be constrained. The county protected most of their territory from change; it restricted new buildings to a quarter-mile radius around the stations and made no changes in single-family zones elsewhere.[15]

Lessons from an earlier failure profoundly influenced the design of the new urban centers. In the 1960s, high-rise office towers had sprouted in an old industrial area known as Rosslyn, across the Potomac from Georgetown. The county laid the district out in the spirit of 1950s urban renewal—single-use office towers amid roads designed for high-speed traffic. It pushed pedestrians off the streets, shunting them onto elevated walkways that led into buildings through unmarked doors at the end of second-floor corridors. Planners and residents, whatever their other differences, were united in revulsion at Rosslyn's ugliness and sterility, and they resolved not to repeat its mistakes.

A decade before the New Urbanist architects would begin their work, plans for the corridor above the Metro line insisted on mixed uses and walkability.

In December 1975, four years before the Orange Line opened, the county board adopted a growth program for the next quarter-century. At its heart was the rebuilding of the Orange Line corridor. Detailed plans for the areas around the stations followed over the next eight years. These documents emerged from lengthy negotiations involving neighborhoods, landowners, planners, and elected officials and won at least grudging assent from all sides.[16]

When the county adopted its new plans, it left low-density suburban zoning in effect. It rezones land only after a developer submits an acceptable design for each building and agrees to pay for a supposedly voluntary "proffer." The voluntary character of the payment is a legal fiction made necessary by Virginia law. The state severely limits local governments' power to impose conditions on developers; the procedure of last-minute rezoning evades this restriction by making the builder choose between "volunteering" to do what the county wants and winding up unable to build at all.

Decision-making in Arlington has avoided the bureaucratic deadlock of Montgomery County. Negotiations focus on the size of the proffer and what it will pay for—the plan already spells out what the developer will be allowed to build. And the builder negotiates directly with the ultimate decision-maker, the county council. Arlington is fairly small—a population of around two hundred thousand—and routine approvals of suburban subdivisions ceased years ago, so the number of new buildings is small enough that council members have time to scrutinize each project individually. Stable land-use policy is also promoted by the continuity of Arlington's liberal Democratic Party leadership; after Ronald Reagan carried the county in 1980, it swung sharply to the left and gave 72% of its votes to Barack Obama in 2008.[17]

As time passed, opposition to growth along the corridor faded away. By 2009, the former leader of the Committee on Optimum Growth insisted that his organization had been not for no growth in the corridor but just for slow growth. The county now intends to urbanize a second run-down corridor, along Columbia Pike, building a streetcar line to make up for the absence of Metro.[18]

In 1989 Maryland governor William Donald Schaefer called for building two light rail lines with state funds. One would cross Baltimore, where Schaefer had long been mayor, from north to south, and the other would run on a recently abandoned 3-mile stretch of freight tracks in Montgomery County outside Washington. The governor, whose motto had always been "do it now," rushed forward headlong to build light rail in his beloved Baltimore. Montgomery County politicians wanted their line too, and they had already purchased the old railroad right of way for that purpose. However, the county's famously protracted planning processes delayed an official decision. By the time they said yes, the funds set aside by Governor Schaefer had disappeared in Baltimore cost overruns and an economic downturn.

The Montgomery light rail route was a transportation planner's dream. Not only did it run between the urban-style downtowns of Bethesda and Silver Spring, the county's two largest job centers, but at each end it would connect to a branch of the new Washington Metro. It could be built at ground level without running into traffic—three major roads crossed over the old tracks on bridges. But the proposal faced lavishly funded opposition. The right of way ran beside wealthy Chevy Chase neighborhoods and, worst of all, through the middle of the golf course of the exclusive Columbia Country Club.

The state, having given up on the idea of building with its own money, began environmental studies to qualify for federal grants. But in 1994, a light rail opponent was elected county executive and the new county council was closely split. Planning work halted and most observers thought the project was dead.

A small group of activists, myself among them, did not give up. The Action Committee for Transit (ACT) had organized in 1986 when the freight line closed. Its few dozen members proselytized for light rail before any audience they could find, relying on elected officials to provide political firepower. After the election setback, Harry Sanders, the group's founder and a former leader of the state's Common Cause, realized a new strategy was needed. He set about organizing a broader alliance in support of the transit line. Only a threadbare coalition could be assembled at first. Business groups gave merely token support; their attention was elsewhere, on a long-running struggle over whether to build an expressway called the Intercounty Connector farther out in the suburbs. The most active allies were recruited among homeowners living near the Washington Beltway—there had been talk for years of widening this crowded highway that runs parallel to the light rail route, and neighborhood leaders feared the project would resurface unless transit was built in the corridor.

The battle over light rail settled into a war of attrition. Opponents sought to turn a bicycle trail, planned from the beginning to run alongside the tracks, into an obstacle to light rail. They convinced the county to build an "interim" graveled trail and then made their slogan "save the trail." The two sides battled for support of environmentalists and bicyclists. Retired ACT members haunted the state capital, watching for killer amendments hidden in the state budget by Columbia Country Club's lobbyists.

Activists were drawn to the light rail issue by the sheer injustice of the situation. The merits of the project first led them to sign on as supporters and attend an occasional meeting. Learning more about the issue, they realized that this transit line, which would benefit so many, had been stopped by the power and money of a country club that was carefully keeping itself out of the limelight. I was one of those who gradually became more committed. When Harry Sanders decided to spend his time on coalition organizing, he asked me to serve as president of ACT. I accepted on the soon-forgotten promise that I wouldn't have to do much work.

It was clear that overcoming the country club's money and connections would require not just majority support—that already existed—but a near-consensus strong enough to overwhelm the opposition. Coalition-building was one part of that; another was winning the battle of public opinion. This required moving beyond a "good government" appeal and making light rail a populist issue by putting Columbia Country Club in the spotlight.

Over the next dozen years, the country club's role was highlighted with leaflets, signs, and media events in front of the "members only" entrance. After research uncovered behind-the-scenes string-pulling, this message reached a large audience through high-profile exposés in the *Washington Post* and *New York Times*. At one point I ran into the club's lobbyist at a political event. "My mother doesn't like what you say about me," he said with a half-smile. For perhaps the only time in my life, I came up with an instant comeback. "Your mother should love what we say. All we ever talk about is how highly paid you are."

Another element of the strategy was countering the opponents' campaign contributions by mobilizing the prorail majority among the voters. The success of the Washington Metro system gives transit proponents a great tactical advantage—supporters can be targeted by passing out leaflets at the stations. Before the 1998 primary election, ACT members distributed twenty thousand scorecards that rated candidates on light rail and other transit issues. The new county council had a six-to-three majority for the light rail line, with one member crediting the scorecard for his margin of victory. The day after the new council was sworn in, it voted to ask the state to resume planning work.

Meanwhile, the State Highway Administration had restarted studies of adding more lanes to the Beltway. Required by federal law to consider transit alternatives, the study in early 1997 added an additional option suggested by ACT. This was an extended version of the Bethesda-Silver Spring light rail

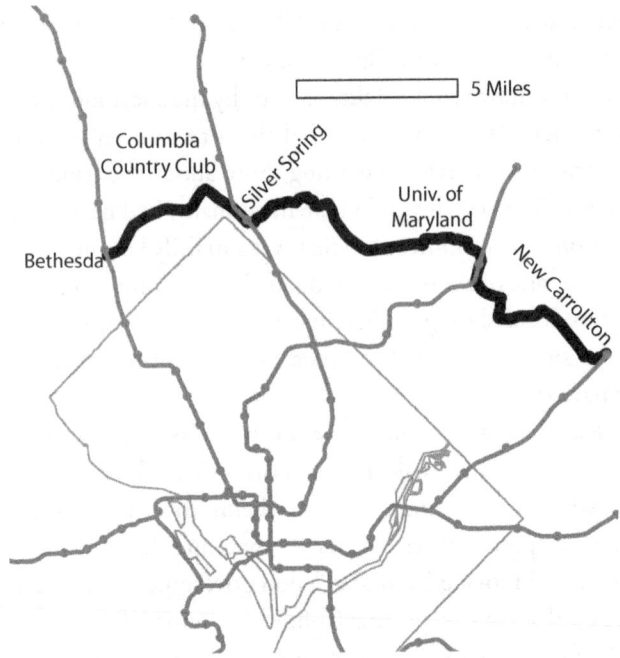

5 Miles

Columbia
Country Club

Silver Spring

Univ. of
Maryland

Bethesda

New Carrollton

The planned route of the Purple Line outside Washington, DC.

line, continuing eastward into neighboring Prince George's County and passing through the campus of the University of Maryland. The terminus of this
route was soon fixed at New Carrollton, where it could connect to Amtrak
trains to New York as well as another Metro branch. With five other colors
already spoken for on the map of the Washington Metro, the project became
known as the Purple Line.

As the Beltway study proceeded, transit options became its focus. Engineers
were finding that widening the highway would be difficult and extraordinarily
expensive, and Governor Parris Glendening's pursuit of his smart growth
agenda brought a higher priority to transit. A political battle was raging over
the Intercounty Connector after the governor stopped work on the highway
in 1999; environmental groups that had earlier hesitated to offend their members in Chevy Chase now lined up behind the light rail line as a major transportation project they could favor.

Expanding the smaller proposal into the Purple Line made light rail even
more popular among the electorate, but the noisy opposition of the county's
most affluent precincts drowned out this quiet support. Even the Purple Line's
most ardent backers underestimated the public's enthusiasm for it. A flyer

showing its route inserted into Washington's iconic five-color subway map was well received, so in March 2001 ACT threw all its resources into passing out thirty thousand copies at Metro stations. Hope that the flyer would attract a few new members turned into astonishment when 120 coupons were clipped out and mailed back with $10 dues checks.

This success inspired a turn to the Purple Line's other established base of grass-roots support. Volunteers distributed the leaflet door to door in communities along the Beltway. Accompanying each copy was a letter from a leader of the neighborhood's civic association, explaining why light rail was needed to stave off the threat of highway widening. The favorable response from homes close to the noisy interstate was expected, but surprisingly just as many new members joined at the far end of the neighborhoods. So the campaign moved on to other areas, reaching more than fifty thousand homes over five years and recruiting over a thousand new members.

Seeking to assemble the widest possible majority, advocates avoided portraying the Purple Line as a social justice issue and emphasized that it would help nearly everyone. It was easy to personalize the benefits. Transit riders saw instantly that they would gain access to attractive destinations. Others could identify with drivers stuck in Beltway congestion; the light rail would give them a way to bypass the traffic jams.

Governor Glendening now swung strongly behind the Purple Line. In October 2001 he gave the route along the old tracks a high-profile endorsement, rejecting alternatives that opponents had put forward to obfuscate the issues. Business no longer saw the transit project as pie in the sky and entered the fray in force. Planning went into high gear, but the victory was short-lived. In 2002 Maryland elected a Republican governor, Robert Ehrlich, who opposed the light rail line.

Ehrlich, under heavy pressure from business lobbies, did not kill the project outright. He chose instead to "obfuscate, alter, study and delay," as his own appointee to the Metro board later put it. Planners put light rail on hold and looked at a low-cost bus route that would bypass the country club. At the same time, the new governor moved quickly ahead to build the Intercounty Connector at a cost of more than $2 billion. This expensive roadway gobbled up funds that might have been used for the Purple Line, but at the same time it strengthened the project's political position. With the highway no longer in question, the transit line became the top transportation priority of suburban business groups.

In 2006 Governor Ehrlich was defeated for reelection by Martin O'Malley, mayor of Baltimore and a Purple Line backer. By now an extraordinary coalition

Gov. Parris Glendening announces plans to build the Purple Line in 2001. Behind him is an Action Committee for Transit banner reading "We don't travel in golf carts and Mercedes—We need the Purple Line."

had lined up behind the project. It included business, labor, environmentalists, ethnic minorities, and many neighborhood associations. Outspoken support emerged even in the Chevy Chase neighborhoods where opposition was strongest. An endorsement from the Washington Area Bicyclist Association undercut the "save the trail" slogan. Most of the few remaining opponents among elected officials now reversed their positions, and the councils and executives of both counties gave their unanimous backing.

The consensus was reinforced in 2010 by a rematch election for governor. By now Columbia Country Club's place in the Purple Line debate was firmly fixed in the public mind. Ehrlich had allowed himself to be quoted saying that "it will not go through the Country Club," and O'Malley had the rare political pleasure of championing a populist cause that won him business support. The Purple Line was at the center of the election campaign, the only specific issue that Washington-area business groups pointed to in their out-of-character endorsement of the Democratic candidate. O'Malley swept to a landslide victory.

Planning for the new light rail line now moved ahead, as swiftly as complex engineering problems and an equally complex federal approval process allowed. In March 2013, the Maryland legislature raised the gasoline tax by 20 cents per gallon, ensuring that the state could pay its share of construction costs. In June, Columbia Country Club dropped its opposition, settling for a shift of the tracks 12 feet to one side so that tees can stay where the golfers want them. The project still needs federal funding, but signs are favorable; the Purple Line is expected to carry 74,000 riders per day, far more than competing projects of similar scope. If all goes according to plan, the Purple Line will break ground in 2015 and go into full operation in 2020.[19]

Portland, Arlington, and the Purple Line were smart growth successes in years when efforts elsewhere often fell short. Do these narratives have common features that might explain their outcome?

Each of these stories begins with initiatives led both from above and from below, from elected leaders and the grass roots. But they then take different courses. In Portland and Arlington, elites were the strongest backers of smart growth; the battle for the Purple Line was long led from the grass roots. Oregon's growth boundaries have been vulnerable to referendum challenges when opponents personalized the issue in ways that voters identified with. In Maryland, it was the supporters of light rail who succeeded, after much struggle, in framing the benefits of light rail—and the motives of the opponents—in vivid, easily understandable images.

But all three share one crucial element. Smart growth advocates win by thinking big. The larger vision inspires the public to override parochial objections. The entire polity chooses its future course; smaller localities lose the veto rights that suburban land tenure ordinarily grants. In Portland, the growth boundary created a coalition for infill development. In Arlington, it was the rejuvenation of an entire corridor. The struggle for the Purple Line summoned enthusiasm that a shorter rail line could not muster, mobilizing a new generation of advocates for urbanism. Harry Sanders of the Action Committee for Transit loved to quote Daniel Burnham: "Make no little plans...."

14

The Politics of Smart Growth

As the experiences of Portland, Arlington, and the Purple Line show, big ideas do not bring change by themselves. For the activism of the committed few to overcome an entrenched status quo, it must be backed up with mass support. Only a political movement, with a practical program and the strength to put it through, can turn vision into reality. Democracy is the means for moving smart growth from aspiration to reality.

Majorities, in a democracy, are not made by altruism alone; they gather when idealism is harnessed to self-interest. The victories of the New Deal and the civil rights movement rested on the organization of workers and African Americans behind demands for justice. Urbanists, likewise, can succeed only by mobilizing constituencies that link their prosperity and social standing to the fulfillment of their vision.

Even a majority achieves little unless its numbers are translated into political power. In our unequal society, there are many things the majority wants and does not get. Raising the minimum wage, making the rich pay more taxes, and putting Wall Street bankers on trial—all are more popular than urbanism. Urbanists, often, are surprised and frustrated by the slow pace of progress. They are entitled to frustration but not to surprise. Change requires politics, and politics requires strategy.

A winning coalition may seek to change the world, but it must be put together in the world as it is. Today's movements for urban revival cannot be launched, as those of an earlier generation were, off the momentum of antifreeway and environmental campaigns. The ideology of localism that propelled the movements of the 1970s was well suited to those negative goals, but it is a poor fit to the positive vision of smart growth.

Portland and Arlington succeeded by building new coalitions. It was not easy; they faced a twofold challenge after their freeways were canceled. There was the difficult intellectual task of developing a new model of growth, one that defied long-established doctrines of city planning. Then came an equally daunting political task. The new course, which bore fruit only slowly, had to be sustained by enduring political majorities.

Many others now seek to copy the achievements of these two cities. In some ways, the imitators have an easier job. With the flowering of the New Urbanism, the design principles that Arlington worked out by trial and error can be learned from textbooks. The market demand for city living has brought the political backing of business interests. And a mass constituency for urbanism has grown in a postsuburban generation. But there are new obstacles as well. Nimby sentiment has hardened since the seventies, and an organized opposition to smart growth has emerged from right-wing think tanks.

How advocates will organize depends on circumstances. The mass urbanist politics of a Portland can sprout where there is fertile soil. Big cities often have urbanist constituencies in waiting, capable of becoming an electoral force. San Francisco cyclists came together when "critical mass" rides filled the streets in the early 1990s. Ten years later, they had a five-thousand-member association that politicians feared to offend.[1]

Where the political climate is conservative and nearly everyone drives, activist organizations are likely to stay small. Yet small advocacy groups can have influence far out of proportion to their numbers when their ideas excite bigger constituencies. Rachel Flynn, the imaginative planning director of Richmond, Virginia, won wide support among residents for a pedestrian-oriented revival of the city's central neighborhoods.[2]

In suburbs, smart growth proponents occupy a strategic political position. The constant battle between developers and neighborhoods keeps local officials in a bind, forcing them to choose between resistance to growth and the need for a healthy local economy. Giving each side half a loaf satisfies no one. A middle way based on a positive program can be an attractive alternative to unsatisfactory compromises based on raw power.

With the backing of a disinterested organization of local residents, politicians find this approach much easier to pursue. Here the advocates' greatest asset is not numbers but credibility. Independence, presence in the community, and transparent finances are the foundations of that credibility. Ongoing associations, even with just a few members, are more effective than ad hoc campaigns. Support for "good" development is more believable when there is a track record of opposing the "bad," and vice versa.

Whatever the political environment, smart growth advocates find it tricky to maintain alliances. The need to fight on two fronts forces them to negotiate their way between two overlapping coalitions. When working to curb sprawl development and highway-building, they join with environmentalists and rural and exurban nimbys. Then they turn to builders, business groups, and low-income housing advocates to overcome nimby opposition to transit and infill.

Such maneuvers pose problems for established organizations with wider agendas than land use. Environmental groups, especially, face inner tensions when they work with builders. Their staff and leadership see nimbys as an obstacle to weaning suburbs from the automobile, but the membership—much of it housed in expensive suburban subdivisions—can be reluctant to follow. A volunteer citizens group, running on a small budget but free of these constraints, is sometimes more effective than a well-funded project run by an existing organization.

Direct limits on the building of automobile-dependent sprawl remain on the smart growth program. The outward push of development continues, albeit with greatly weakened force after the collapse of the real estate boom. Successes may be limited in the short term, but the movement relies on an alliance between urbanists and opponents of outer-suburb growth in the outer suburbs.

In the long run, the partisans of urban revitalization and rural preservation are natural allies. Those who seek to preserve farms and forests are sure to be accused of strangling the economy; they need to be able to say where housing and stores should go instead. Urbanists, similarly, need to demonstrate their independence of developer allies by working against "bad" projects. Beyond that, coalitions give both sides a reason to look beyond the issues at hand and broaden their thinking.

The program of these coalitions must be carefully crafted. The fallout of the clampdown of the 1970s shows that growth controls can backfire if not well designed. Statewide growth boundaries have been proven effective in

Oregon, but they seem beyond reach elsewhere at the moment. Local ordinances will be easier to enact, but they have their limitations. Curbs on office parks are hard to enforce at a time when governments, desperate for jobs and tax revenue, eagerly yield to the desires of employers. Restrictions on stores and housing lose their punch when development leaks across town and county boundaries. Still, merely slowing building in the exurbs may be enough to stop it, by buying time until long-term market trends take effect. And even when the prospects of victory are dim, taking a stand has educational value.

The reverse side of the sprawl control coin is infill development. Of all the elements of smart growth, it may be the most popular in the abstract. In brick and concrete, however, it is often fiercely controversial.

The politics of infill depends on location. Big-city downtowns almost always welcome new buildings—the economic benefits are vast, and the neighbors are few. Where the overflow from downtown can be channeled into empty old industrial districts, things for the most part still go smoothly. But when new structures are to be inserted into neighborhoods near existing homes, infill becomes a much more complicated matter.

It is in the favored quarter, where jobs cluster near expensive housing, that the economic incentives for new urban-style development are greatest. Here the promise of large profits puts the political muscle of big real estate developers behind smart growth. In jurisdictions large enough that near-neighbors are not the only voters, the developers usually find friends among politicians—not just conservatives but also liberals who see an opportunity to win business backing that they would otherwise seek in vain.

But the politicians seek to strike a balance. Favored-quarter neighborhood activists are rarely willing to endorse new buildings—in wealthy suburbs, the residents who like growth least rise to the top of homeowner groups. Even when nimbys are politically outmatched, there is a strong desire to appease them with concessions. The dominant political coalitions will be endangered if disputes become so inflamed that elections turn on development issues.

Arlington's Rosslyn-Ballston corridor runs along the edge of the favored quarter, and its political strategy has often been emulated. It amounts to a bargain between neighborhoods and developers. Big new buildings can go up, but they are carefully confined to small districts around the rail stations. Single-family homeowners far from transit are "protected" because development is channeled away from them. Neighborhoods closer in get amenities paid for by the builders, and the new arrivals are often forbidden to park on streets within their boundaries. Arlington introduced residential permit parking in the 1970s, with districts carefully gerrymandered to exclude apartment buildings.

With this program, local officials reach out to rank-and-file homeowners over the heads of civic association leaders. Civic activists, like most believers in a cause, are inclined to think that what they want for themselves is good for everyone, and even if they live far from train stations they instinctively ally themselves with nimbys closer in. Their followers, however, are more likely to take the self-interested tack of "better over there than near me" and support infill development that isn't in their own back yards.

Infill plans do get support from some neighborhood leaders. Some of them simply agree that smart growth is for the good. Others remain unconvinced by urbanist arguments but see development as inevitable. They resign themselves to what they cannot stop and seek to negotiate what concessions they can from the developers

The Arlington compromise squeezes growth into a tight radius. High-rises near the station are surrounded by single-family houses on suburban lots. This does not reproduce the old streetcar suburbs, where side streets lined with one- and two-family houses packed closely together feed customers to stores along the trolley line. New urbanist planners would surely prefer to build fewer high-rises and spread the same floor space over a larger area by scattering row houses and apartment buildings through neighborhoods.

But the political forces at work in upper-income suburbs rarely allow such mixing. Advocates and planners who might want to insert small apartment houses into single-family neighborhoods face fierce opposition from well-organized homeowner groups. Proponents of change have only the force of their convictions; scattered-site development spreads its profits too thinly to generate a self-interested lobbying force. From the urbanist point of view, the dense high-rise nodes that go up in these suburbs are a second best, but they are usually the best attainable in the circumstances.

In less affluent suburbs, infill does not have big-business muscle behind it and must find a different path. Here Portland is the outstanding success story. The impetus was the state's growth boundary law, which requires the border to be moved out if zoning rules inside the boundary do not allow enough building to house all the new residents expected within the next twenty years.

Portland did not have Arlington's opportunity to limit its smart growth to the vicinity of rail stations. The favored-quarter suburbs to the city's west did rezone some land around the new light rail line, but they were willing to take only so many newcomers. The only area with enough room to house the city's growing population was the old streetcar suburbs on the less affluent east side. In that part of the city, high-rise building was not an option. There the light rail stations, built alongside interstate highways, were not attractive sites for dense urban centers.

To preserve its growth boundary, Portland had to squeeze more people into low-rise residential neighborhoods. The city did this by allowing smaller lots and two-family houses in one-family zones. New rules were pushed through by an unlikely coalition of urbanists, environmentalists, and homebuilders, driven together by the state's growth boundary law.

Other cities have found it hard to duplicate this alignment of forces. Some have added row houses and apartments to middle-income neighborhoods—New York City in particular gained population the same way in the 1990s. But there the zoning was already in place, left over from the permissive past. Portland's rewrite of its zoning code was, in its time, unique.

In the 2010s Portland has begun to find imitators. So far changes elsewhere are more modest, and they still prove highly controversial. But there may be a wider political opening for this model of urbanization in the aftermath of the crash of 2008.

In the wake of the housing bubble, many declining inner suburbs face a situation like Portland's east side during the lumber recession of the 1980s. Despite economic stress, they remain attractive places to live, and close-in locations make it practical to commute by bus. Dividing houses into two apartments would help owners pay their mortgages and give tenants affordable rentals. But duplex conversion, when not banned altogether, is made difficult and expensive by zoning obstacles like requirements for added off-street parking and house-by-house approval.

As urbanists seek to ease these rules, they may be able to build alliances that extend beyond the transit riders and young city dwellers who constitute their usual political base. Immigrants, by definition newcomers, are among those disadvantaged by exclusionary zoning. But the effects of zoning on the overall housing market are slow and indirect; immigrants face difficulties nearer at hand, and they rarely get involved in land-use matters. Duplex conversion, which offers immediate relief for the pressing problem of housing affordability, could be the one zoning issue that rouses low-income ethnic constituencies.

In city centers as on the fringe, the larger the area that makes a decision, the more easily a majority for smart growth can be assembled. When built-up areas allow nearby neighbors to decide on infill, they deny any voice to the beneficiaries of the development—the people who would live, work, shop, and walk around in the newly urbanized areas. Farther out, the grant of zoning power to small towns yields similarly undemocratic results. Farmers allow themselves to sell their land to tract developers, and the buyers of the expensive new houses then keep out the less affluent who would like to follow them.[3]

Local governments zealously defend their zoning powers, and full transfer to a higher level of government is rarely feasible and often undesirable. But the antisnob zoning laws passed by a few states in the 1970s had a real effect in forcing single-family suburbs to let in less expensive housing and allow apartment buildings. In recent years more modest reforms have again proved possible. Some states encourage recalcitrant suburbs to accept transit-oriented development, and others penalize towns that allow too much sprawl.

Statutes need not be as strong as Oregon's growth boundary law to recast local political debates. California's Napa Valley wine country provides a striking example. A strongly antigrowth electorate defeated a 2008 referendum aimed at derailing a New Urbanist development on an old factory site. A state law that dates to 1980 requires every county to accept its share of affordable housing, and voters feared that rejecting the project would undermine rules that protect vineyards from development.[4]

Another route to change is through federal laws that encourage more rational land use. These laws work through regional bodies known as Metropolitan Planning Organizations, or MPOs. The MPOs are supposed to coordinate land use with transportation planning. But they are typically governed by a board composed of local elected officials, and they rarely challenge local land-use decisions.[5] Portland is the one city where voters elect the MPO, and its experience shows that an elected regional body, once it exists, tends to attract more power. Direct election of MPOs might be an attainable reform elsewhere, especially as the growing affluence of urban downtowns and the changing racial composition of both cities and suburbs calm suburban fears of metropolitan government.

15

Democratic Urbanism

Creating denser cities is just the beginning of the unmaking of sprawl. What fills in the urban spaces must be truly urban.

The needed changes are many, and they will not be easy. The roots of sprawl go deep, permeating the subsoil of American life. Thousands of mundane decisions about streets, sidewalks, houses, schools, stores, and civic buildings shape the suburban landscape. Some are made under the watchful eyes of snob zoning, others are negotiated at the regulatory toll booth, and not a few reflect the profit-and-loss calculations of fiscal zoning.

Policy directives will only slightly shift the outcome of these choices—the landowners, neighbors, and government officials who make them will continue to pursue their own agendas. Nor can public participation exert much influence—activists and volunteers, unless they live in the immediate vicinity, rarely find the time to inject themselves into these everyday decisions. Only structural change—altered institutions and incentives that give rise to different systems of control—can transform the behavior of the interest groups concerned with local real estate.

Our inherited patterns of land-use governance mix different economic systems, and new arrangements will involve new mixtures. A helpful way to think about reform is to list the elements that might go into those mixtures.

The economist János Kornai classified the ways economic activity is organized into five mechanisms. The market, where buyer and seller negotiate as equals before the law, is of course one. Another is bureaucratic coordination, which passes information up and down a hierarchy. This was Kornai's main concern; his scholarly aim was to understand Soviet communism. He adds three other mechanisms: self-governance, with decisions made by voting; ethical coordination, gifts given without expectation of return; and family coordination.[1]

In the organization of American land use all five mechanisms are present, and the common stable patterns combine elements of more than one. Even in the snob zoning of a small suburb, self-governance lays out the zones and the market decides whether anything gets built in them. On the scale of a metropolis, economics, politics, law, and sociology are entangled in an intricate net.

Weaknesses in the governance of land use are widely recognized, and there is no lack of proposals for change. But reformers, all too often, seek only to perfect the mechanism closest at hand. Planners put forth better plans, economists rail against overregulation, and local activists insist that nearby property owners should have the last word. Isolated changes can bring unexpected consequences as a tug at one thread ripples across the web.

A restructured governance of land use would, ideally, set each mechanism to the tasks it does best. Markets are most effective in catering to a diversity of tastes; owners of buildings should be able to alter their use as consumers make new demands. Only bureaucrats can do the boring work of making sure potholes are patched and sewers don't overflow; they need the budgets and the authority to get their jobs done. Voting gives everyone a say in policy choices; the people as a whole have the right to make the big decisions.

In all the complexity of land use governance, this last principle stands out: the reestablishment of popular sovereignty. All deserve a voice in determining the common future. The principle of one person, one vote must replace the restricted voting of suburban land tenure. The vagaries of a war of snobbery against greed should not shape our cities.

Zoning, covenants, and historic preservation, as now organized, all function to maintain the status quo. Of the three, zoning has the most pervasive influence.

One basic element of reform is the elimination of zoning's openly undemocratic features. When the public votes on rezoning, suffrage should be based on residence rather than landownership. Tenants should receive the same notice of proposed changes as landlords. Associations should be recognized as representing neighborhoods only if they accept renters as equal members with homeowners. The more zoning boards are democratic in form, the greater the ability of the unrepresented to organize politically and change their practice.

But that is only a beginning. New Urbanist planners have undertaken a fundamental rethinking of zoning. They call for complete replacement of current ordinances with what they call the form-based code. It regulates the size, shape, and placement of buildings instead of specifying the uses inside them as a zoning code does.[2]

On the surface the form-based code aims at the substance of the rules rather than procedure, but in practice it alters power relationships. The bureaucracy and the neighbors lose control of the insides of buildings and gain more influence over their outsides; builders and their customers make the opposite exchange. Mixed-use buildings, no longer exceptions, are no harder to approve than single-use buildings and are no more liable to neighborhood obstruction. Citizens who wish to preserve sprawl no longer possess means of influence that those who wish to challenge it lack.

Charles Siegel, a transit activist in Berkeley, California, would take the democratization of zoning much farther. Siegel has an anarchist streak, but he is also a pragmatist and among the few who have thought carefully about governance and sprawl. If cities were left to grow without rules, he points out, today's automotive dominance would only perpetuate itself. Instead of abolishing regulation entirely, he therefore seeks to replace prescriptive rules with a framework that enables spontaneity and complexity to flourish. Instead of leaving planning to experts, he would have the political process set limits on the nature of development.

Siegel has some specific suggestions for his grass-roots legislators. He would limit the number of floors in buildings—three or four stories where we wish to imitate streetcar suburbs, six for urban neighborhoods—and require a little bit of empty space for light and air. He insists on small blocks and would put a cap on how much land one owner could control. Most of all, rules are needed to tame the automobile and prevent it from corroding the fabric of the city. He would do this with area-wide speed limits. In city centers, cars might be banned entirely; urban neighborhoods would limit speed to 10 or 15 miles an hour; suburbs would allow drivers to go 20 or 25. A centrally planned network of rapid trains would tie the entire city together.[3] Even if this sketch seems utopian, it has value in showing a coherent direction for change.

Especially pertinent is Siegel's call for divided ownership of land. It offers a practical cure for the lack of character that plagues even the best New Urbanist projects. A single owner who controls an entire shopping district can offer tenants immunity from nearby competition in exchange for higher rents. Each store on the property winds up in a distinct market niche. The merchant who can afford to pay the most rent is the one who fills the niche most efficiently, and that is usually a chain store with standardized merchandise. Thus the stultifying sameness of enclosed shopping malls—and the eerie mall-like feeling that even well-designed New Urbanist suburbs can exude.

A contrasting dynamic sets in when adjoining buildings have different owners. Stores in the same line of business are let in. Head-to-head competition drives merchants to cut prices, raise quality, and add distinctive traits to their goods. Trades cluster into specialized centers that draw customers from throughout the metropolis. Competition and proximity are potent drivers of innovation, infusing a far wider area with economic vitality.[4] And the rich fabric of differentiated neighborhoods makes the city much more than the sum of its streets—it was the supremely specialized business districts of mid-twentieth-century Manhattan that turned Jane Jacobs into an urbanist.

Current planning practice, even among New Urbanists, tilts strongly toward unified control. Master plans promote *land assembly*. When cities condemn land for redevelopment, they most often seek a single buyer for the entire property. If the project is too big for one company, a *master developer* is put in charge. Landowners are not the only decision-makers enticed by the monopoly profits that single ownership can bring—local government is relieved of infrastructure costs, neighbors appeased by suburban-style amenities, politicians showered with campaign contributions. But the city itself, economically weaker and deprived of urban texture, is the worse.

Even when common ownership is not imposed by fiat, zoning laws encourage it. Some places allow mixed-use development only on large lots. Elsewhere, the expense of seeking approvals is so great that small-scale projects are unfeasible. If rules were friendlier to diversity of ownership, infill projects could be more like old downtowns, given life and color by their smaller property owners. Simpler rules can build more complex cities.

Simpler, as Siegel emphasizes, is more democratic as well. When the public has clear choices, it can decide among them. Complexity transfers power away from voters, either to planners or to the private interests most directly concerned. Streamlining approval processes democratizes zoning.

More often than not, when infill is built in today's suburbs, each building is a political decision. Either a locality waits to rezone until the owner is ready to build, or the zoning requires a case-by-case approval to build anything big enough to give the builder a profit. This, in large jurisdictions especially, yields a profoundly undemocratic governance of land use. The near neighbors have leverage to extract concessions, and citizens with a less direct interest lack motivation to counter them.

The more democratic practice is to adopt area-wide plans after public debate and immediately rezone all land for its intended use. Because plans attract the interest of a broader public than single buildings, the landowners and neighbors must share their influence. Power flows to the voters of the larger area.

A practical objection to this procedure is that governments lose the power to make developers pay for infrastructure and amenities. But there is another way to extract money from developers: taxation. Taxation is more democratic because the money raised is spent in the open, as part of the city budget. The entire population has a voice. When developer contributions are worked out behind the scenes, the biggest benefits go to the people with the power to say no. These, most often, are small groups of wealthy homeowners who live near the most profitable new buildings.

If anything in the world of land use is an affront to democracy, it is the private government of the homeowner association. At best, those too poor to own real estate are denied a vote; at worst, future generations are bound irrevocably by the whims of the developer who created the association. Always, the rights of residents to free speech, artistic self-expression, and free movement are at risk.

The "planned communities" of the 1960s and 1970s are aging, and the dead hands of deed covenants now weigh down on their inhabitants. They fix land uses in place; they ban mixed uses and upstairs apartments. These rules, often nearly impossible to alter, preclude the infill strategies that enlivened the inner-ring suburbs of Arlington and Portland.

The homeowner associations, designed for permanent prosperity, are ill fitted for economic decline. Distressed homeowners stop paying fees, and assessments go up on the neighbors. Foreclosure, the association's ultimate remedy to collect unpaid assessments, is useless when houses are mortgaged for more than they are worth—the bank, which normally gets paid before the association, will take all the money if the property is sold. Rising fees squeeze the owners who keep paying, and the entire community falls into a cycle of decay.

Obsolete rules and straitened budgets are symptoms of a fundamental defect. Homeowner associations are governments, not private organizations. The principles of constitutional government, arrived at through centuries of struggle, should apply to them. Mandatory payments for the upkeep of common services should be treated as taxes, worthy of priority payment before private debts like mortgages. Covenants on land use, density, and design of buildings should expire after a fixed lifetime, replaced by zoning regulations that can be kept up to date. (This seemingly radical innovation is a return to the legal doctrines of the nineteenth century, put in place to prevent just the sort of problem associations now face.) And community governments, whatever their form or origin, should be controlled by their citizens, with fundamental freedoms protected and voting rights extended to tenants and homeowners alike.[5]

Critics of homeowner associations are many, but their focus tends to be narrow. They limit their complaints to the most obnoxious rules or get bogged down in the minutiae of individual disputes. Incumbent board members and the for-profit management firms that associations hire to run their operations defend the status quo. With heavy lobbying in state capitals, they have managed so far to stave off reform by agreeing to cosmetic changes. But there is a large constituency for change among homeowners who revile the unresponsive, nitpicking boards of their associations. Framing the issue within the broader debate over smart growth and democratic control of land use would encourage state legislatures to remedy the underlying defects of private government.

Historic preservation is the third pillar of suburban land tenure. Its prevailing doctrines are an open invitation to thinly disguised nimbyism. Vaguely defined categories can, with enough ingenuity and political influence, be stretched to fit almost any old building. In Santa Monica, California, civic groups tried to make a half-empty trailer park a historic landmark. Their goal was to block a 486-unit apartment complex near a future light rail station. This was the rare case where the Landmarks Commission had no choice but to turn them down. Its jurisdiction was limited to the concrete pads, the commission declared; it was powerless to protect the trailers.[6]

The preservationists' core concept, historic and architectural "significance," is a catch-all that lumps together two distinct categories: the landmark and the merely old. There are good arguments for protecting both sorts of buildings, but they are of different orders.

True landmarks are places of such exceptional importance—sites of historic events, great works of architecture, and such—that total protection is merited. But divorcing significance from artistic merit leaves no basis for identifying architectural landmarks. In the end, aesthetic judgments are still made—they are unavoidable—but they are made behind the scenes by insiders, allowing criticism from the public to be brushed off.

Old things that are not landmarks deserve protection too, but of a different sort. The heritage of the architectural past lies in ordinary-looking styles—what architects call *vernacular*. To preserve a style, buildings must survive, but what matters is how many and not which ones. No single structure is essential.

Because cities are living organisms and not architectural museums, some old buildings must be torn down. This imperative is recognized in practice by preservation authorities, but their theory distinguishes only the historic from the not historic. Without a basis for choosing among old structures, they fall back on the rule of first come, first served. The wealthiest and most influential neighborhoods show up first, and it is their old buildings that stay. Urbanist theory suggests the opposite—demolish the ordinary when it sits on expensive real estate and preserve architectural styles on less valuable land. The old buildings that remain would be what Jane Jacobs thought they should be, low-rent settings for the economic diversity that makes cities thrive.

There are old neighborhoods where the historic fabric itself merits preservation, but even here some new building should be allowed. The current preservation system creates dead zones that wall off the past—even when, as in the case of Washington's Cleveland Park district, the defining characteristic said to make it historic is a mixture of different ages and styles. Rapid change can destroy the distinctive traits of city neighborhoods, but stopping construction hardly ensures the survival of historic character. Today's upscale Greenwich Village is not the place that drew in the John Reeds and Jane Jacobses.

The heritage of the past is most alive when it is embedded in a living environment. One way to mix old and new might be with quotas on destruction of threatened building styles. A city would limit how many Victorian frame houses could be demolished each year, how many Sears Craftsman houses, how many buildings in each historic district. The permits might be given out first come, first served, or if demand were high they could be auctioned off. In each category, a minimum number of structures would have to be preserved— no more permits when the limit is reached. Setting quotas in the open balances the aesthetic judgments of the entire city against the political pull of nimby neighborhoods. San Francisco would surely retain most of its wooden Victorians, Los Angeles might get by with some dingbats here and there, and the entire country could probably make do with just a handful of original McDonald's golden arches.

Many of the changes suggested here would run afoul of the legal principles that now underpin land use regulation. The status quo rests on a series of legal fictions—the police power, the master plan, voluntary consent to covenants, historical significance—that make reform hard to discuss rationally and harder to enact. The persistence of these doctrines, in the face of their patent unreality, reflects the need to reconcile the system of suburban land tenure with the law's obsolete concept of private property.

As the law sees it, land is something with value in itself. In the days when real estate was bought to grow corn or cut lumber, this was an eminently sensible doctrine. But today life is otherwise. Urban land, as distinct from useful buildings that might sit on it, has little intrinsic worth. It acquires value to the extent that the rules allow something to be built there or that a buyer thinks the rules can be changed to let something be built.

In legal theory and public consciousness, owners still have an inherent right to use their land. But in practice that right disappeared years ago and was replaced by suburban land tenure. Today no one seeks to reverse that evolution—those most insistent on protecting property rights are often the fiercest partisans of snob zoning. Legal doctrines should be based on facts and not obsolete theories.

This does not mean that judges can step back and let governments do whatever they wish—but they should protect the underlying purposes that private property serves rather than any abstract right. Rules that bar interference with the zoning that happens to be in place purport to protect property owner against arbitrary actions of government, but they do so by freezing in place the equally arbitrary decisions made years before. The balance between a farmer's desire to subdivide land and city dwellers' wish to limit sprawl should be struck by today's electorate rather than the voters who lived in a small town long ago. The rights of landowners, like the rights of neighbors, must be weighed against the will of the majority.

A real need that property rights serve is to protect against unfairness of local governing bodies. A perfect balance between the individual and the public interest will be impossible to find. But the goal of improving on the current situation is hardly daunting. Ensuring that homeowner associations can no more abridge rights than local governments would be a good start.

Another useful function of land ownership is to create markets that offer choice to consumers and promote economic growth. In the mixed economy of land use, some markets serve these ends and others don't. Property rights serve no larger social purpose when they restrict consumer choice and protect status at the expense of economic activity. This, most often, is the effect when homeowners enforce rules written by long-dead developers.

When good policy collides with legal fiction, it is the law that should change. Suburban land tenure is deeply rooted in the American psyche and will not soon disappear. But the law should recognize it as a political claim that can be outvoted. It should not be a legal entitlement.[7]

Reconciling a new legal structure with existing constitutional law will require ingenuity. But lawyers are rich in ingenuity. Those who undertake this task will have to reconcile conflicting goals, and imperfections are inevitable. Still, it will not be hard at all to do better than the current arrangement. Jurisprudence that reflects reality could enlarge popular sovereignty and at the same time offer more choice to consumers and more rights to individuals.

The democratization of land use is only the end of the beginning of the battle against sprawl. Even with form-based codes, new street design standards, and better governance, the detailed work of building will remain to be done by specialists. Architects, planners, builders, and engineers can be empowered to create more livable cities, but how well they do it will be up to them.

Humanizing the landscape of strip malls and edge cities is not a simple task. Fortunately, many thinkers are at work on solutions. A good introduction for general readers is *Suburban Nation* by Andres Duany, Elizabeth Plater-Zyberk, and Jeff Speck. Professionals can turn to books like Galina Tachieva's *Sprawl Repair Manual* and *Retrofitting Suburbia* by Ellen Dunham-Jones and June Williamson.

The worse the sprawl, it turns out, the harder it is to fix. Successful transit-oriented downtowns, in Arlington, Portland, and elsewhere, take advantage of existing grid street patterns. New buildings can arrive one by one, and sidewalks that are already walkable become livelier as more people walk on them. In more recently built suburbs, where the superblock layout funnels traffic onto six- and eight-lane arterials, this sort of gradual upgrade is nearly impossible. There are few pedestrians on the unpleasant highways, so the existing structures face away from them and occupants of new, more urban buildings have nowhere to walk to. When someone suggests a new road connection, objections are swift and loud. In this environment any through street becomes a traffic sewer—a complete grid would be better for everyone, but no one benefits by going first.

To overcome the twin hurdles of politics and traffic, entire neighborhoods must be redesigned at once. In the automobile-era suburbs of Washington, where superblock road designs predominate, this work has already begun. Under Montgomery County's White Flint plan, a new street grid will criss-cross what are now parking lots. Across the Potomac River, planners have undertaken the formidable task of rebuilding Tysons Corner after the Metro arrives there in 2014.

The street network around the White Flint Metro station (entered at dots), Montgomery County, Maryland. Left in 1988 and right as planned for 2020 (with pedestrian connections dashed).

These thorough makeovers are so expensive that only wealthy sections of the favored quarter can afford them. The new street networks are never as dense and well connected as in older cities, and they emerge only over decades. White Flint got a head start from an earlier master plan that began to open passageways through the superblocks. Even so, the grid will take a dozen years to fill out, and it will not connect to adjacent subdivisions. The new Tysons, with two wide roads through its heart that are already nearly impassible for pedestrians, could be stillborn. Its planners were unable to overcome local traffic engineers' insistence that more people always need more roads, and they agreed to add more lanes of speeding traffic to its already wide central highways.

Such hindrances continue to obstruct urban transformation, even where the manifest need to rebuild has opened purses. In places the way forward is known but the will is lacking; elsewhere planners face conundrums that no one has yet solved. And rebuilding edge cities is only part of the task; less costly fixes will have to be devised for the exurbs of the last housing boom, whose premature decay has already begun.

If the citizenry continues to demand change, these intellectual roadblocks may be overcome along with the political and economic obstacles. Unsolved problems will find answers and better responses will emerge to difficulties thought already overcome. Public mobilization does not just erect a political framework; it inspires further progress. Democracy has a way of unleashing human creativity.

16

Affordable Housing in an Ownership Society

Affordability is an issue that bedevils urbanists. When neighborhoods revive, say critics of smart growth, the people who live in them are the losers. Rents shoot upward, forcing out low-income tenants. Soon the middle class is priced out too. Home values skyrocket, and their owners can't afford the tax bills. Stores stocked with everyday necessities are replaced by trendy boutiques, and then the boutiques give way to chain stores. Diversity fades into the stodgy uniformity of rootless affluence.

This is a familiar story, and it has elements of truth. But what drives up the cost of urban living is not revitalization so much as the obstacles in its way. Good transit reaches only a small portion of the metropolis, and there good schools and safe streets are often lacking. Affluent neighborhoods near rail lines keep housing scarce with single-family zoning, parking minimums, and height limits. Where sections of the city improve, pent-up demand collides with scarcity, and prices rise.

Whatever the trigger for gentrification may be, moreover, the damage it does is less severe than critics claim. It helps residents in some ways as it hurts them in others. Homeowners troubled by higher taxes still gain wealth from rising house prices. Many renters live in public housing or are under rent control, and others stay on in aging apartments while landlords resist the lure of redevelopment to hold out for even higher prices. In the meantime, renters and homeowners alike enjoy the improvements that come with the arrival of more affluent neighbors.

But if affordability is a weak argument *against* smart growth, it is still a problem *for* smart growth. Tenants can be victims of a process that creates enormous value for others. In a world of zoning, covenants, and historic districts, this is hardly the natural working of a free market. Land use law takes pains to shelter homeowners from the intangible "impacts" of nearby stores and apartments, yet it gives tenants no protection against the very tangible harm of higher rents.

The disappearance of affordable housing from reviving neighborhoods hurts the poor most, but the whole city suffers with them. The demand for urban living, in many cities, is dammed up between the barriers of poverty and crime on one side, and suburban land tenure on the other. It has great force when it breaks through. Once an area begins to improve, housing prices shoot up and the population turns over rapidly. A zone of affluence emerges, separated by invisible walls from the surrounding poverty. Gentrification, bottled up in small spaces, destroys the mosaic of mixed uses and mixed incomes sought by many of those who initiate the process. Active intervention on behalf of affordability preserves diversity. It makes for a more livable city as well as a fairer one.

The most direct and efficient way to keep housing affordable is rent control. Rent control is of course less popular among landlords than among tenants, so it has long been a subject of fierce debate.

Mainstream economists tend toward skepticism about price controls of any sort, and rent control has been a particular target of the conservative wing of the profession. The case against rent control has changed little over the years. It is, in essence, that fixing rents destroys the incentive to create more affordable housing by building new homes or splitting up existing ones. The classic statement is a 1946 pamphlet commissioned by the National Association of Real Estate Boards and written by Milton Friedman and George Stigler. Writing at a time of postwar housing shortage, Friedman and Stigler laid heavy stress on the splitting. "Until there is sufficient new construction," they argued, "this doubling up is the only solution."[1]

Whatever merit such contentions may have in the abstract—and there are strong counterarguments—they have little relevance to the housing market as it actually exists. The logic of unfettered competition presupposes that owners of capital assets seek to maximize their property's value and utility. This theory breaks down when the goal is to gain prestige by letting fewer people live on each acre of land. The competitors aim not to use their own assets more productively but to prevent their neighbors from using theirs.

Thus, competition in the real estate market is tightly fettered. The very purpose of zoning rules is to reduce the supply of apartments. The realtors' trade association, which paid for the Friedman and Stigler pamphlet, also helped draft the model planning act of 1928. Their open intent, in promoting planning, was to raise house prices by limiting supply. The realtors' passion was not free markets, but high rents.[2]

Zoning, with its insistence on single-family "character," steps in with particular force when someone tries to follow Milton Friedman's advice. Homeowners with unused rooms break the law if they create another dwelling unit. New entrants into the housing market—demobilized soldiers in 1946, immigrants and recent college graduates today—have no access to empty living space.

When houses cannot be divided, removing rent controls adds nothing to the supply of homes. The only legal way to double up is to move in with your parents, and rent ceilings don't stop parents from taking in their children. All deregulation does is take money from tenants and put it in landlords' pockets.[3] A vote on rent control, with single-family zoning on the books, does not decide whether the government will set rents. It chooses whether to raise them up with one law or hold them down with another.

When shortages are most severe, tenants are most in need of protection, but that is when rent control is least effective. It is a dam that protects only when the flood does not rise too high. If the market rent climbs far above the controlled rent, tenants and landlords alike exploit the gap. They sublet, pay "key money," and otherwise do business off the books. To keep controls working, new housing must satisfy the demand.

Most of the world today, and the United States in the past, have believed that the profit motive cannot produce an adequate supply of affordable housing. Many countries initially responded as the New Deal did, with housing built by cities or by public agencies. With the passage of time, it became clear that ownership by centralized government agencies brought problems of its own. While the sterility that George Orwell and Jane Jacobs observed in public housing can be blamed on modernist planning theories, the remedies for that ill—variety, flexibility, and personal initiative—are not easily applied by large bureaucracies.

In the years since the 1970s, western Europe has sought to combine the virtues of individual and common ownership. The urban housing market has

Nonprofit housing in the Netherlands, built at the sidewalk with stores on the ground floor.
(Courtesy of Pamela Lindstrom.)

evolved in the direction of market socialism. Apartments are rented and sold in an open market, while cooperatives and nonprofits compete in the building of new structures. The land under the buildings remains in government hands, owned by the city or controlled to limit the scope of individual profit.

Public attitudes and power relationships would need to change enormously before the United States could move toward such a system. And there is a further obstacle. Even if the federal government offered funding for public housing on the scale of the past, the problem of siting the housing in a city of status-seeking neighborhoods would remain to be overcome.

But urbanists cannot neglect government and nonprofit housing. The existing stock of public housing is irreplaceable for those who live there. And the neighborhoods around housing projects benefit too, by retaining economic diversity as they gentrify. When buildings must be torn own, due to age and wear or to insufficient density, new public housing should replace them. And, however distant the prospect, the country needs a revived national program of housing construction.[4]

Prosperous communities, if they have the political will, can add to their affordable housing even without federal aid. The rent on apartments for the middle class (but not the poor) can usually pay for construction and upkeep. The reason apartments are so expensive in upscale neighborhoods is not so much the cost of construction as the scarcity of opportunities to build. Scarcity value is embodied in land prices, but local governments own much land and can deploy their regulatory powers to obtain the use of other land. The vast demand for less expensive housing can hardly be sated by such means, but what is built is immensely valuable to its inhabitants and the neighborhoods around them.

In few places are tenants numerous and well organized enough to enact rent control, and in the absence of federal money only so much new affordable housing can be built. It can be hard even to preserve what now exists.

This issue comes to the fore in rapidly gentrifying neighborhoods. Here urbanist thinking offers some potential remedies. A flat-out ban on new off-street parking would channel new housing away from the top end of the market.[5] Unrestricted conversion of single-family houses to duplexes would let owners stay in place and benefit from rising values while adding to the supply of less expensive rentals. Both measures would guide change rather than trying to halt it altogether.

Tenant advocates often fall back instead on a purely defensive approach and oppose new construction in the neighborhood. This strategy rests on a seemingly straightforward logic. Real estate prices are always a matter of location—buildings are expensive because they're near expensive buildings—so keeping out new buildings, which will always charge a higher rent than the older ones around them, helps keep housing affordable.

The means of stopping development is a political coalition of tenants and nimby homeowners. This alliance is surely an odd basis for left-wing politics, but a school of academic theory justifies it as such. The idea is that neighborhoods are defending themselves against an exploitative and nearly all-powerful "growth machine." The fuel that drives the machine is profit, derived from the excess of the "exchange value" realized when land is redeveloped over the "use value" enjoyed by its current residents.[6] This logic dovetails nicely with the greedy developer mantra of more conservative suburban homeowners.

Growth machine theory has the merit of focusing on the exercise of political power, something that is glossed over in much establishment writing about land use. It explains, moreover, why urban renewal and downtown expressways were so hard to stop in the 1950s and 1960s. But the theory is less useful in current circumstances. For one thing, it exaggerates the power of the growth machine. Developers would surely, if allowed, build their high-rises in prestigious close-in neighborhoods like Beverly Hills, Grosse Pointe, and Georgetown. Condos would be easier to sell there than in the run-down areas where local governments now let them build.[7] For another, the concept of use value misconstrues the motivation for resistance to growth. Nimbys acquire higher status by means of conspicuous waste; what zoning protects is not the use of land but its disuse.

A variant of this theory that emphasizes the role of lower-income neighborhoods as centers of resistance to capitalism is popular among neo-Marxist writers. Aiming to understand the global forces behind recent economic trends, they focus on the role of banks and real estate developers in urban change and downplay the role of individual gentrifiers. The single-family zoning of suburban homeowners has little relevance to their concerns and is often taken for granted.

The focus on gentrification shifts the political base for affordable housing. Tenants themselves do not mobilize on the abstract issue of future land use as they do for the immediate protection of rent control. Meanwhile, support grows more intense among the gentrifiers themselves—for some grass-roots advocates of affordable housing, opposition to gentrification begins with a desire to keep the neighborhood just the way it was when they moved in. Sympathy for low-income residents comes only afterward.[8]

At their worst, local struggles against gentrification have less to do with the poor than with protecting the brand image of poverty in a newly hip neighborhood. Local activists seize on neo-Marxist theory to denounce all change as the evil machinations of the multinational elite. Here there is an echo of prosprawl libertarians like Randal O'Toole and Joel Kotkin. One group hails nimbys as enemies of the urban cultural elite; the other welcomes them as partners in the struggle against global capital. Either way, the rhetoric serves a similar purpose. It provides a rationale for alliances that would otherwise be hard to square with the locally fashionable political ideology.[9]

Identifying gentrification as the underlying issue brings the issues of transportation and development to the fore. Other things in poor neighborhoods keep wealthy newcomers out too—crime and bad schools, for example— but it is hard to argue for their preservation. An activist may think, as one Chicagoan told an interviewer, that crime helps keep his neighborhood from becoming "too nice," but few longtime residents agree.[10] Targeted instead are light rail lines and new buildings on vacant land. In themselves they displace no one, but as triggers of change they seem as threatening as condo conversions and they are much easier to stop.

For tenants, who certainly have a direct concern for affordability, coalitions with nimbys lead to a dead end. Changing city neighborhoods cannot be preserved as low-rent refuges unless the demand for urban living is soaked up somewhere else. New urban downtowns would have to be built in the wealthy areas where CEOs live and jobs cluster. But the alliance with nimbys makes it impossible to challenge snob zoning within the same political jurisdiction. And by legitimating resistance to change, it reinforces the status quo elsewhere.

The wealthy inevitably play the exclusion game more effectively than the poor. Pent-up demand is funneled into the surviving remnants of an older urbanism. The price of the existing housing stock soars. This dynamic of gentrification has gone furthest in San Francisco, where soaring housing costs accompany tight building limits. The best-paid jobs are in Silicon Valley office parks, so reverse commuters' cars crowd the streets of once-poor neighborhoods.

Housing is least affordable in the wealthiest suburbs and city neighborhoods, which price out the middle class along with the poor. Minimum-wage workers are not the only ones forced into long commutes; teachers and firefighters can't afford to live near their jobs either.

A common remedy in such areas is what is known as inclusionary zoning. These rules require builders to rent or sell a certain portion of new housing at prices that middle-income people can pay. More than one hundred localities have adopted them. Some places require affordable housing in all new housing; elsewhere builders who comply earn a *density bonus*—the right to put bigger buildings on their land.[11]

Inclusionary zoning is usually an add-on to existing zoning codes, and that has been a weakness. Zoning's original purpose was to keep low-priced dwellings out, and pasting in new text does not undo the exclusionary workings of the rest of the ordinance. Parking minimums are a particular burden; an affordable apartment near a subway station has no need for a $50,000 underground parking space. Exempting affordable housing from such rules—or repealing them altogether—builds more homes at less cost.

Condominium fees are another obstacle. In high-end condos, doormen, athletic clubs, and such extras drive up the monthly charge. Here again, car-free living can be the remedy. The condo association might own the garage and finance itself by renting out spaces, or it could assess fees on parking spaces rather than living spaces. Residents of affordable units would escape paying for unneeded luxuries if they went without a car or parked off the premises.

The number of affordable apartments inclusionary zoning can build is small compared to the need, but its political significance is great. By allowing people of modest means to live everywhere, it breaks through the suburban cycle of competitive exclusion. The real estate market, driven by the cost of land and the influence of local nimbys, when left to itself pushes low-income housing toward less expensive sections of town. Absent inclusionary zoning, homeowners in those areas will complain that they are stuck with what no one else will take. Giving all areas a share of officially designated affordable housing smooths the way for other means of mixing income levels and combining land uses.

Inclusionary zoning has little point unless houses are expensive and new buildings are going up. After the housing bubble, such success is more the exception than the rule. Cleveland, Detroit, and Buffalo are full of walkable neighborhoods where the supply of housing exceeds the demand. There no one worries about affordability.

There are, too, places in the middle, where the boom is long gone yet housing remains maddeningly expensive. Decay and affordability can be problems simultaneously. Such middle-range neighborhoods can be found in inner suburbs of relatively prosperous cities. Here the legalization of two-family houses would help deal with both threats.

Another type of middle-income suburb, the McMansion exurb, poses a less tractable problem. Although their economic settings vary, ranging from relative prosperity to the calamities of Las Vegas, Phoenix, and southwest Florida, all are at risk of the cycle of decay endured by inner cities in the 1950s and 1960s. House prices fall, public services go downhill as tax revenues decline, and an influx of lower-income residents magnifies the resulting loss of status. Some areas on the outskirts of San Francisco and Washington may soon see a flight of the affluent in search of good schools and safe neighborhoods in the inner city.

Exurban decline, if it starts to feed on itself, may prove hard to stop. When streetcar suburbs went downhill, they still offered an inexpensive place to live. With stores in walking distance and buses to downtown, no one needed a car. Zoning was permissive and covenants long forgotten, so big old Victorian houses were broken up into affordable apartments and rooming houses. Slums like the South Bronx did collapse, but many neighborhoods built before the First World War sustained themselves as healthy, livable working-class communities.

Failed exurbs will find this path hard to follow. Expensive commuting cancels out low rents. Zoning forbids the breakup of big houses into rental apartments, and covenants occasionally forbid rentals altogether. Some subdivisions are already half-empty, and complete abandonment could become a long-term trend.

One California exurb, the city of Merced, may have stumbled into a way out of this dilemma. A new state university with 5200 students has room for only 1600 in the dorms, so the students have taken to renting empty McMansions. These living arrangements do not run afoul of zoning rules because the structure is not divided into separate apartments. Five students may pay $200 a month each and share a five-bedroom house that once went for more than half a million dollars. A sophomore does his homework in the Jacuzzi; a senior fills a walk-in closet with baseball caps and T-shirts. The university sends free buses to student-heavy subdivisions.[12]

Few outer suburbs are endowed with Merced's student population, but many have families of modest means in search of better homes. If the law allowed it, five- and six-bedroom houses could be split into two or three apartments. Long-distance commutes will never be cheap, but their cost can be kept within reason by running commuter trains or buses from park-and-ride lots. Where affordable housing is scarce and the destination is a dense downtown full of jobs, subdividing may be a way out in the exurbs too.

Tenants, in a country where most people own their homes, enter politics in a position of weakness. For owners, housing affordability is a two-edged sword. They are both sellers and buyers, and as sellers they like high prices. They want, moreover, their neighbors' houses to be expensive—it is a matter of status and of real estate prices too.

Advocates for affordable housing are left with a stark political choice between two strategic alliances.

One approach is to preserve the existing stock of low-cost housing with strict rent control that blocks demolition of affordable units. Only when new supply cushions it against market demand can such a system endure. The supply can come from public or nonprofit housing built on vacant land or, in the absence of federal housing subsidies, by opening up residential neighborhoods to construction of new housing. This strategy has had successes, in cities from New York to Santa Monica, but they require the right political and ideological circumstances. Public debate must be open to ideas of the left. And low-income voters must be well organized, in unions or political parties, strong enough to be the senior partners in the inevitable alliance with the nimbys.

When tenants don't have enough strength to make rent control a realistic possibility, alliances with nimbys can easily boomerang. Tenant votes go to slow growth candidates who, when elected, make new housing harder to build. In the absence of new urban places, affluent would-be urbanites flood into the walkable neighborhoods that already exist and bid up prices there.

Renovations and condo conversions eat up the affordable housing in these old city districts.

Affordable housing proponents can avoid this outcome by dealing with the other side in the developer–nimby wars. They lend their support to new development in exchange for inclusionary zoning and easing of limits on rental apartments in houses. This strategy promises much less to renters than the benefits of rent control. But it has a chance of success in many more places.

Neither local strategy can promise more than partial success. Before affordable and livable housing can be built for all, the political environment must change both nationally and locally. Financing must come from the federal government, and zoning boards must allow infill development without arm-twisting by developers. Both are long-term quests. But they are goals that cannot be abandoned.

17

On Track toward Livable Cities

Great cities, Daniel Burnham understood, are built from plans with "magic to stir men's blood." A century after his passing, that maxim has lost none of its force. Today it is the inheritance of sprawl that stalls the renewal of cities and stymies the renovation of suburbs. Change comes only when the public is roused to impose its will.

Trains, like nothing else in cities, possess Daniel Burnham's magic. When discussion of new rail lines starts, ideas bubble up from the grass roots. Fierce debates erupt over where the tracks should go. The public joins the discussion because change is not abstract. Those near the route see how their daily lives will be affected, and others can put themselves in their shoes.

If a project is put to a public vote, volunteers mobilize. Supporters living along the future tracks counter the inevitable nimbys. Environmental groups, slow to speak out when infill development is at issue, wax enthusiastic. Coalitions of unusual breadth come together, uniting labor, business, ethnic neighborhoods, and conservationists. Polls show that trains are popular.

Trains provoke this interest and engagement because they are much more than transportation. The urban rebirth of the last thirty years has been a rail renaissance. New York, Boston, Chicago, and Philadelphia have revived around their subways; change comes fastest not to the prettiest or safest neighborhoods but to those with the best rail connections.[1] Washington and

Portland have been remade by their new train lines. In Los Angeles, Denver, and San Francisco, skimpy rail networks that reach suburbs just here and there have sufficed to revive once-fading downtowns.

As they remake cities, rail lines bring rethinking. By elevating public space, they reject the suburban ideal of isolation. A visible challenge to the driver's ingrained belief that a car is the only normal way to move around, they affirm in steel and concrete that city dwellers no longer rank below suburbanites. Grass-roots advocacy for urbanism begins, almost always, with a railroad.

Rail transit is not merely a conveyance. It is the political and mental key that opens the door to urban change.

In economics, as in politics, rail transit is central to urban revival. Financing alone cannot revive the ailing postbubble housing market, because the supply of dwelling places is ill-matched to the demand. Suburban McMansions are a drag on the market; what consumers seek are apartments and townhouses in the new transit-oriented urban centers. But there are simply not enough places to build the housing that is in demand; few cities have a transit network large enough to open up the needed land.

Money spent on new urban rail lines thus stimulates the economy twice. The direct impact of construction dollars is followed by the redevelopment that transit brings.

Rail construction is important, too, for housing affordability. New homes near train stations are expensive, in many cities, simply because there are so few places they can go. The demand for apartments near transit exceeds the supply of places to put them. If land near rail stations loses scarcity value, new transit-oriented housing will be more affordable for the middle class.

Nothing else the federal government could do would help cities as much as a drastic increase in funding for subways and light rail. Beyond the direct benefits of transportation, jobs, and pollution control, rail transit has a multitude of political and economic spinoffs. Urban trains are good for the body, the spirit, and the pocketbook, and they should be a top priority of national policy.

Rail transit has its critics, and not just among the right-wing defenders of sprawl. One persistent line of attack is technocratic. Proponents of *bus rapid transit*, or BRT—buses that board like trains and move faster than other traffic by running in their own lanes or getting more green lights—assert that they can provide the same quality of transportation as light rail for much less money. They point to successes in Latin America and elsewhere overseas.[2]

These claims run up against a strong public preference for rail over bus, and they have come under withering criticism from light rail proponents. When there are stops at traffic lights, busways carrying heavy passenger loads are slower than light rail.[3] Rail advocates also dispute the claims of cost savings, and they point out that the ride is smoother and more comfortable by train. Americans, they argue, will not accept the crowding that enables buses in low-income countries to carry large passenger loads.[4]

Cost, speed, and ridership all matter, but urban revival depends on what is outside the vehicle as much as who is inside it. Here busways fall short; they do not fit as well on city streets. To move as many people as three-car trains that are five minutes apart, buses have to run every minute or so. It is easy to cross the street between trains that pass by every five minutes; a bus lane that carries the same number of riders has frequent traffic that is a barrier to those on foot. And if the passenger load is too heavy for downtown streets, the trains can be put underground, while bus tunnels are hard to build, expensive, and unpleasant. Flexibility is touted as an advantage of busways—buses can leave the reserved lane when convenient and enter traffic—but in densely built-up places with many transit riders it is trains that are more adaptable.

In any case, the debates of specialists about the tangible pros and cons of transit modes do not shape public opinion. The intensity of the public preference for rail has a different cause. Rail has high status. Buses do not. Second-class transportation, people feel, will only make their city second-class.

As the bus proponents see it, these attitudes are irrational prejudices that should not distort public policy. But status shapes cities just as money does; ignoring it is the opposite of realism. No one would tell Los Angeles and Washington that they are wasting money by redeveloping old factory districts, because high-rises could have been built without subsidies by rezoning Brentwood and Georgetown. Comparing a light rail line that emerges from a contentious political battle to a bus route no one asked for is like picking the spot for a new office tower without checking whether neighbors will object to the zoning change.

Yet that is what transit planners are required to do. The federal bureaucracy, hostile to rail since the Ronald Reagan administration, helps lead the push for bus rapid transit. Until the rules were changed in 2010, it ranked projects solely on their cost-effectiveness as means of transportation.[5] The Federal Transit Administration now gives some weight to the potential of a project to spur land development, but the bias toward buses remains.

At the local level, where the politics of transportation planning mostly play out, rail-bus debates are unavoidable. Budgets are always limited, and spending too much money on rail lines with too few riders can cripple transit agencies. But here the rationale for bus rapid transit is usually to spend less, not to get more for the same money. Once this choice is made, flexibility becomes BRT's Achilles' heel. A city decides to cut costs by building a rail-like busway; the engineers go to work; the savings turn out less than hoped. The easy way out is to drop the train-like features of the bus lane. The promises are rapid, but the bus is slow.

Some BRT advocates disown the run-of-the-mill bus lines that emerge from this sequence of bait and switch; Robert Poole, of the libertarian Reason Foundation, embraces them. "BRT," he writes, "aims to provide performance and service qualities comparable to those of rail transit but at a cost that is considerably lower than that of light rail systems." But bus rapid transit, he tells those who are thinking of actually building it, does not need to move rapidly. He advises cities to operate what he calls "BRT-lite"—a bus painted a special color, running in regular traffic lanes but making fewer stops.[6]

A similar reversal of positions occurs when transit agencies try to move regular buses faster. The arguments for what are called *bus priorities* are based on efficiency—crowded roadways carry more people when buses get lanes to themselves and traffic lights let them through first. This is the same kind of thinking that recommends BRT as a substitute for rail. But the right-wingers who laud BRT when light rail is on the agenda have little interest in this kind of efficiency. Quick to condemn wasteful spending when it goes to rail, they fall silent when motorists benefit from waste. They now put status ahead of efficiency; buses may be a cheaper way to move, but they rank low in the suburban pecking order.

On those infrequent occasions when bus rapid transit does come to pass, the vehicle's inferior standing quickly asserts itself. Cleveland built a high-profile BRT on Euclid Avenue with traffic lights that turned green when a bus approached. As soon as the line opened, drivers on cross streets complained, and the "signal preemption" was turned off within weeks. Boston, in the 1970s, relocated its aging Orange Line on land cleared for a canceled interstate. The low-income neighborhoods traversed by the old elevated tracks were promised light rail as a replacement. Instead they got a pair of bus lanes dubbed the Silver Line. When it snows, which is not a rare event in Boston, plows clear the car lanes and pile up snow where the buses go—the opposite of what happens on the light rail Green Line.[7]

Another group of rail critics concern themselves with equity rather than efficiency. They willingly concede that rail provides a better quality of travel—in

Boston's Silver Line bus rapid transit route after a snowstorm, with buses in mixed traffic because bus lanes are not plowed.
(Courtesy of Jeremy Marin.)

fact, the premise of their argument is that buses are transport for those who can't afford to drive. New rail lines, they contend, draw off money better spent on the poor and give the middle class a luxury ride at the expense of the more deserving.

This thinking crystallized when the Bus Riders Union of Los Angeles was formed in 1993. The city's rail revival was faltering in the face of construction problems and political infighting, while a swelling population of immigrants jammed buses. The regional transit agency faced a giant budget hole and chose to plug it by raising fares and cutting bus service. The new organization sued, charging a violation of civil rights laws, and won a settlement that brought new buses, less rush-hour crowding, and lower fares.

The Bus Riders Union's hostility to rail transit emerges from a broader political analysis. Its founders believe that white America is hopelessly corrupted by racism. They thus put race at the center of their politics and treat economics as secondary. This perspective offers little prospect of creating a majority within this country for change, and they therefore give priority to supporting Third World revolutions by mobilizing the minority poor.[8] They have no desire to elect allies to office—that would only reinforce the illusion of American democracy—but seek to extort concessions from the power structure by means of lawsuits and disruption.[9]

From this point of view, conflict between bus passengers and middle-class commuters is not something to avoid. It mirrors the larger struggle between oppressed racial minorities and the white population. The Bus Riders Union has no use for vehicles where poor and middle class ride together. It blurs the cleavages of race and poverty that it organizes around.

The hard work of the Bus Riders Union and the buses its lawsuits have put on the street have won it admirers across the country. Few imitators share the group's ideology, but many copy its transit program by setting buses against trains.

But bus instead of rail is a false choice. Trains, in the long run at least, are rarely financed at the expense of buses. Rail lines are paid for with higher taxes or fewer roads, and they help finance buses by winning political support for transit. Once the stations open, bus routes feed into them and their newly walkable surroundings. This attracts the middle-class ridership that buses lack elsewhere.

And trains appeal to drivers as well as their own riders, assembling majorities that buses cannot achieve on their own. In Virginia's sprawling Hampton Roads region, the planning body asked residents what kind of transport tax dollars should be spent on. Light rail was supported by 57% of those who answered the poll, slightly more than highway construction, although only 2% said they usually get around on transit. Heavy rail got 37% and buses only 22%.[10] Even the Bus Riders Union in Los Angeles piggybacked on rail—the improvements its lawsuit won were paid for by a tax passed to build Metro lines.

New York, San Francisco, and Washington, with their subway and streetcar lines, show the spinoff effect of trains. Buses crowd the streets, much more so than in cities without rail. In transportation, as in other domains, the poor do best when they share public services with the middle class. Social Security and Medicare thrive; even their enemies pretend to be their protectors. Welfare programs wither away, political punching bags for their opponents, and buses that serve only the poor suffer the same fate.

Few states finance transit as they do roads. The entire state bears the burden of rural highways, but outside the highly urban states of New Jersey and Maryland the cost of trains and buses is borne disproportionately by big-city taxpayers. New rail lines require local tax increases which, very often, go before the voters in a referendum.

This hurdle—one that highways are rarely made to cross—is not a low bar. A strong case must be presented to an electorate that is inevitably suspicious of higher taxes. Success comes easiest when a route and budget are on the table—voters, very sensibly, want to know what they will get for their money. As transit grows more popular, majorities are easier to assemble. In 2000 and 2001, local taxes for transportation won passage about half the time; a decade later three-quarters were approved.

Winning these elections requires a broad coalition of support. Most successful transit campaigns bring together labor, business, and environmentalists. Labor almost invariably supports new rail lines in principle, but its active mobilization does not always follow; firm commitments to union construction and operation of the future rail system are needed up front. Business backing is crucial because money is so powerful in American politics. Few transit referenda win without the help of downtown real estate interests, and blessings by business umbrella groups can deter funding of the opposition. Environmentalist endorsements, while not always essential, are valuable too. They add votes, they can bring volunteers, and they defuse the arguments of nimby opponents. Grass-roots transit advocacy groups, although they rarely match the numerical strength of their allies, play a central role. Their track record of disinterested advocacy adds credibility that backers with a financial interest lack, and they are often the backbone of volunteer efforts.[11]

These diverse coalitions can be hard to hold together. The most troubling question, usually, is whether to combine transit and highway spending in a package. This is a choice that must be approached pragmatically. How much of the money does transit get, and will the money bring real change? The perfect should never be the enemy of the good, but some spending packages merely perpetuate the status quo.

New rail lines are the centerpiece of transportation reform, but they are hardly the end of it. Transit does not compete with the automobile on a level playing field when cars get enormous hidden subsidies. No subsidy is bigger than free parking, something suburban zoning codes effectively require. All the parking spaces in the United States, taken together, are worth more than the country's cars and trucks, and 99% of them are given away.[12]

Parking is a core element of sprawl. Not only does free parking subsidize driving, but it also makes it hard to create walkable downtowns. Parking lots and garages deaden sidewalks and gobble up land. Density can be preserved by putting parking underground, but that drives up the price of city housing and may not be affordable at all.[13]

Change is difficult. Drivers' instincts and emotions rebel against it; the car culture demands free and easy parking. Former Santa Monica planning commissioner Frank Gruber marvels at local nimbys who detest five-story apartment houses yet enthuse over plans for a seven-story public garage. "Parking is like sex," he observes. "If you have to pay for it, it's not right."[14]

Still, many motorists have parking fears that are rationally grounded, and this segment of opinion can be won over. As Donald Shoup shows in his book *The High Cost of Free Parking*, the key reform is setting the price of parking at a level that makes it easy to find a space—what has become known as *performance parking*. Drivers gain in convenience as they lose in cash. Shoup has put his theories into practice by successfully repricing parking meters in Pasadena, Redwood City, and other California suburbs.[15]

But performance parking is only a first step. Limiting demand so that it matches supply does not stop the creation of too much supply. Pressure to build excess parking comes from many sources.

Single-family neighborhoods often ask for extra parking when high-rises go up nearby. They want assurance that newcomers won't park on "their" streets. In old streetcar suburbs, parking is scarce and this is a practical concern. Elsewhere the issue is social status; there are plenty of spaces along the curb, but the prestige of the subdivision would suffer if alien automobiles were allowed into them.

Underground parking can appease these demands, but it is expensive and only attracts more traffic. Instead, homeowners are often given exclusive rights to park on neighborhood streets. Occupants of new buildings are denied parking permits, either by rule or by gerrymandering the borders of the parking districts. A policy that in effect marks apartment dwellers' cars with a scarlet A is surely discriminatory. But it is much less unfair to be forbidden to park in the neighborhood than not to be allowed to live there at all. If people are more important than cars, parking discrimination is a price worth paying to overcome housing discrimination.

Parking at stores is another tricky issue. Merchants in the new suburban mixed-use developments love cheap parking for their customers. Some pay for it themselves and give it away; others push for public garages. Either way, customers who arrive on foot subsidize those who drive. And the pedestrians have no choice but to pay; they are a captive market that has nowhere else to go. This is one more subsidy for motorists, unfortunate but often necessary. Driving to suburban malls is massively subsidized, and storefront businesses must compete. As the suburban downtowns grow into true urban centers, they will eventually have to be weaned from their dependence on excess parking. It will be a difficult task, and one that must await its proper time.

What can be done now is to remove parking minimums from zoning codes. That would be significant progress; everyone loses when money is spent to build parking that the builders don't want. But deregulation is no panacea—the forces that push for subsidized parking are strong, so even the parking the builders want is too much.[16] Thus, much remains to be learned about parking policy. Are maximums a good idea? Should parking be taxed to recover the street-building costs it imposes on local governments? Should merchants be forbidden to bundle it with other goods they sell and required to add a charge for customers who park? Research into such questions has scarcely begun.

Streets are not just transportation arteries. As Jane Jacobs understood, they are stages for the most human of all activities—living together as social animals. At their best, people on foot crowd them, meeting by plan and by chance with neighbors, acquaintances, and strangers. New Urbanist designers have learned to fit buildings comfortably into cities, but the streets have not kept up with the structures. Roadways are still built for the automobile, with wide lanes and fast-moving cars.

The obstacle here is not ignorance but lack of will. A new breed of traffic engineers has figured out the design of walkable streets. Portland, with its bike lanes and traffic calming, gave an early demonstration of their art, but imitators have been few and sluggish. Even the cities with the highest subway ridership in the country, New York and Washington, were slow to follow suit. Only after 2005 did they begin to redesign downtown streets for bicycles and pedestrians. Elsewhere the car is still king. There is at most a grudging bow to "complete streets"—bike lanes on the sides of roads, brick crosswalks, and here and there a "pedestrian zone" that proves everyplace else is an automobile zone.

The problem here is political, and rail is the political remedy. The bureaucrats who control road design fear the consequences if they rock the boat too soon, and they fear them with reason. Sharing roadways with pedestrians and bicycles challenges motorists' sense of entitlement. Only when voters pour out of trains on foot, matching the drivers in vehemence and number, can the demand for walkability be heeded without dread of electoral revenge.

The long drive into sprawl has reached a dead end. America needs trains to carry it back out. For our cities to fulfill their urban potential, winning a new transportation policy—in the nation, in the states, and locally—is the central political task.

Transit advocates come to that task with special burdens, but also with unusual strengths. They begin at a disadvantage when they try to convince politicians of the rightness of their reasoning. Elected officials drive constantly to visit with their constituents, and this experience inclines them to see things from the motorist's point of view.

But in politics the force of argument counts for less than the force of votes. And train riders have built-in advantages when they come together to exert political power. The driver, traveling alone, is pushed toward individualism and consumerism, while mass transit brings people to a common place where they can discuss their problems and join forces. Places where people walk and ride the train are places that stimulate political activism.[17]

Once riders organize, they have strength beyond their numbers. Activists connect easily with their base—when they pass out flyers at the station, they are targeting their supporters with laser-like precision. Rail commuters, some evidence suggests, even vote more often than drivers in low-turnout local elections. An auto commuter may not know there's an election, while someone who takes the train regularly probably shook the hand of all the candidates.[18]

The strengths of the train rider, when seized on, far outweigh the weaknesses. Railroads are much more than steel and concrete. They build cities by growing their economies, by enlivening their streets. They empower us all to break our national addiction to sprawl and take our future into our own hands.

Afterword

The desires for worldly goods and for the respect of others are basic human urges that few individuals can overcome. Neither impulse, surely, will soon vanish, but each can be made to serve good ends or bad. They can find an outlet in destructive egoism, or they can be channeled so that the striving of each contributes to the welfare of all.

The quest for material gain contributes most to the common good when it is a collective rather than an individual enterprise. Large business organizations have brought the world vast improvements in productivity and advances in technology. In unions, the push for higher wages creates industrial civilization's greatest force for equality, democracy, and mass enlightenment.

But the last forty years have seen a shift away from cooperation and toward individual money-making. Organized labor grows weaker. Businesses operate, more and more, to enrich their managers alone.

The search for honor and prestige, by contrast, is most socially useful when it is a quest for individual prominence. Then it inspires philanthropy and innovation, motivating the talented to be creators of the arts and sciences and the merely wealthy to be their patrons. In a collectivity, the desire for respect easily goes astray. It leads to invidious distinctions of race, wealth, or ancestry.

Today we privilege the worst side of both these urges. Suburban land tenure empowers zoning boards, homeowner associations, and historic districts in the pursuit of collective status-seeking. The quest for permanence and exclusivity imposes conformity, stifles self-expression, and discourages the display of excellence.

Meanwhile, individual gain supplants common prosperity as a motive force for building. Immediate profit matters more than long-term value. The shopping mall and the master developer replace the business district of small landowners who cooperate as they compete. Bond-market manipulation finances real estate, and houses become assets to flip rather than homes to grow old in.

The making of the places where we live is far too complex an undertaking to be other than a social endeavor. How we oversee it determines what and where we build. Today our governance of land use sanctions individual greed and collective snobbery and denies us the power to mold the human landscape to our intentions. The selfish motives of gain and preferment can never be banished from human life, but we must harness them to work for the betterment of all. Surely we can do that, if we organize ourselves to build the communities we desire.

Acknowledgments

My greatest debt for the development of the ideas in this book is to my colleagues in the Action Committee for Transit. Its members have been a constant support, balancing idealism with practicality while working together in harmony and mutual support. I could not possibly name all who deserve thanks, but among those worthy of special mention are Nick and Carole Brand, Jean Buergler, John Carroll, Jim Clarke, Ronit Dancis, Bee and Brian Ditzler, Jon Elkind, John Fay, Ruth Fort, Tom Fuchs, Greg Gagarin, Bruce Gilson, the late Ted Gordon, Neil Greene, Jon Gubits, Carl Henn (whose premature loss continues to be felt), Kathy Jentz, Tracey Johnstone, Quon Kwan, Alan Lauer, Richard McArdle, Jessica Mitchell, Harvard Morehead, Kristen Mosbæk, Rodolfo Perez, Dan Reed, Richard Reis, Eleanor Rice, Hans Riemer, Barbara Sanders, Greg Sanders, Miriam Schoenbaum, David Sears, Tina Slater, Tom Stecher, Ed Tennyson, Ted Van Houten, Wes Vernon, Cavan Wilk, Bill Wilson, and especially Cindy Snow. I learned much from Richard Hoye, and I owe most of all to ACT's founder Harry Sanders, whose loss we all regret constantly.

I must also thank the activists in other organizations that I have worked with on the issues of transportation and land use. Among them are David Alpert of Greater Greater Washington; Webb Smedley, Ralph Bennett, and Wayne Phyillaier of Purple Line Now; Cheryl Cort, Kelly Blynn, and Stewart Schwartz of the Coalition for Smarter Growth; Craig Simpson, Jimmy Allen, and Jackie Jeter of Amalgamated Transit Union Local 689; Karren Pope-Onwukwe and Todd Reitzel of Prince George's Advocates for Community-Based Transit; Robbyn Lewis of the Red Line Now PAC; Dolores Milmoe, Diane Cameron, and Neal Fitzgerald of the Audubon Naturalist Association; John Wetmore of Perils for Pedestrians; and Dru Schmidt-Perkins of 1000 Friends of Maryland. I learned much from civic activists in Montgomery County, including Richard Arkin, Jack Bonsby, Peter Galvin, Margo Kelly, Dan Wilhelm, and the late Stuart Rochester. No less deserving of gratitude are the dedicated public servants who have overseen the Purple Line in its long odyssey: Glenn Orlin, Henry Kay, Ernest Baisden, and Mike Madden. The ideas here are, of course, mine, and I am sure all of those I thank will find things to disagree with.

Another source of ongoing inspiration has been *Dissent* magazine. Many of the ideas in this book were first developed in articles, from which some text has been adapted. These include "Bureaucracy and Markets" (Fall 1995), "Suburbs, Status and Sprawl" (Winter 2001), and "Stuck in Traffic" (Summer 2006).

I am obliged as well to many for help directly in the writing of this book. I had useful discussions with Arlington County Supervisor Chris Zimmerman, Nick Caston, Pamela Lindstrom, and my daughter Estye Fenton. Rick Rybeck, Cavan Wilk, Steven Amter, and Wes Vernon read and commented on sections of the manuscript, and David McBride and Sarah Rosenthal of Oxford University Press did much to help perfect it. Terry Owens of the Maryland Transit Administration; David Kessler of the Bancroft Library, University of California; and Duane Lucia of the West End Museum helped me locate photographs. Dan Malouff earns special thanks for drafting all the maps.

Notes

Chapter 1

1. Carl J. Guarnieri, *The Utopian Alternative: Fourierism in Nineteenth-Century America* (Cornell University Press, Ithaca, NY, 1991); Morris Hillquit, *Socialism in the United States* (Funk & Wagnalls, New York, 1903), pp. 78–88.

2. The original source for this quotation, attributed to Mary Ellen Russell, daughter of the "sailor preacher" Father Edward Taylor who was close to Emerson and other transcendentalists, is Thomas Wentworth Higginson, *Part of a Man's Life*, (Houghton Mifflin, Boston, 1904), p. 12. Mrs. Russell's dates are given in her grandson's memoir, Thomas Russell Ybarra, *Young Man of Caracas* (I. Washburn, New York, 1941).

3. Kenneth T. Jackson, *Crabgrass Frontier: The Suburbanization of the United States* (Oxford University Press, New York, 1985), pp. 84–85; Dolores Hayden, *Building Suburbia* (Vintage, New York, 2003), p. 52.

4. Roger Wunderlich, *Low Living and High Thinking at Modern Times, New York* (Syracuse University Press, Syracuse, NY, 1992).

5. John Humphrey Noyes, *History of American Socialisms*, (J.B. Lippincott & Company, New York, 1870), esp. pp. 449–511; Guarnieri, *Utopian Alternative*, pp. 322–326; Hayden, *Building Suburbia*, pp. 52–53; Susan Henderson, "Llewellyn Park, Suburban Idyll," *Journal of Garden History*, vol. 7, pp. 221–243 (1987).

6. Henderson, "Llewellyn Park"; Hayden, *Building Suburbia*, pp. 54–61; Robert Fishman, *Bourgeois Utopias: The Rise and Fall of Suburbia* (Basic Books, New York, 1987), esp. p. 125.

7. Henderson, "Llewellyn Park"; Michael Kazin, *American Dreamers: How the Left Changed a Nation* (Alfred A. Knopf, New York, 2011), p. 55.

8. Henderson, "Llewellyn Park."

9. Henderson, "Llewellyn Park."

10. Jackson, *Crabgrass Frontier*, pp. 79–81.

11. Jackson, *Crabgrass Frontier*, p. 79; Robert M. Fogelson, *Bourgeois Nightmares* (Yale University Press, New Haven, CT, 2005), pp. 40–42; Hayden, *Building Suburbia*, p. 65.

12. Jackson, *Crabgrass Frontier*, pp. 95–97; Fogelson, *Bourgeois Nightmares*, pp. 35, 88–90, 131–137; Fishman, *Bourgeois Utopias*, pp. 144–148; Mary Corbin Sies,

"Paradise Retained: An Analysis of Persistence in Planned, Exclusive Suburbs, 1880–1980," *Planning Perspectives*, vol. 12, pp. 165–191 (1997).

13. Sam Bass Warner Jr., *Streetcar Suburbs: The Process of Growth in Boston (1870–1900)*, 2nd ed. (Harvard University Press, Cambridge, MA, 1978); Hayden, *Building Suburbia*, pp. 71–88.

14. Warner, *Streetcar Suburbs*, pp. 46–66, 75–79.

15. Henry James, *The Bostonians* (Penguin Classics edition, London, 1986), pp. 52, 55.

16. William M. Offutt, *Bethesda: A Social History* (Innovation Game, Washington, DC, 1995), pp. 74–77; Carl Abbott, *Greater Portland: Urban Life and Landscape in the Pacific Northwest* (University of Pennsylvania Press, Philadelphia, 2001), p. 87.

17. Warner, *Streetcar Suburbs*, pp. 144–151.

18. Warner, *Streetcar Suburbs*, p. 122; Fogelson, *Bourgeois Nightmares*, pp. 40–41.

19. Warner, *Streetcar Suburbs*, p. 122; Fogelson, *Bourgeois Nightmares*, pp. 54–59.

20. Fogelson, *Bourgeois Nightmares*, pp. 60–66; William S. Worley, *J. C. Nichols and the Shaping of Kansas City* (University of Missouri Press, Columbia, 1990), pp. 30–36.

21. Worley, *J. C. Nichols*, pp. 61–70, 78–80, 116–117, 122–144, 164–174, 232–263; Fogelson, *Bourgeois Nightmares*, pp. 108–109; J. C. Nichols, "Subdivision: The Realtor Must Anticipate the Future Needs of His City," *National Real Estate Journal*, Oct. 24, 1921, quoted in Jane Holtz Kay, *Asphalt Nation* (University of California Press, Berkeley, 1997), p. 180; J. C. Nichols, "Subdivision Practices," *National Real Estate Journal*, Nov. 4, 1938, http://www.umkc.edu/WHMCKC/publications/JCN/JCNPDF/JCN053.pdf, accessed December 21, 2011.

22. Worley, *J. C. Nichols*, pp. 91–93; Fogelson, *Bourgeois Nightmares*, pp. 118–130. Inspired: Cheryl Caldwell Ferguson, "River Oaks: 1920s Suburban Planning and Development in Houston," *Southwestern Historical Quarterly*, vol. 104, pp. 191–228 (2000).

23. Fishman, *Bourgeois Utopias*, pp. 146–147; Sies, "Paradise Retained." Quotation from Charles Cheney, quoted in Robert Fogelson, *The Fragmented Metropolis: Los Angeles 1850–1930* (Harvard University Press, Cambridge, MA, 1967), p. 324 fn.

24. Thorstein Veblen, *The Theory of the Leisure Class*, chapter 6.

25. Michael Jones-Correa, "The Origins and Diffusion of Restrictive Covenants," *Political Science Quarterly*, vol. 115, pp. 541–568 (2001); Fogelson, *Bourgeois Nightmares*, pp. 95–103, 125–131.

26. Jackson, *Crabgrass Frontier*, pp. 160–171, 174–177; Hayden, *Building Suburbia*, pp. 115, 118–120, 127.

27. Marc A. Weiss, *The Rise of the Community Builders: The American Real Estate Industry and Urban Land Planning* (Columbia University Press, New York, 1987), pp. 73, 114–116; John Kenneth Galbraith, *The Great Crash, 1929* (Houghton Mifflin, Boston, 1955), pp. 3–7.

28. Weiss, *Community Builders*, pp. 70–72.

29. Weiss, *Community Builders*, pp. 12, 54–58, 65–72, 79–87; Marc A. Weiss, "The Real Estate Industry and the Politics of Zoning in San Francisco, 1914–1928,"

Planning Perspectives, vol. 3, pp. 311–324 (1988); Mel Scott, *American City Planning Since 1890* (University of California Press, Berkeley, 1969), pp. 76, 152–163.

30. Christopher Silver, "The Racial Origins of Zoning in American Cities," in June Manning Thomas and Marsha Ritzdorf, eds., *Urban Planning and the African American Community: In the Shadows* (Sage Publications, Thousand Oaks, CA, 1997), pp. 23–42; Jones-Correa, "Racial Covenants"; Fogelson, *Bourgeois Nightmares*, pp. 98–99; Seymour I. Toll, *Zoned American* (Grossman, New York, 1969), pp. 262–263.

31. Keith D. Revell, "Regulating the Landscape: Real Estate Values, City Planning, and the 1916 Zoning Ordinance," in David Ward and Olivier Zunz, eds., *The Landscape of Modernity: Essays on New York City, 1900–1940* (Russell Sage Foundation, New York, 1992), pp. 19–45; Toll, *Zoned American*, pp. 110–116, 143–166, 172–184; Scott, *American City Planning*, pp. 153–160.

32. The anticipation cannot be documented directly for obvious reasons, but for the behavior following immediately on the adoption of zoning ordinances see Scott, *American City Planning*, pp. 197; Weiss, "Zoning in San Francisco"; Toll, *Zoned American*, pp. 207–210. When zoning arrived, the machines were losing a major source of graft as a result of the slowdown in streetcar expansion.

33. Scott, *American City Planning*, pp. 160–161, 192–198, 227–228.

34. Fogelson, *Bourgeois Nightmares*, pp. 155–159; Kenneth Baar, "National Movement to Halt the Spread of Multifamily Housing, 1890–1926," *Journal of the American Planning Association*, vol. 58, pp. 470–482 (1992); William M. Randle, "Professors, Reformers, Bureaucrats and Cronies: The Players in *Euclid v. Ambler*," in Charles M. Haar and Jerold S. Kayden, eds., *Zoning and the American Dream* (Planners Press, Chicago, 1989), pp. 31–59, see pp. 49–50. For an anthropological description of the animus against apartments, written in the 1970s but reflecting long-persisting attitudes, see Constance Perin, *Everything in Its Place: Social Order and Land Use in America* (Princeton University Press, Princeton, NJ, 1977), pp. 32–70.

35. Baar, "National Movement"; Marc A. Weiss, "Urban Land Developers and the Origins of Zoning Laws: The Case of Berkeley," *Berkeley Planning Journal*, vol. 3, pp. 7–25 (1986); Scott, *American City Planning*, pp. 161–162, 192–193; Richard F. Babcock, *The Zoning Game: Municipal Practices and Policies* (University of Wisconsin Press, Madison, 1966), pp. 3–6, 115; Raphael Fischler, "Health, Safety and the General Welfare—Markets, Politics and Social Science in Early Land-Use Regulation and Community Design," *Journal of Urban History*, vol. 24, pp. 675–719 (1998).

36. Jones-Correa, "Racial Covenants"; Evan McKenzie, *Privatopia: Homeowner Associations and the Rise of Residential Private Government* (Yale University Press, New Haven, CT, 1994), pp. 56–74.

37. Fogelson, *Bourgeois Nightmares*, pp. 206–207; Weiss, *Community Builders*, pp. 68–72; Worley, *J. C. Nichols*, pp. 126, 132–139.

38. Michael Lewyn, "How Overregulation Creates Sprawl (Even in a City Without Zoning)," *Wayne Law Review*, vol. 50, pp. 1171–1207 (2004); Teddy M. Kapur, "Land Use Regulation in Houston Contradicts the City's Free Market

Reputation," *Environmental Law Reporter*, vol. 34, pp. 10045–10063 (2004); John Mixon, "Four Land Use Vignettes from Unzoned(?) Houston," *Notre Dame Journal of Law, Ethics & Public Policy*, pp. 159–185 (2010); Babcock, *Zoning Game*, pp. 25–28; David G. McComb, *Houston: A History* (University of Texas Press, Austin, 1981), pp. 96–97, 99, 156–160.

39. See McKenzie, *Privatopia*, pp. 122–149.
40. Conservative economists who interpret zoning as a collective property right include Robert H. Nelson, *Zoning and Property Rights* (MIT Press, Cambridge, MA, 1977); William A. Fischel, *The Economics of Zoning Laws: A Property Rights Approach to American Land Use Controls* (Johns Hopkins University Press, Baltimore, 1985); Peter Gordon, F. Frederic Deng, and Harry W. Richardson, "Private Communities, Market Institutions, and Planning," in N. Verma, ed., *Institutions and Planning* (CUPR Press, New Brunswick, NJ, 2007).
41. Babcock, *Zoning Game*, pp. 12, 140–142.
42. Only a few scholars have asked why there is such fine sorting by social status in American suburbs. The question is usually addressed, when it is, in the context of a comparison with Europe. The most plausible answer, other than historical accident, comes from Ernst Freund, quoted in Toll, *Zoned American*, pp. 266–267; Herbert J. Gans, "The Failure of Urban Renewal," *Commentary*, April 1965, pp. 29–37. They suggest that greater sorting occurs here because the more fluid class structure of this country leaves Americans deprived of other markers of status. Another European inheritance from feudalism may also be relevant; the lord's manor was surrounded by peasant hovels, so bourgeois residences that imitated it did not need spatial separation from the urban poor. Other deterministic explanations are less convincing. Robert Fishman, *Bourgeois Utopias*, pp. 104–107, 118–121, contends that the bourgeoisie had the same urge for social separation in Europe as in America. He explains the suburbanization of the middle class in the United States and Britain, but not in France, by political democracy and inherited legal doctrines. These factors do not account for the early twentieth-century revolution in American land tenure law. Michael N. Danielson, *The Politics of Exclusion* (Columbia University Press, New York, 1976), p. 23, points to the local control of zoning in the United States; this does not explain restrictive covenants and exclusionary zoning within cities. Perin, *Everything in Its Place*, esp. pp. 32–44, 108–124, looks not to Europe but to pre-industrial societies. She suggests that American culture associates different housing arrangements with different stages of life and that taboos against mixing of life stages are universal features of human culture.

Chapter 2

1. Babcock, *Zoning Game*, pp. 30–31, 116–120, 185; Fogelson, *Bourgeois Nightmares*, p. 112.
2. Fogelson, *Bourgeois Nightmares*, pp. 158–159; Scott, *American City Planning*, p. 154.
3. Randle, "The Players."

4. Toll, *Zoned American*, pp. 122–140; Scott, *American City Planning*, pp. 95–100, 117–127.

5. Weiss, *Community Builders*, pp. 54–67; Worley, *J. C. Nichols*, pp. 89–92.

6. Scott, *American City Planning*, pp. 84–88; Toll, *Zoned American*; Herbert Gans, *People, Plans and Policies* (Columbia University Press, New York, 1991), pp. 124–130.

7. Scott, *American City Planning*, pp. 97, 152; Weiss, *Community Builders*, pp. 56–60, 64–72.

8. Randle, "The Players"; Baar, "National Movement"; Toll, *Zoned American*, pp. 199–200.

9. Scott, *American City Planning*, pp. 192–195; Toll, *Zoned American*, pp. 203–204, 268.

10. Toll, *Zoned American*, pp. 168–171; Scott, *American City Planning*, pp. 152–153.

11. Michael Allan Wolf, *The Zoning of America* (University Press of Kansas, Lawrence, 2008); Arthur V. N. Brooks, "The Office File Box—Emanations from the Battlefield," in Haar and Kayden, *Zoning and the American Dream*, pp. 3–30; Randle, "The Players"; Scott, *American City Planning*, pp. 238–240. Quotation from *Euclid v. Ambler*.

12. Scott, *American City Planning*, pp. 193–195, 242–248; Weiss, *Community Builders*, pp. 72–78; Marc A. Weiss, "Planning Subdivisions: Community Builders and Urban Planners in the Early Twentieth Century," in *Planning and Financing Public Works* (Public Works Historical Society, Chicago, 1987), pp. 21–46; Toll, *Zoned American*, p. 164.

13. Sinclair Lewis, *Babbitt* (Dover, Mineola, NY, 2003), quotations from pp. 30, 51, 58.

14. Peter D. Norton, *Fighting Traffic: The Dawn of the Motor Age in the American City* (MIT Press, Cambridge, MA, 2008), esp. pp. 72–85, 139–141, 185–193, 207–235.

15. Mark S. Foster, *From Streetcar to Superhighway: American City Planners and Urban Transportation, 1900–1940* (Temple University Press, Philadelphia, 1981), pp. 71–78, 110–111, 113; Robert M. Fogelson, *Downtown: Its Rise and Fall, 1880–1950* (Yale University Press, New Haven, CT, 2001), pp. 102–108, 160–182; Ruth Knack, Stuart Meck, and Israel Stollman, "The Real Story Behind the Standard Planning and Zoning Acts of the 1920s," *Land Use Law & Zoning Digest*, February 1996, pp. 3–9.

16. Zachary M. Schrag, *The Great Society Subway: A History of the Washington Metro* (Johns Hopkins University Press, Baltimore, 2006), p. 35.

17. Scott, *American City Planning*, pp. 31-39, 44-57; Charles Moore, *Daniel H. Burnham, Architect, Planner of Cities* (Houghton Mifflin, Boston, 1921), vol. 2, p. 147.

18. Scott, *American City Planning*, esp. pp. 117–127; Foster, *Streetcar to Superhighway*, pp. 33–36, 70–72.

19. Scott, *American City Planning*, pp. 232–237. Country Club District: Fogelson, *Bourgeois Nightmares*, p. 74.

20. Southworth, "Street Standards."

21. Scott, *American City Planning*, esp. pp. 197–198, 214–215, 255–256; Nathan Glazer, *From a Cause to a Style: Modernist Architecture's Encounter with the American City* (Princeton University Press, Princeton, NJ, 2007), p. 175.

22. Weiss, "Planning Subdivisions"; Scott, *American City Planning*, p. 285.

23. Babcock, *Zoning Game*, pp. 32–38.

24. Scott, *American City Planning*, pp. 278–279.

25. Scott, *American City Planning*, p. 250. Mumford developed the same themes in *The City in History* (Harcourt, Brace & World, New York, 1961), esp. pp. 426–434.

Chapter 3

1. Rosalyn Baxandall and Elizabeth Ewen, *Picture Windows: How the Suburbs Happened* (Basic Books, New York, 2000), pp. 46–49; Scott, *American City Planning*, pp. 259–260; McKenzie, *Privatopia*, pp. 45–51. Worley, *J. C. Nichols*, p. 107, points out the similarity of Radburn to the design of the Country Club District fifteen years earlier.

2. Jackson, *Crabgrass Frontier*, pp. 195–203.

3. Jackson, *Crabgrass Frontier*, pp. 203–225; Weiss, *Community Builders*, pp. 141–158; Southworth, "Street Standards." "Retain stability" and "park area": Jackson, p. 208. "Messianic fervor": Weiss, p. 148. Detroit wall: Thomas J. Sugrue, *The Origins of the Urban Crisis: Race and Inequality in Postwar Detroit* (Princeton University Press, Princeton, NJ, 1996), pp. 63–65.

4. Jackson, *Crabgrass Frontier*, p. 195; Baxandall and Ewen, *Picture Windows*, pp. 67–74.

5. Jackson, *Crabgrass Frontier*, pp. 219–230; Sugrue, *Urban Crisis*, pp. 72–88; Joshua B. Freeman, *Working-Class New York: Life and Labor Since World War II* (New Press, New York, 2000), pp. 105–120; Arnold R. Hirsch, "Less than Plessy," in Kevin M. Kruse and Thomas J. Sugrue, eds., *The New Suburban History*, (University of Chicago Press, Chicago, 2006), pp. 33–56.

6. Jackson, *Crabgrass Frontier*, pp. 231–240; Baxandall and Ewen, *Picture Windows*, pp. 117–139; Hayden, *Building Suburbia*, pp. 136–137.

7. Kay, *Asphalt Nation*, pp. 212–214, 241–242.

8. Robert A Caro, *The Power Broker: Robert Moses and the Fall of New York* (Alfred A. Knopf, New York, 1974), esp. pp. 172–220, 896–972, 1026–1039. Owen D. Gutfreund, "Rebuilding New York in the Auto Age: Robert Moses and His Highways," in Hilary Ballon and Kenneth T. Jackson, eds., *Robert Moses and the American City: The Transformation of New York* (W. W. Norton, New York, 2007), suggests that the stoppage of rail expansion was entirely a consequence of federal policy and local public opinion, but as discussed in Chapter 6, other large cities did expand their rail systems during these years.

9. Norton, *Fighting Traffic*, pp. 159–171, 202–206, 234–241; Michael Southworth and Eran Ben-Joseph, "Street Standards and the Shaping of Suburbia," *Journal of the American Planning Association*, vol. 61, pp. 65–81 (1995). Leaded gasoline: Benjamin Ross and Steven Amter, *The Polluters: The Making of Our Chemically Altered Environment* (Oxford University Press, New York, 2010), pp. 33–34.

10. Southworth and Ben-Joseph, "Street Standards."

11. Donald C. Shoup, *The High Cost of Free Parking* (Planners Press, Chicago, 2005), pp. 21–23, 380–382, 607. "Purely aesthetic": Clan Crawford, *Strategy and Tactics in Muncipal Zoning* (Prentice-Hall, Englewood Cliffs, NJ, 1969), p. 84, quoted by Shoup, p. 433.

12. Shoup, *Free Parking*, pp. 21–23, 129–141.

13. Fogelson, *Downtown*, pp. 317–320, 341–350; Scott, *American City Planning*, pp. 285–287, 379–385.

14. Fogelson, *Downtown*, pp. 358–364, 371–377; Scott, *American City Planning*, pp. 380–385, 426–428.

15. Owen D. Gutfreund, *Twentieth Century Sprawl: Highways and the Reshaping of the American Landscape* (Oxford University Press, New York, 2004), pp. 25–59. Moses: Raymond A. Mohl, "Stop the Road: Freeway Revolts in American Cities," *Journal of Urban History*, vol. 30, pp. 674–706 (2004).

16. Fogelson, *Downtown*, pp. 365–370, 378–380; Scott, *American City Planning*, p. 501.

17. Fogelson, *Downtown*, pp. 237–238, reports that downtown real estate interests, when they first became concerned about urban decline, turned to Miller McClintock and Harland Bartholomew for advice. Hilary Ballon, "Robert Moses and Urban Renewal," in Ballon and Jackson, *Robert Moses*, pp. 94–115, recounts Moses' acceptance of the "modernist paradigm of superblock urbanism." Gregory Heller, "The Power of an Idea: Edmund Bacon's Planning Method Inspiring Consensus and Living in the Future," B.A. thesis, Wesleyan University, 2004, pp. 97–101, 107–112, describes the suburban inspiration of the design concepts developed by Philadelphia's influential planning director.

18. Sugrue, *Urban Crisis*, pp. 181–258; Danielson, *Politics of Exclusion*, pp. 125–126; Jim Sleeper, *The Closest of Strangers: Liberalism and the Politics of Race in New York* (W. W. Norton, New York, 1990), pp. 80–90, 116–152.

19. Alyssa Katz, *Our Lot: How Real Estate Came to Own Us* (Bloomsbury, New York, 2009), pp. 1–15; Hillel Levine and Lawrence Harmon, *The Death of an American Jewish Community: A Tragedy of Good Intentions* (Free Press, New York, 1992), pp. 164–180, 194–224.

20. Danielson, *Politics of Exclusion*, pp. 79–106, 213–236.

Chapter 4

1. "The Last Leaf."

2. Christine Stansell, *American Moderns: Bohemian New York and the Creation of a New Century* (Metropolitan Books, New York, 2000), esp. pp. 16–18. In Russian exile communities in Europe, there were forerunners of the Greenwich Village synthesis of advanced politics and art, but they are less relevant for our purposes here than they are in political history.

3. This is explored by Cesar Grana, *Modernity and its Discontents* (Basic Books, New York, 1964), pp. 163–171.

4. Towertown: Harvey Warren Zorbaugh, *The Gold Coast and the Slum: A Sociological Study of Chicago's Near North Side* (University of Chicago Press, Chicago, 1929). Russian Hill: Richard Walker, "Classy City: Residential Realms of the Bay Region," http://oldweb.geog.berkeley.edu/PeopleHistory/faculty/R_Walker/ClassCity.pdf, pp. 20–21. French Quarter: Scott S. Ellis, *Madame Vieux Carré: The French Quarter in the Twentieth Century* (University Press of Mississippi, Jackson, 2009), pp. 24–30.

5. Lewis, *Babbitt*, quotations from pp. 143–144, 30, 33, 139, 65.

6. Ellis, *Madame Vieux Carré*, pp. 43, 71–73; James Albert Gazell, "The High Noon of Chicago's Bohemias," *Journal of the Illinois State Historical Society*, vol. 65, pp. 54–68 (1972); John d'Emilio, *Sexual Politics, Sexual Communities: The Making of a Homosexual Minority in the United States, 1940–1970* (Chicago: University of Chicago Press, 1983), pp. 31–33, 38–39; 180–182; Paul Goodman, *Growing Up Absurd* (Random House, New York, 1960), pp. 63–69.

7. Vance Packard, *The Status Seekers* (David McKay, New York, 1959), quotations from pp. 66, 305, 90.

8. Walker, "Classy City," pp. 20, 29.

Chapter 5

1. William G. Grigsby, *Housing Markets and Public Policy* (University of Pennsylvania Press, Philadelphia, 1963), p. 251. Emphasis in original.

2. Scott, *American City Planning*, pp. 536–541, 592.

3. Anthony Flint, *Wrestling with Moses* (Random House, New York, 2009), pp. 3–28, 90–92; Alice Sparberg Alexiou, *Jane Jacobs, Urban Visionary* (Rutgers University Press, New Brunswick, NJ, 2006), pp. 39–50, 57–65.

4. Jane Jacobs, *The Death and Life of Great American Cities* (Modern Library Edition, New York, 1993). Ballet: pp. 65–71. Four principles: pp. 196–197.

5. Gans, *People, Plans and Policies*, pp. 33–43 (article originally published in 1962).

6. Alexiou, *Jane Jacobs*, pp. 43–50, 68–70; Flint, *Wrestling with Moses*, pp. 22–25; Charles Grutzner, "Shopping Scarce in City Projects," *New York Times*, June 16, 1957; John Sibley, "Village Housing a Complex Issue," *New York Times*, March 23, 1961.

7. George Orwell, *The Road to Wigan Pier* (Harcourt Brace Jovanovich, New York, 1958), pp. 65–74, quotations from pp. 71, 182.

8. Jacobs, *Death and Life*, p. 482.

9. Bruce Brugmann and Greggar Sletteland, *The Ultimate Highrise: San Francisco's Mad Rush Toward the Sky...* (San Francisco Bay Guardian, San Francisco, 1971), esp. p. 223.

10. See, e.g., Charles Grutzner, "Rise of the Urban Region: A Study of New Way of Life," *New York Times*, January 27, 1957; "City Told to Aid People, Not Cars," *New York Times*, April 21, 1958; Harrison E. Salisbury, "Study Finds Cars Choking Cities as 'Urban Sprawl' Takes Over," *New York Times*, March 3, 1959; Cabell Phillips, "Capital Uneasy on Traffic Plan," *New York Times*, October 22, 1961. Subway collapse: Caro, *Power Brokers*, pp. 930–933.

11. Jacobs, *Death and Life*, pp. 325–326, 334.
12. Gans, "Failure of Urban Renewal."
13. Warren Weaver, "Science and Complexity," *American Scientist*, vol. 36, pp. 536–544 (1948).
14. Jacobs, *Death and Life*. Habits of mind: p. 574. High-energy: p. 577.

Chapter 6

1. Salisbury, "Cars Choking Cities". History of word: George R. Hess, "Just What Is Sprawl, Anyway?," *Carolina Planning*, vol. 26, no. 2, pp. 11–26; Bruegmann, *Sprawl*, p. 119.
2. Emma Harrison, "Rebirth of Family Seen in Suburbs," *New York Times*, March 21, 1958; Wilfred Owen, "In Defense of the Automobile," *New York Times*, October 16, 1960.
3. "Statement by Nixon on Housing Program," *New York Times*, September 29, 1960.
4. Sugrue, *Origins of the Urban Crisis*, pp. 57–88; Martin Meyerson and Edward Banfield, *Politics, Planning and the Public Interest* (Free Press, Glencoe IL, 1955).
5. Fogelson, *Downtown*, pp. 239–240, 318–320, 340–380; Herbert J. Gans, "The Failure of Urban Renewal," in James Q. Wilson, ed., *Urban Renewal: The Record and the Controversy* (MIT Press, Cambridge, MA, 1966), pp. 537–557; Ballon, "Moses and Urban Renewal."
6. Caro, *Power Broker*, pp. 965–983; Chester Hartman, "The Housing of Relocated Families," *Journal of the American Institute of Planners*, vol. 30, pp. 266–286 (1964).
7. Herbert J. Gans, *The Urban Villagers: Group and Class in the Life of Italian-Americans* (Free Press, New York, 1962), pp. 282–287, 291–304, 308–318; Thomas H. O'Connor, *Building A New Boston: Politics and Urban Renewal, 1950-1970* (Northeastern University Press, Boston, 1993), pp. 26–28, 50–52, 61–65, 125–137, 141–142; Walter McQuade, "Boston: What Can a Sick City Do," in Wilson, *Urban Renewal*, pp. 259–277.
8. Barry Bluestone and Mary Huff Stevenson, *The Boston Renaissance: Race, Space, and Economic Change in an American Metropolis* (Russell Sage Foundation, New York, 2000), pp. 82–86; O'Connor, *New Boston*, pp. 182–188, 215–219.
9. Flint, *Wrestling with Moses*, pp. 61–92; Robert Fishman, "Revolt of the Urbs: Robert Moses and His Critics," in Ballon and Jackson, *Robert Moses*, pp. 122–129.
10. Flint, *Wrestling with Moses*, pp. 138–178; Caro, *Power Broker*, pp. 850–894.
11. William Issel, " 'Land Values, Human Values, and the Preservation of the City's Treasured Appearance': Environmentalism, Politics, and the San Francisco Freeway Revolt," *Pacific Historical Review*, vol. 68, pp. 611–646 (1999); Mohl, "Stop the Road"; Katherine M. Johnson, "Captain Blake versus the Highwaymen: Or, How San Francisco Won the Freeway Revolt," *Journal of Planning History*, vol. 8, pp. 56–83 (2009); Joseph Rodriguez, *City against Suburb: The Culture Wars in an American Metropolis* (Praeger, Westport, CT, 1999), pp. 21–46.

12. Schrag, *Great Society Subway*, pp. 36–44, 119–128, 134–141.

13. Alan Lupo, Frank Colcord, and Edmund P. Fowler, *Rites of Way: The Politics of Transportation in Boston and the U.S. City* (Little Brown, Boston, 1971), pp. 1–111; Chester Hartman, *Between Eminence and Notoriety: Four Decades of Radical Urban Planning* (Center for Urban Policy Research, New Brunswick NJ, 2002), p. 19.

14. Mohl, "Stop the Road." Other cities in which plans for urban interstate networks were drastically cut back include Baltimore, Cleveland, New Orleans, and Philadelphia. There were more limited highway cancellations in many other cities, including even Houston, Los Angeles, and Detroit.

15. Schrag, *Great Society Subway*, pp. 180–182; Federal urging: Gutfreund, *Twentieth-Century Sprawl*, pp. 32–34.

16. Mohl, "Stop the Road"; Lupo, *Rites of Way*, pp. 162–166, 215–218; Jacob Kobrick, "Let the People Have a Victory: The Politics of Transportation in Philadelphia, 1946–1984," Ph.D. thesis, University of Maryland, 2010, pp. 193–227, 254–292; Tom Lewis, *Divided Highways: Building the Interstate Highways, Transforming American Life* 2nd ed. (Cornell University Press, Ithaca, NY, 2013), pp. 179–210.

17. Eric J. Plosky, "The Fall and Rise of Pennsylvania Station: Changing Attitudes Toward Historic Preservation in New York City," M.S. Thesis, Massachusetts Institute of Technology, 1999.

18. See Suleiman Osman, *The Invention of Brownstone Brooklyn: Gentrification and the Search for Authenticity in Postwar New York* (Oxford University Press, New York, 2011), pp. 220–230, 253, 262–265, 273–275.

19. Jewel Bellush and Murray Hausknecht, "Planning, Participation, and Urban Renewal," in Bellush and Hausknecht, eds., *Urban Renewal: People, Politics, and Planning* (Anchor Books, Garden City, 1967), pp. 278–286; Susan S. Fainstein, *The Just City* (Cornell University Press, Ithaca, NY, 2011), pp. 65–67, 75–78; Lupo, *Rites of Way*, pp. 161–162. Boyd: Mohl, "Stop the Road."

20. Lupo, *Rites of Way*, pp. 220–222; information from transit systems' websites. Bus-only lanes were also introduced on the streets of many cities in the late 1950s and 1960s; only some of these have survived. See Asha Weinstein Agrawal, Todd Goldman, and Nancy Hannaford, "Shared-Use Bus Priority Lanes on City Streets: Case Studies in Design and Management," Mineta Transportation Institute, Report No. CA-MTI-12-2606, April 2012, pp. 6–9, http://transweb.sjsu.edu/PDFs/research/2606-shared-use-bus-priority-lanes-city-streets.pdf, accessed April 25, 2012.

21. Stephen Zwerling, *Mass Transit and the Politics of Technology: A Study of BART and the San Francisco Bay Area* (Praeger, New York, 1974), pp. 20–31, 39–44, 65–68; Office of Technology Assessment, "Assessment of Community Planning for Mass Transit: Volume 8-San Francisco Case Study," Report OTA-T-23, February 1976; Johnson, "Captain Blake"; Rodriguez, *City against Suburb*, pp. 47–54.

22. Schrag, *Great Society Subway*.

23. Gulf Reston Inc., "A Brief History of Reston," http://www.restonmuseum.org/main_/rht_briefHistory.htm.

24. Margaret Pugh O'Mara, "Uncovering the City in the Suburb," in Kruse and Sugrue, *New Suburban History*, pp. 57–79; Jon C. Teaford, *Post-Suburbia: Government and Politics in the Edge Cities* (Johns Hopkins University Press, Baltimore, 1997), pp. 50–54; Bluestone and Stevenson, *Boston Renaissance*, pp. 92–94.

25. McKenzie, *Privatopia*, pp. 81–93.

26. Max Neutze, *The Suburban Apartment Boom: Case Study of a Land Use Problem* (Resources for the Future, Washington, 1968), pp. 8, 86–90; McKenzie, *Privatopia*, pp. 94–96.

27. Data from U. S. Bureau of the Census, "New Privately Owned Housing Units Started: Annual Data," http://www.census.gov/const/www/newresconstindex. html, accessed July 8, 2011.

28. Neutze, *Suburban Apartment Boom*, pp. 52–57, 67–72, 84–85; Danielson, *Politics of Exclusion*, pp. 103–104.

29. Shoup, *Free Parking*, pp. 142–143; Mike Davis, *City of Quartz: Excavating the Future in Los Angeles* (Vintage, New York, 1990), p. 176. The term dingbat first appeared in print in Reyner Banham, *Los Angeles: The Architecture of Four Ecologies* (Harper & Row, New York, 1979), pp. 157–159.

30. Babcock, *Zoning Game*, pp. 6–11, 91; Patricia Burgess, "Of Swimming Pools and 'Slums,'" in Mary Corbin Sies and Christopher Silver, *Planning the Twentieth-Century American City* (Johns Hopkins University Press, Baltimore, 1996), pp. 212–239; Alan Mallach, "The Tortured Reality of Suburban Exclusion: Zoning, Economics, and the Future of the Berenson Doctrine," *Pace Environmental Law Review*, vol. 4, pp. 37–130 (1986).

31. Danielson, *Politics of Exclusion*, pp. 72–74; Babcock, *Zoning Game*, pp. 9–11.

32. Osman, *Brownstone Brooklyn*, pp. 8–9, 82–118, 189–219.

33. Cameron Logan, "The Constituent Landscape: History, Race and Real Estate in Washington, D.C, 1950-1990," Ph.D. thesis, George Washington University, 2008, pp. 97–108; John F. Bauman, "The Paradox of Post-War Urban Planning: Downtown Revitalization versus Decent Housing for All," in Daniel Schaffer, ed., *Two Centuries of American Planning* (Johns Hopkins University Press, Baltimore, 1988), pp. 231–264. Yorkville: Glazer, *From a Cause to a Style*, pp. 167–168, 172–173. Society Hill: Alan Ehrenhalt, *The Great Inversion and the Future of the American City* (Alfred A. Knopf, New York, 2012), p. 142. Osman, *Brownstone Brooklyn*, pp. 82–102, describes artists and writers, some complaining that Greenwich Village has been taken over by tourists and poseurs, in the lead when gentrification of Brooklyn Heights peaked in the 1950s, but he notes that the first arrivals in the 1940s were bankers and insurance managers. The non-bohemian style persisted in the South; the revival of downtown Wilmington, North Carolina, in the 1960s and 1970s is described by Julia Anne Yannetti, "From Downtown Revitalization to Suburban Preservation in Wilmington, North Carolina," M.A. Thesis, University of North Carolina, Wilmington, 2010, pp. 45–56. In New Orleans, in the first half of the twentieth century, bohemians and elite gentrifiers were sometimes allies and sometimes opponents; see Ellis, *Madame Vieux Carré*, pp. 18–19, 22–26, 42–44.

Chapter 7

1. Gans, "Failure of Urban Renewal."

2. Jones-Correa, "Racial Covenants"; McKenzie, *Privatopia*, pp. 70–75; Davis, *City of Quartz*, pp. 161–163; Spear, *Black Chicago*, pp. 208–212; Weiss, "Zoning in San Francisco"; Sugrue, *Urban Crisis*, pp. 44–45; Kevin Fox Gotham, "Urban Space, Restrictive Covenants and the Origins of Racial Residential Segregation in a US City, 1900–50," *International Journal of Urban and Regional Research*, vol. 24, pp. 616–633 (2000).

3. Whyte, *Organization Man*, pp. 287–291; Babcock, *Zoning Game*, p. 42.

4. Numerous observers, coming from different points of view, agree on the occurrence of a qualitative change and its timing: Davis, *City of Quartz*, pp. 174–180; Danielson, *Politics of Exclusion*, pp. 37–39, 64–66; Brugmann and Sletteland, *Ultimate Highrise*, p. 92; Michelle J. White, "Self-Interest in the Suburbs: The Trend Toward No-Growth Zoning," *Policy Analysis*, vol. 4, pp. 185–203 (1978); Teaford, *Post-Suburbia*, p. 173; Christopher B. Leinberger, *The Option of Urbanism: Investing in a New American Dream* (Island Press, Washington, DC, 2008), p. 131; William A. Fischel, "An Economic History of Zoning and a Cure for its Exclusionary Effects," *Urban Studies*, vol. 41, pp. 317–340 (2004). Peter Siskind, "Suburban Growth and Its Discontents," in Kruse and Sugrue, *New Suburban History*, pp. 161–182, puts the change slightly earlier, in the late 1960s.

5. William Fulton, *The Reluctant Metropolis: The Politics of Urban Growth in Los Angeles* (Johns Hopkins University Press, Baltimore, 1997), pp. 51–62; Davis, *City of Quartz*, pp. 188–210; Teaford, *Post-Suburbia*, pp. 174–186; Madelyn Glickfeld and Ned Levine, *Regional Growth . . . Local Reaction: The Enactment and Effects of Local Growth Control and Management Measures in California* (Lincoln Institute of Land Policy, Cambridge, MA, 1992), pp. 5–8.

6. Scott, *American City Planning*, pp. 240–241.

7. Davis, *City of Quartz*, pp. 170–180; Logan, "The Constituent Landscape," p. 133; Robert Bruegmann, *Sprawl: A Compact History* (University of Chicago Press, Chicago, 2005), p. 241, n. 15.

8. Glickfeld and Levine, *Regional Growth*, pp. 13–14, provide a more detailed catalog of growth control techniques.

9. S. Mark White and Elisa Paster, "Creating Effective Land Use Regulations through Concurrency," *Natural Resources Journal*, vol. 43, pp. 753–779 (2003).

10. Montgomery County, the home of the most-studied APFO, had to exempt the area around the White Flint Metro station in 2011 to make transit-oriented development possible there. See also Charles E. Connerly, Timothy Stewart Chapin, and Harrison T. Higgins, *Growth Management in Florida: Planning for Paradise* (Ashgate, Aldershot, UK, 2007), pp. 211–223. Pendall, "Do Land-Use Controls Cause Sprawl?," finds that APFOs promote density, but his definition of APFO appears to be different from that used here, and his evidence, a statistical analysis, is less than definitive.

11. Louise Nelson Dyble, "Revolt against Sprawl: Transportation and the Origins of the Marin County Growth-Control Regime," *Journal of Urban History*, vol.

34; pp. 38–66 (2007); Richard A. Walker, *The Country in the City: The Greening of the San Francisco Bay Area* (University of Washington Press, Seattle, 2007), pp. 88–95.

12. John M. DeGrove, *Planning Policy and Politics: Smart Growth and the States* (Lincoln Institute of Land Policy, Cambridge, 2005), pp. 11–15; Richard F. Babcock and Charles L. Siemon, *The Zoning Game Revisited* (Lincoln Institute of Land Policy, Cambridge, 1985), pp. 135–157, 235–254; Maryland Association of Counties, "PlanMaryland: 1974 Land Use Legislation Fights Still Echo Today," http://conduitstreet.mdcounties.org/2011/07/11/plan-maryland-1974-l and-use-legislation-fight-still-echoes-today/, accessed August 20, 2011.

13. R. Pendall, "Do Land-Use Controls Cause Sprawl?," *Environment and Planning B: Planning and Design*, vol. 26, pp. 555–571 (1999).

14. Compare Plosky, "Pennsylvania Station," pp. 33–45, to Logan, "Constituent Landscape," pp. 120–134. Logan, p. 252, states that "historic districts were quite explicitly designated in the 1970s to control the rate and nature of change." Quotations from Plosky, p. 51; Robin Elizabeth Datel, "Preservation and a Sense of Orientation for American Cities," *Geographical Review*, vol. 75, pp. 125–141 (1985).

15. Wendy Swallow, "Group Seeks to Save Park and Shop," *Washington Post*, November 9, 1985; Elizabeth Kastor, "Panic in Cleveland Park," *Washington Post*, April 23, 1986.

16. Cleveland Park Historic District, National Register of Historic Places Registration Form, March 19, 1987, quotation from Section 8, p. 40; Logan, "Constituent Landscape," pp. 294–296; Swallow, "Save Park and Shop"; Kastor, "Panic in Cleveland Park"; Eve Zibart, "Cleveland Park Given Historic Designation," *Washington Post*, November 20, 1986.

17. Logan, "Constituent Landscape," p. 7; "Introduction to the Historic Preservation Guidelines," District of Columbia Historic Preservation Office, n.d.; Fogelson, *Bourgeois Nightmares*, pp. 89–92, 161–164; Worley, *J. C. Nichols*, pp. 135–137, 142.

18. Babcock, *Zoning Game*, p. 116; Davis, *City of Quartz*, p. 204.

19. Fulton, *Reluctant Metropolis*, pp. 177–199; Davis, *City of Quartz*, pp. 171–172.

20. Davis, *City of Quartz*, pp. 180–185.

21. Danielson, *Politics of Exclusion*, pp. 88–92; Kenneth Forton, "Expanding the Effectiveness of the Massachusetts Comprehensive Permit Law by Eliminating Its Subsidy Requirement," *Boston College Environmental Law Review*, vol. 28, no. 4 (2001); John J. Tarrant, *The End of Exurbia* (Stein and Day, New York, 1976), pp. 61–63. A somewhat similar law was enacted in California in 1980.

22. David L. Kirp, John P. Dwyer, and Larry Rosenthal, *Our Town: Race, Housing, and the Soul of Suburbia* (Rutgers University Press, New Brunswick, NJ, 1996), pp. 112–118; Siskind, "Suburban Growth."

23. Flint, *Wrestling with Moses*, pp. 131–135.

24. Stefan Bradley, *Harlem vs. Columbia University: Black Student Power in the Late 1960s* (University of Illinois Press, Champaign, IL, 2009), pp. 39–62, 67–101; http://morningsidepark.org/park/history.php, accessed September 25, 2013. Quotation from Jacobs, *Death and Life*, p. 143.

25. Peter Dreier, John Mollenkopf, and Todd Swanstrom, *Place Matters: Metropolitics for the Twenty-First Century*, 2nd ed. (University Press of Kansas, Lawrence, 2004), pp. 180–183; 204–206; Brugmann and Sletteland, *Ultimate Highrise*, esp. pp. 58–59, 194–202.

26. Osman, *Brownstone Brooklyn*, pp. 226–231, 272–280; G. William Domhoff, "Why San Francisco Is Different: Progressive Activists and Neighborhoods Have Had a Big Impact," September 2005, http://sociology.ucsc.edu/whorulesamerica/local/san_francisco.html, accessed July 4, 2011; Japonica Brown-Saracino, *A Neighborhood That Never Changes: Gentrification, Social Preservation, and the Search for Authenticity* (University of Chicago Press, Chicago, 2009), pp. 51–79, 189–192.

27. Marsha Prior and Robert V. Kemper, "From Freedman's Town to Uptown: Community Transformation and Gentrification in Dallas, Texas," *Urban Anthropology*, vol. 34, pp. 177–216 (2005); Jason Hackworth, *The Neoliberal City: Governance, Ideology, and Development in American Urbanism* (Cornell University Press, Ithaca, NY, 2007), pp. 153–163.

28. Brown-Saracino, *Neighborhood That Never Changes*, gives a perceptive portrait of what she calls "social preservationists."

29. "Neighbors of Ashby BART Statement of Principles," http://nabart.com/nabart.html, accessed July 4, 2011.

30. Brugmann and Sletteland, *Ultimate Highrise*, p. 201; Zelda Bronstein, "The Stealth Plan to Bicycle-ize Marin Avenue," *Berkeley Daily Planet*, December 10, 2004; "Save the Alameda," January 14, 2010.

31. See, e.g., William A. Fischel, "Why Are There NIMBYs?," *Land Economics*, vol. 77, pp. 144–152 (2001); Gordon, "Private Communities."

32. Perin, *Everything in Its Place*, pp. 137–144. Edward L. Glaeser and Bryce A. Ward, "The Causes and Consequences of Land Use Regulation: Evidence from Greater Boston," *Journal of Urban Economics*, vol. 65, pp. 265–278 (2009) show empirically that zoning in the Boston area greatly reduces property values. Robert Cervero and Michael Duncan, "Neighbourhood Composition and Residential Land Prices: Does Exclusion Raise or Lower Values?," *Urban Studies*, vol. 41, pp. 299–315 (2004) similarly find that separation of land uses lowers property values in California's Silicon Valley.

33. Davis, *City of Quartz*, pp. 174–180; Danielson, *Politics of Exclusion*, p. 55.

34. Walker, *The Country in the City*, pp. 92–94, 99–107.

35. Thomas Frank, *The Conquest of Cool: Business Culture, Counterculture, and the Rise of Hip Consumerism* (University of Chicago Press, Chicago, 1998).

36. "City of Los Altos Single-Family Residential Design Guidelines, New Homes & Remodels," http://www.ci.los-altos.ca.us/commdev/planning/documents/ResidentialDesignGuidelines.pdf, accessed May 27, 2013.

37. Osman, *Brownstone Brooklyn*, pp. 195–202, 205, 209; Logan, "Constituent Landscape," pp. 122–131, 159–160; Brown-Saracino, *Neighborhood That Never Changes*, pp. 8, 145–179.

38. Glickfeld and Levine, *Regional Growth... Local Reaction*, pp. 21–27.

39. Greenwich: Danielson, *Politics of Exclusion*, pp. 59–60. Chevy Chase: Manuel Perez-Rivas, "Posh Md. Area In Throes of Growing Pains; Friendship Heights' Future Is Subject of Intense Debate," *Washington Post*, July 1, 1996.

40. Lydia Sullivan, quoted by Dan Reed, *Just Up the Pike*, http://www.justupthepike. com/2011/02/plan-preserves-kensingtons-assets-while.html, accessed July 14, 2011, emphasis in original.

Chapter 8

1. Vehicle miles traveled from http://www.fhwa.dot.gov/policyinformation/statistics/2009/vmt421.cfm, accessed July 15, 2011.

2. James A. Dunn, Jr., *Driving Forces: The Automobile, Its Enemies, and the Politics of Mobility* (Brookings Institution, Washington, DC, 1998), pp. 35–39; Brian D. Taylor, "Public Perceptions, Fiscal Realities, and Freeway Planning," *APA Journal*, vol. 61, pp. 43–56 (1995); Martin A. Sullivan, "Gas Tax Politics—Part I," Tax Analysts, September 22, 2008, http://www.taxhistory.org/thp/readings.nsf/Art Web/5DDB79194769C2BF852574D5003C28D5?OpenDocument, accessed July 13, 2011.

3. Federal Highway Administration, "Highway Taxes and Fees—2008" and "Highway Taxes and Fees—1998," available at http://www.fhwa.dot.gov/ohim/ hwytaxes/2008/index.cfm, accessed July 13, 2011. The Consumer Price Index increased by 32% from 1998 to 2008.

4. Benjamin Ross, "Stuck in Traffic: Free-Market Theory Meets the Highway Lobby," *Dissent*, vol. 53, no. 3, pp. 60–64 (Summer 2006).

5. "Effectiveness of 'Children at Play' Warning Signs," Wisconsin Dept. of Transportation, April 27, 2007, http://wisdotresearch.wi.gov/wp-content/ uploads/tsrchildrenwarningsigns.pdf, accessed December 12, 2013; Russell Carter, "Kids Cited for Playing on Sidewalk in OK Town," KFOR-TV, September 18, 2010, http://www.kfor.com/news/local/kfor-news-mustang-ordinance-story,0,5279078. story, accessed July 2, 2011.

6. Norreen McDonald, Austin Brown, Lauren Marchetti, and Margo Pedroso, "U.S. School Travel 2009: An Assessment of Trends," *American Journal of Preventive Medicine*, vol. 41, pp. 146–151 (2011); Lenore Skenazy, "A Principal Calls CPS after Mom Lets Daughter, 10, Ride City Bus to School," *Free-Range Kids* blog, http://www.freerangekids.com/a-principal-calls-cps-after-mom-lets-daughter-10-ride-city-bus-to-school/, accessed November 18, 2012.

7. Andres Duany, Elizabeth Plater-Zyberk, and Jeff Speck, *Suburban Nation: The Rise of Sprawl and the Decline of the American Dream* (North Point, New York, 2000), pp. 66–69. 8½ minutes: Benjamin Ross, *Greater Greater Washington*, January 14, 2013, http://greatergreaterwashington.org/post/ 17341/8half-minutes-to-cross-the-street/.

8. Duany, *Suburban Nation*, pp. 69–70. Reflective clothing: http://www.walkinginfo. org/why/tips_walking-safely.cfm; http://www.harttma.com/Community/Road Safety/PedestrianSafety.aspx, accessed August 20, 2012.

9. "Truck Lines Gird for Rail Combat," *New York Times*, June 28, 1953.

10. "Capitol Delivery," *New York Times*, January 20, 1975; Robert Sherrill, "Raising Hell on the Highways," *New York Times Magazine*, November 27, 1977.

11. Dunn, *Driving Forces*, p. 38; Ernest Holsendolf, "Legislation to Raise the Gas Tax by 5 Cents Is Introduced to Senate," *New York Times*, November 30, 1982;

Jerry Knight, "A Tradeoff for the Truckers," *Washington Post*, December 12, 1982; Matthew L. Wald, "The Bigger the Truck, the More Controversy," *New York Times*, July 18, 1997.

12. Stephen Kinzer, "New York Fights U.S. to Exclude Longer Trucks," *New York Times*, January 27, 1983; Federal Highway Administration, "Federal Size Regulations for Commercial Motor Vehicles," FHWA-HOP-04-022, October 2004, pp. 1–2, 12.

13. Bureau of the Census, "New Privately Owned Housing Units." Apartments are defined by the Census Bureau as buildings with five or more units; townhouses count as single-family homes.

14. McKenzie, *Privatopia*, pp. 11–12, 103–105, 127, 129–132, 164–165; Paula A. Franzese and Steven Siegel, "Trust and Community: The Common Interest Community as Metaphor and Paradox," *Missouri Law Review*, vol. 72, pp. 1111–1157 (2007).

15. Edward J. Blakely and Mary Gail Snyder, *Fortress America: Gated Communities in the United States* (Brookings Institution, Washington, 1999); Rich Benjamin, "The Gated Community Mentality," *New York Times*, March 29, 2012.

16. Teaford, *Post-Suburbia*, pp. 87–96; Elizabeth Kneebone, "Job Sprawl Revisited: The Changing Geography of Metropolitan Employment," Brookings Institution, April 2009. Union avoidance: Dreier, *Place Matters*, p. 118; Sugrue, *Urban Crisis*, p. 128; Fogelson, *Downtown*, p. 195.

17. Robert Lang, *Edgeless Cities: Exploring the Elusive Metropolis* (Brookings Institution, Washington, DC, 2003), pp. 90–94; Harry J. Holzer and Michael A. Stoll, "Where Workers Go, Do Jobs Follow? Metropolitan Labor Markets in the US, 1990–2000," Brookings Institution, December 2007; Leinberger, *Option of Urbanism*, pp. 35–40; Teaford, *Post-Suburbia*, pp. 162–172.

18. William H. Whyte, *City: Rediscovering the Center* (University of Pennsylvania Press, Philadelphia, 2009 [first published 1989]), pp. 286–289; Jackson, *Crabgrass Frontier*, pp. 268–269; Leinberger, *Option of Urbanism*, pp. 37–38; Joel Garreau, *Edge City: Life on the New Frontier* (Anchor, New York, 1992), pp. 91–93. See also Danielson, *Politics of Exclusion*, pp. 141–148; O'Mara, "Uncovering the City."

19. Leinberger, *Option of Urbanism*, pp. 42–44; Hayden, *Building Suburbia*, pp. 154–158.

20. Barry Ritholtz, "Case Shiller 100 Year Chart (2011 Update)," http://www.ritholtz.com/blog/2011/04/case-shiller-100-year-chart-2011-update/, accessed November 12, 2011.

21. Alan Ehrenhalt, *The Great Inversion and the Future of the American City* (Alfred A. Knopf, New York, 2012), pp. 90–112; Sugie Lee and Nancey Green Leigh, "The Role of Inner Ring Suburbs in Metropolitan Smart Growth Strategies," *Journal of Planning Literature*, vol. 19, pp. 330–346 (2005).

22. Katz, *Our Lot*, pp. 54–73.

23. Yves Smith, *Econned: How Unenlightened Self Interest Undermined Democracy and Corrupted Capitalism* (Palgrave, New York, 2010), pp. 236–240, 247–251, 253–263; Katz, *Our Lot*, pp. 78–128.

24. Leinberger, *Option of Urbanism*, pp. 49–62.

25. Katz, *Our Lot*, pp. 130–131; Associated Press, "Pools Become Mosquito Havens in Foreclosure," April 22, 2009, http://www.msnbc.msn.com/id/30344932/ns/technology_and_science-science/t/pools-become-mosquito-havens-foreclosure/, accessed July 16, 2011.

Chapter 9

1. Siskind, "Suburban Growth," describes sharp political swings in the 1960s and 1970s in Montgomery County, Maryland, Fairfax County, Virginia, and the Town of Ramapo in New York. Similar accounts can be found for Marin County, California, in the 1960s in Dyble, "Revolt against Sprawl" and for Loudoun County, Virginia, in the late 1990s and early 2000s in Anthony Flint, *This Land: The Battle over Sprawl and the Future of America* (Johns Hopkins University Press, Baltimore, 2006), pp. 186–188.
2. Sies, "Paradise Retained"; Teaford, *Post-Suburbia*, pp. 18–24.
3. Dennis P. Sobin, *Dynamics of Community Change: The Case of Long Island's Declining "Gold Coast"* (Ira J. Friedman, Port Washington, NY, 1968), pp. 29–38, 99–104, 108–110, 151–156.
4. Teaford, *Post-Suburbia*, pp. 14–18, 60–69, 96–108, 201–204.
5. Hayden, *Building Suburbia*, pp. 138–141; "John S. Todd, Father of the City of Lakewood, A History," http://www.lakewoodcity.org/civica/filebank/blob-dload.asp?BlobID=3305, accessed Aug. 28, 2011, esp. p. 33.
6. Kapur, "Land Use Regulation in Houston"; Mixon, "Land Use Vignettes."
7. Ross and Amter, *The Polluters*, pp. 78–81. Berkeley, California, had a similar motivation when it established industrial zones within its boundaries in 1916. The zones enabled Standard Oil and other polluting industries to ignore the objections of working-class neighbors when they located their factories. See Weiss, "Case of Berkeley."
8. Hector Becerra, "Vernon Mayor and Ex-official Are Indicted," *Los Angeles Times*, November 15, 2006; "A Steep Fall for Patriarch of Tiny, Industrial Vernon," *Los Angeles Times*, May 29, 2009; Hector Becerra, Sam Allen, and Kim Christensen, "Vernon a Tightly Controlled Fortress," *Los Angeles Times*, September 18, 2010.
9. Steve Volk, "Turf Wars: Neighbors Gone Wild," *Philadelphia Magazine*, June 2010.
10. P. Michael Saint, Robert J. Flavell, and Patrick F. Fox, *NIMBY Wars: The Politics of Land Use* (Saint University Press, Hingham, MA, 2009) p. 116.
11. Whyte, *City*, p. 241 has a similar description of planners who stand aside.
12. Babcock, *Zoning Game*, p. 141; Paul Schwartzman, Ruben Castaneda, and Cheryl W. Thompson, "Jack Johnson, Prince George's County Executive, and His Wife, Leslie, Arrested," *Washington Post*, November 13, 2010; David Daddio, " 'Dernoga Money' Stymied College Park Growth," *Greater Greater Washington*, http://greatergreaterwashington.org/post/10191/dernoga-money-stymied-college-park-growth/, accessed January 21, 2012.
13. Christopher Niedt, "Gentrification and the Grassroots: Popular Support in the Revanchist Suburb," *Journal of Urban Affairs*, vol. 28, pp. 99–120 (2006).

14. The large and muddy academic literature on this subject has much confusion between snob zoning and fiscal zoning. Economists, professionally concerned with money, often mistake status-seeking for defense of property values.

15. Dreier, *Place Matters*, pp. 111–112; Fulton, *Reluctant Metropolis*, pp. 255–281.

16. János Kornai, *The Socialist System: The Political Economy of Communism* (Princeton University Press, Princeton, NJ, 1992), esp. pp. 127–130, 176.

17. The project is now moving forward by annexing the land to the adjoining city of Rockville, which has simpler approval processes.

Chapter 10

1. Babcock, *Zoning Game*, p. 47 suggested at the time that cultural change was an element in the 1960s apartment boom.

2. For a comprehensive count of sitcom settings, see Michael Ray Fitzgerald, "Sitcoms and Suburbia: The Role of Network Television in the De-Urbanization of the U.S., 1949–1991," M.S. Thesis, University of Florida, 1997, esp. pp. 68–74, 87.

3. See Veblen, *Theory of the Leisure Class*, chapter 6.

4. Dan Hoffman, "Mowing with Goats," http://googleblog.blogspot.com/2009/05/mowing-with-goats.html, accessed July 23, 2011; Marty Englert, "Goats the New Chickens," *United Press International*, January 29, 2010.

5. Data from National Golf Foundation, http://secure.ngf.org/cgi/faqa.asp, accessed December 17, 2012.

6. Perin, *Everything in Its Place*, pp. 42–44, 55–59, analyzes this attitude from an anthropological perspective.

7. Bret Rappaport, "Green Landscaping: Greenacres," *John Marshall Law Review*, vol. 26, no. 4 (1994); Steven Kurutz, "The Battlefront in the Front Yard," *New York Times*, December 20, 2012.

8. Montgomery County Council, June 11, 2013, http://montgomerycountymd. granicus.com/MediaPlayer.php?view_id=6&clip_id=5289, accessed June 14, 2013, quotations from testimony of Hessie Harris at 28:02.

9. Belmont, California, Municipal Code, Chapter 5, Article IV, "Regulation of Pygmy Goats."

10. Ehrenhalt, *Great Inversion*, esp. pp. 3–8, 40–88, 137–144.

11. Ehrenhalt, *Great Inversion*, pp. 67–71; Soni Sangha and Vivian Yee, "As Beer Garden Extends Welcome to Juice-Box Set, Some Barflies Jeer," *New York Times*, August 2, 2012.

12. Jason Hackworth and Neil Smith, "The Changing State of Gentrification," *Tijdschrift voor Economische en Sociale Geografie*, vol. 92, pp. 464–477 (2001).

13. John Thomas, "Residential Construction Trends in America's Metropolitan Regions, 2010 Edition," U.S. Environmental Protection Agency Report, January 2010, pp. 10, 19. Big apartment buildings are those with at least twenty units. Figures for New York City exclude Staten Island, which is more suburban than the rest of the city.

14. Flint, *This Land*, pp. 61–78. Manifesto: http://www.cnu.org/charter, accessed August 3, 2011.

15. Leinberger, *Option of Urbanism*, pp. 106–112.

16. Edwin Slipek, "Inward and Upward," *Style Weekly* (Richmond, VA), January 29, 2013.

17. Matthew Dickens and John Neff, *2011 Public Transportation Fact Book* (American Public Transportation Association, Washington, 2011), Appendix A, pp. 1–2; Steven E. Polzin, Xuehao Chu, and Nancy McGuckin, "Exploring Changing Travel Trends," http://onlinepubs.trb.org/onlinepubs/conferences/2011/NHTS1/Polzin2.pdf, accessed August 27, 2011.

18. Kytja Weir, "Vehicle Registrations Drop in District," *Washington Examiner*, April 14, 2009.

19. John Pucher, "Renaissance of Public Transport in the United States?," *Transportation Quarterly*, vol. 56, pp. 33–49 (2002); Washington ridership based on unpublished data furnished by WMATA.

20. Sam Roberts, "More Commuters Are Going against the Flow, and Out of the City," *New York Times*, November 7, 2005; Charles V. Bagli, "Regretting Move, Bank May Return to Manhattan," *New York Times*, June 8, 2011. The Washington Metro has ridership trends similar to the New York commuter rail lines.

21. Gregory L. Thompson, "Defining an Alternative Future: Birth of the Light Rail Movement in North America," *Proc. 9th National Light Rail Transit Conference*, Transportation Research Circular E-C058, November 2003, pp. 25–36; Robert C. Post, *Urban Mass Transit: The Life Story of a Technology* (Greenwood, Westport CT, 2007), pp. 137–139; John W. Schumann, "Status of North American Light Rail Transit Systems: Year 2009 Update," *Proc. Joint International Light Rail Conference*, Los Angeles, April 19–21 2009, Transportation Research Circular E-C145.

22. Dunn, *Driving Forces*, pp. 42–43; Jack McCroskey, *Light Rail and Heavy Politics* (Tenlie Publishing, Denver, 2003), pp. 65–107.

23. Gregory L. Thompson, "Taming the Neighborhood Revolution: Planners, Power Brokers, and the Birth of Neotraditionalism in Portland, Oregon," *Journal of Planning History*, vol. 6, pp. 214–247 (2007); Ruth Hultgren, "How It Happened," http://www.friendsoflightrail.org/history/documents/How%20It%20Happened.pdf, accessed August 7, 2011; Fulton, *Reluctant Metropolis*, pp. 135–150.

24. Jason Henderson, *Street Fight: The Politics of Mobility in San Francisco* (University of Massachusetts Press, Amherst, 2013), pp. 54–86; http://www.preservenet.com.

25. Barbara McCann, *Completing Our Streets: The Transition to Safe and Inclusive Transportation Networks* (Island Press, Washington, DC, 2013), pp. 22–29, 32–33.

26. Michael M. Grynbaum, "New York Traffic Experiment Gets Permanent Run," *New York Times*, February 11, 2010; "Broadway Is Busy, with Pedestrians, if Not Car Traffic," September 5, 2010.

27. DeGrove, *Planning Policy and Politics*, pp. 20–23, 27–28.

28. DeGrove, *Planning Policy and Politics*, pp. 262–275; Gerrit-Jan Knaap and John W. Frece, "Smart Growth in Maryland: Looking Forward and Looking Back," *Idaho Law Review*, vol. 43, pp. 445–473.

Chapter 11

1. David Brock, *The Republican Noise Machine: Right-Wing Media and How It Corrupts Democracy* (Crown, New York, 2004), pp. 44–67.
2. Flint, *This Land*, pp. 153–163; Bruegmann, *Sprawl*, p. 157.
3. Lewis, *Babbitt*, p. 65; Baxandall and Ewen, *Picture Windows*, pp. 90–96; 103–112; Babcock and Siemon, *Zoning Game Revisited*, p. 215.
4. Wendell Cox, *War on the Dream: How Anti-Sprawl Policy Threatens the Quality of Life* (iUniverse, New York, 2006); Bruegmann, *Sprawl*, p. 153; Joel Kotkin, "California Wages War on Single-Family Homes," *Forbes Magazine*, July 26, 2011.
5. Bruegmann, *Sprawl*, p. 87. Bruegmann's justification of zoning is on pp. 105–107.
6. Cox, *War on the Dream*, pp. 128–130; Flint, *This Land*, p. 157. Criticisms of Cox and O'Toole are summarized by Tod Litman, "Evaluating Rail Transit Criticism," http://www.vtpi.org/railcrit.pdf, accessed August 22, 2011, and Todd Litman, "Rail Transit In America: A Comprehensive Evaluation of Benefits," http://www.vtpi.org/railben.pdf, accessed March 2, 2012, pp. 44–55.
7. Joel Kotkin, *The Next Hundred Million: America in 2050* (Penguin, New York, 2010), pp. 35, 38–40, 77–78, 233–234.
8. http://www.perc.org/articles/article402.php, accessed August 10, 2011.
9. Gordon, "Private Communities." See also Peter Gordon and Harry Richardson, "Exit and Voice in U.S. Settlement Change," http://www-bcf.usc.edu/~pgordon/pdf/exit_voice.pdf, accessed July 3, 2012, which lauds newly incorporated suburban governments as "less likely to be prompted to extend standing to large numbers of 'stakeholders' at the expense of property owners." Gordon and Richardson try to justify their rejection of democratic governance by contending that economic welfare will be maximized by local governing bodies that compete to supply "collective goods." But their argument contradicts itself. After conceding that free-market competition among individuals is inefficient, they reason from the premise that competition among local governments *will* necessarily be efficent. No justification is offered for this premise, even though competition among governments faces the problems of agency in addition to the problems that affect competition among individuals.
10. Flint, *This Land*, pp. 182–184.
11. Flint, *This Land*, pp. 172–173; 182–184; 202; Nancy Chapman and Hollie Lund, "Housing Density and Livability in Portland," in Connie P. Ozawa, ed., *The Portland Edge: Challenges and Successes in Growing Communities* (Island Press, Washington, DC, 2004), pp. 206–229.
12. Flint, *This Land*, pp. 136–139.
13. Donna Holt, "Smart Growth—Is It Really Smart?," http://www.rightsidenews.com/2011031522005/life-and-science/energy-and-environment/smart-growth-is-it-really-smart.html, accessed December 12, 2013.
14. Leslie Kaufman and Kate Zernike, "Activists Fight Green Projects, Seeing U. N. Plot," *New York Times*, Feb. 3, 2012. Quotation from http://www.postsustainabilityinstitute.org/what-is-un-agenda-21.html, accessed September 25, 2013.

15. See Edward Glaeser, *Triumph of the City: How Our Greatest Invention Makes Us Richer, Smarter, Greener, Healthier, and Happier* (Penguin, New York, 2011); Michael Lewyn, *A Libertarian Smart Growth Agenda: How to Limit Sprawl Without Limiting Property Rights* (Lambert, Saarbrücken, 2012); and Stephen Smith's blogging on *Market Urbanism.*

16. Paul M. Weyrich and William S. Lind, *Moving Minds: Conservatives and Public Transportation* (Free Congress Foundation, Alexandria, VA, 2009), quotation from p. 15.

17. B. Bruce-Briggs, *The War against the Automobile* (E. F. Dutton, New York, 1977); James Q. Wilson, "Cars and Their Enemies," *Commentary*, July 1997; James Q. Wilson, "The War on Cars," *Slate*, January 15, 1998, http://www.slate.com/id/3670/entry/24043/, accessed August 14, 2011; Randal O'Toole, "The Coming War on the Automobile," *Liberty*, vol. 11, no. 4, pp. 25–30 (March 1998); Stephen Moore, "The War against the Car," *Wall Street Journal*, November 11, 2005; Wendell Cox, "Washington's War on Cars and the Suburbs," Heritage Foundation Special Report SR-79, June 17, 2010; Eric de Place, "The 'War on Cars': A Brief History of a Rhetorical Device," http://www.grist.org/article/2011-01-06-war-on-cars-a-history, accessed August 14, 2011.

18. Christopher N. Osher, "Bike Agenda Spins Cities toward U.N. Control, Maes Warns," *Denver Post*, August 4, 2010; John Cassidy, "Battle of the Bike Lanes," http://www.newyorker.com/online/blogs/johncassidy/2011/03/battle-of-the-bike-lanes-im-with-mrs-schumer.html, accessed December 12, 2013.

19. Speed cameras: Petula Dvorak, "In Montgomery County, Cameras Are Frequent Victims of Accelerated Tempers," *Washington Post*, November 5, 2011. Permit parking: Joel Kotkin, "The War against Suburbia," *American*, January 21, 2010, http://www.american.com/archive/2010/january/the-war-against-suburbia, accessed August 15, 2011. Crosswalks: Dan Neil, "Pedestrian Detection," *Wall Street Journal*, January 21, 2011.

20. Elise Hitchcock, "Pedestrian Convicted of Vehicular Homicide in Own Child's Death," *Atlanta Journal-Constitution*, July 14, 2011; David Goldberg, "Protect, Don't Prosecute, Pedestrians," *Washington Post*, August 4, 2011. After her case got national attention, Nelson was eventually allowed to plead guilty to jaywalking and pay a $200 fine.

21. Wendell Cox, "The Real Test for Congestion Charging is Whether It Will Choke Off Jobs," *Telegraph*, February 17, 2003; Wendell Cox, "The London Congestion Charge: Separating the Hype from Reality," *Public Purpose*, June 2005, http://www.publicpurpose.com/pp87-lcc.pdf, accessed August 14, 2011. In the first article, written before the charge was imposed, Cox wrote that "congestion pricing makes all the economic sense in the world, but it remains to be seen whether it makes economic sense in central London." In the second, he wrote that "the problem is that the conditions that have produced traffic reduction and modest public transport impacts in London exist in few other places in the world."

22. Sam Staley, "Bloomberg vs. the Cars," http://reason.org/blog/show/bloomberg-vs-the-car; Sam Staley, "Is the End of Transponders Near," http://reason.org/blog/show/is-the-end-of-transponders-near, accessed August 14, 2011.

23. Randal O'Toole, "Using Markets to Enhance Mobility," http://www.cato-unbound.org/2011/04/06/randal-otoole/using-markets-to-enhance-mobility/, accessed August 14, 2011; Stephen Smith, "Virginia Land Use Law: Marc Scribner from CEI Responds," http://marketurbanism.com/2011/02/07/virginia-land-use-law-marc-scribner-from-cei-responds/, accessed August 21, 2011. Scribner also fears that allowing dense development will cause condemnation of private land for redevelopment, something not authorized by the legislation at hand.

24. George Will, "High Speed to Insolvency," *Newsweek*, February 27, 2011; Kotkin, "War against Suburbia"; Randal O'Toole, *The Vanishing Automobile and Other Urban Myths: How Smart Growth Will Harm American Cities* (Thoreau Institute, Bandon, OR, 2001), pp. 481–492.

Chapter 12

1. George Orwell, "Politics and the English Language," in *Orwell: A Collection of Essays* (Houghton Mifflin Harcourt, Orlando, FL, 1981), pp. 156–170.

2. Babcock, *Zoning Game*, pp. 48, 115. Perin, *Everything in Its Place*, pp. x, 81–83, emphasizes the lack of frankness in discussions of land use.

3. Site Plan 82004005A, Gables Rothbury Square, heard by Montgomery County Planning Board, July 14, 2011.

4. Exemplary at one time could refer to any example, but this usage was essentially extinct a century ago.

5. Sean Howell, "The Manhattanization of Menlo Park?" *Almanac* (Menlo Park, CA), October 20, 2009.

6. The city of West Palm Beach, Florida, has issued a policy on neutral transportation language: http://www.8-8ocities.org/Articles/City%20Transportation%20Language%20Policy.pdf, accessed October 5, 2011.

7. Researchers use a variety of definitions of conflict and rarely state them explicitly. A pedestrian prevented from leaving the sidewalk by a legal automobile movement never counts as a conflict.

8. John Townsend, quoted in Courtland Milloy, "Speed Cameras: Traffic Enforcement or Highway Robbery?" *Washington Post*, September 11, 2012.

9. This line of thinking is taken to an extreme by Tara Roeder, who argues that New Urbanist efforts to mix income levels are a racist attack on minority and working-class communities. "American Spaces: New Urbanism's Fascist Rhetoric," *Consortium: A Journal of Crossdisciplinary Inquiry* (2011).

Chapter 13

1. Abbott, *Greater Portland*, pp. 79–97, 140–142, 148–149; Gregory L. Thompson, "Taming the Neighborhood Revolution: Planners, Power Brokers, and the Birth

of Neotraditionalism in Portland, Oregon," *Journal of Planning History*, vol. 6, pp. 214–247 (2007).

2. Carl Abbott, "Centers and Edges: Reshaping Downtown Portland," in Ozawa, *Portland Edge*, pp. 164–183; Thompson, "Neighborhood Revolution."

3. "Introduction," in Carl Abbott, Deborah Howe, and Sy Adler, eds., *Planning the Oregon Way: A Twenty-Year Evaluation* (Oregon State University Press, Corvallis, 1994), pp. xi–xiv; Gerrit Knaap, "Land Use Politics in Oregon," ibid., pp. 3–23; Abbott, *Greater Portland*, pp. 161–162.

4. Ethan Seltzer, "It's Not an Experiment: Regional Planning at Metro, 1990 to the Present," in Ozawa, *Portland Edge*, pp. 35–60; Abbott, *Greater Portland*, pp. 166–170; DeGrove, *Planning Policy and Politics*, pp. 19–22, 26.

5. Abbott, *Greater Portland*, pp. 157–160; DeGrove, *Planning Policy and Politics*, pp. 23–24.

6. William G. Robbins, *Landscapes of Conflict: The Oregon Story, 1940–2000* (University of Washington Press, Seattle, 2004), pp. 293–301; Knaap, "Land Use Politics."

7. Deborah Howe, "The Reality of Portland's Housing Market," in Ozawa, *Portland Edge*, pp. 184–205. Howe reports that the median inflation-adjusted rent in the city grew by 8.8% in the 1970s and 2.2% in the 1980s. Individual tenants saw even smaller increases, if not decreases—if the rent in every existing unit stays the same, the average rent will go up because new units, which typically have much higher rents than old ones, enter the market. Of the total Portland rental housing stock, approximately 18% was less than ten years old in 1979 and 5% was that new in 1989.

8. Howe, "Portland's Housing Market"; Steven Johnson, "The Myth and Reality of Portland's Engaged Citizenry and Process-Oriented Governance," in Ozawa, *Portland Edge*, pp. 102–117.

9. Seltzer, "Not an Experiment"; Sy Adler and Jennifer Dill, "The Evolution of Transportation Planning in the Portland Metropolitan Area," in Ozawa, *Portland Edge*, pp. 230–256; Nancy Chapman and Hollie Lund, "Housing Density and Livability in Portland," ibid., pp. 206–229; DeGrove, *Planning Policy and Politics*, pp. 23–30.

10. Flint, *This Land*, pp. 172–186, 202.

11. Abbott, *Greater Portland*, pp. 175–176; Chapman and Lund, "Housing Density"; Flint, *This Land*, p. 182.

12. Adler and Dill, "Evolution of Transportation Planning"; "Building Future Transportation Leadership Seminar Proceedings: Success Factors from Portland," TriMet, January 24, 2008, esp. pp. 12–22. Ridership in Portland and Washington is calculated from unlinked trips reported to the American Public Transportation Association for the first quarter of 2011.

13. Robert Brosnan, "30 Years of Smart Growth: Arlington County's Experience with Transit Oriented Development in the Rosslyn-Ballston Metro Corridor," July 2008, http://www.arlingtonva.us/departments/CPHD/planning/power-point/rbpresentation/rbpresentation_060107.pdf, accessed October 15, 2011.

14. "Arlington's Smart Growth Journey," http://arlington.granicus.com/Media Player.php?view_id=4&clip_id=1206, accessed October 15, 2011; Schrag, *Great Society Subway,* pp. 122–127, 134–141.

15. Schrag, *Great Society Subway,* pp. 130–131, 223–227; Mark R. Parris, "The Rosslyn-Ballston Corridor: Early Visions," Arlington County Planning Department, February 1989.

16. Parris, "Early Visions"; "Arlington's Smart Growth Journey."

17. Brosnan, "30 Years of Smart Growth." This analysis is also based on discussions with people active in Arlington politics.

18. "Arlington's Smart Growth Journey."

19. This section is written mostly from the author's experiences. Written sources on the history of the Purple Line include a newsletter archive at http://actfortransit. org/archives/publications/; Jo-Ann Armao, "Montgomery Trolley Plan Travels on a Bumpy Track," *Washington Post,* October 15, 1989; Josh Kurtz, "Purple Line Has Taken a Circuitous Path," *Gazette* [Gaithersburg, MD], March 24, 2000; Katherine Shaver, "Glendening Stokes Rail Fight; Decision to Build Purple Line Inside Beltway Fires Up Duncan," *Washington Post,* October 30, 2001; Gretchen Morgenson, "With a Gift, Fannie Mae Puts on Golf Shoes," *New York Times,* September 29, 2002; Catherine Dolinski, "Ehrlich Drawing the Line," *Gazette,* August 27, 2003 ("will not go through"); Katherine Shaver, "Fortunes Shift for East-West Rail in Md.: Purple Line Stalled as Connector Hums toward Construction Under Ehrlich," *Washington Post,* January 16, 2005; Robert J. Smith, "Will the Purple Line Be Built?" *Washington Post,* July 6, 2006 ("obfuscate, alter"); Katherine Shaver, "Purple Line Foes Offer No Ideas, and No Names," *Washington Post,* July 13, 2008; Katherine Shaver, "Format of Purple Line Up to Voters," *Washington Post,* October 8, 2010.

Chapter 14

1. Henderson, *Street Fight,* pp. 115–120.

2. Thad Williamson, "Justice, the Public Sector, and Cities," in Clarissa Rile Hayward and Todd Swanstrom, eds., *Justice and the American Metropolis* (University of Minnesota Press, Minneapolis, 2011), pp. 177–197.

3. See Fischel, *Economics of Zoning Laws,* pp. 209–216.

4. Louisa Hufstader, "Pipe Dreams," *Northbay Business Journal,* December 2008. According to rumor, the referendum was initially financed by developers who wanted to overturn the ban on building on vineyards.

5. Elisabeth R. Gerber and Clark C. Gibson, "Balancing Regionalism and Localism: How Institutions and Incentives Shape American Transportation Policy," *American Journal of Political Science,* vol. 53, pp. 643–658 (2009); Arthur C. Nelson, Thomas W. Sanchez, James F. Wolf, and Mary Beth Farquhar, "Metropolitan Planning Organization Voting Structure and Transit Investment Bias: Preliminary Analysis with Social Equity Implications," *Transportation Research Record,* vol. 1895, pp. 1–7 (2004); Fulton, *Reluctant Metropolis,* pp. 155–174.

Chapter 15

1. Kornai, *Socialist System*, pp. 91–109.
2. Duany, *Suburban Nation*, pp. 221–224.
3. Charles Siegel, *Unplanning: Livable Cities and Political Choices* (Preservation Institute, Berkeley, CA, 2010), esp. pp. 69–92.
4. Glaeser, *Triumph of the City*, makes this point strongly and perhaps overstates it.
5. Franzese and Siegel, "Trust and Community," offer a more detailed program of reform that addresses these problems without making homeowners associations into governments.
6. Jason Islas, "Santa Monica's Village Trailer Park Gets Celebrity Boost," *Lookout News*, May 23, 2012, http://www.surfsantamonica.com/ssm_site/the_lookout/news/News-2012/May-2012/05_23_2012_Santa_Monicas_Village_Trailer_Park_Gets_Celebrity_Boost.html. For anti-growth basis of opposition to this project, see http://www.smclc.net/PDF/VTP/VTP5-21-12.pdf. Both accessed July 15, 2012.
7. Fischel, *Economics of Zoning Laws*, recommends moving in the opposite direction by making zoning a property right that can be bought and sold. Fischel is realistic and thoughtful in his analysis of zoning as it is now, but his recommendations for change too often rest on the unexamined premise that the object of zoning is economic welfare.

Chapter 16

1. Milton Friedman and George Stigler, "Roofs or Ceilings? The Current Housing Problem" (1946), http://www.fee.org/library/books/roofs-or-ceilings-the-current-housing-problem/, accessed November 12, 2011; Brian Doherty, *Radicals for Capitalism: A Freewheeling History of the Modern American Libertarian Movement* (Public Affairs, New York, 2007), pp. 191–193.
2. Weiss, "Planning Subdivisions."
3. Another objection to rent control is that it gives incumbent tenants an unfair advantage over newcomers to town, who wind up paying a higher price for their own apartments because so much housing has been kept off the market. But the same argument can be made against homeownership, which also grants preferential use of houses to their incumbent occupants. Critics of rent control rarely call for the abolition of private property.
4. See Glazer, *Cause to a Style*, pp. 165–191.
5. Henderson, *Street Fight*, pp. 91, 99–104.
6. John Logan and Harvey Molotch, *Urban Fortunes: The Political Economy of Place* (University of California Press, Los Angeles, 1987) is the basic source for this theory. Similar analyses are found in Jason Hackworth, *The Neoliberal City: Governance, Ideology, and Development in American Urbanism* (Cornell University Press, Ithaca, NY, 2007); Sidney Plotkin, *Keep Out: The Struggle for Land Use Control* (University of California Press, Berkeley, 1987), esp. pp. 7–11.

7. Logan and Molotch, *Urban Fortunes*, pp. 120–123, suggest that these areas are protected by mutual solidarity among the builders and that doing so is functional to the growth machine because the availability of fancy places to live makes the city more attractive to outside investors. A city's fancy neighborhoods are surely an economic asset, but it does not follow that developers avoid building in them for that reason. Many upscale neighborhoods have had to work hard to stop development.

8. Brown-Saracino, *Neighborhood That Never Changes*, pp. 118–120, 127–130.

9. Brown-Saracino, *Neighborhood That Never Changes*, pp. 252–253, discusses political motivations for the reticence of neo-Marxists about nimbys.

10. Brown-Saracino, *Neighborhood That Never Changes*, pp. 93, 234–235.

11. Heather Schwartz, "Housing Policy Is School Policy: Economically Integrative Housing Promotes Academic Success in Montgomery County, Maryland," Century Foundation, 2010, p. 4, http://tcf.org/assets/downloads/tcf-Schwartz.pdf, accessed November 11, 2011.

12. Patricia Leigh Brown, "Animal McMansion: Students Trade Dorm for Suburban Luxury," *New York Times*, November 13, 2011.

Chapter 17

1. Ehrenhalt, *Great Inversion*, pp. 40–88.

2. Annie Weinstock, Walter Hook, Michael Replogle, and Ramon Cruz, "Recapturing Global Leadership in Bus Rapid Transit: A Survey of Select U.S. Cities," Institute for Transportation & Development Policy, May 2011, http://www.itdp.org/documents/20110526ITDP_USBRT_Report-HR.pdf, accessed November 29, 2011.

3. Alan Hoffman, "Advanced Network Planning for Bus Rapid Transit: The 'Quickway Model' as a Modal Alternative to 'Light Rail Lite,'" Federal Transit Administration report, February 2008, pp. 57, 77–78.

4. Litman, "Rail Transit in America," pp. 40–43; "'Bus Rapid Transit' or 'Quality Bus'? Reality Check," Light Rail Now, http://www.lightrailnow.org/facts/fa_brt007.htm, accessed November 29, 2011; "Bus Rapid Transit—Not for New Jersey," New Jersey Association of Railroad Passengers, http://www.nj-arp.org/Assets/bus%20rapid%20transit%20-%20not%20for%20nj.pdf, accessed December 12, 2013.

5. ."Success Factors from Portland," pp. 51–60; Yonah Freemark, "US Government Plans Overhaul of New Start Funding Guidelines, Reducing Importance of Cost-Effectiveness," *Transport Politic*, http://www.thetransportpolitic.com/2010/01/13/us-government-plans-overhaul-of-new-start-funding-guidelines-reducing-importance-of-cost-effectiveness/, accessed November 26, 2011.

6. Robert Poole and Kenneth Orski, "Hot Networks: A New Plan for Congestion Relief and Better Transit," Paper 305, Reason Foundation, 2001, www.rppi.org/ps305.pdf,; Robert Poole, "Better Busways Don't Require Exclusive Lanes," *Gwinnett Gazette*, December 2, 2011.

7. Karen Farkas, "HealthLine Buses Moving Slower Than Expected on Euclid Avenue," *Cleveland Plain Dealer*, July 6, 2010; Massachusetts Sierra Club,

"MBTA's Silver Line—Taxpayers Get Less for More," http://www.sierraclubmass. org/issues/conservation/silverline/slreport.pdf, accessed March 4, 2012.

8. In its organizing strategy, the group's leader Eric Mann wrote, "the focus has been on building 'independent social movements' that are antiracist, rooted in the working class of color, and fighting various manifestations of racism and national oppression." Eric Mann, "A Race Struggle, a Class Struggle, a Women's Struggle All at Once: Organizing on the Buses of L.A.," *Socialist Register*, vol. 37, pp. 259–263 (2001); Eric Mann, "Building the Anti-Racist, Anti-Imperialist United Front: Theory and Practice from the L.A. Strategy Center and Bus Riders Union," http://www.thestrategycenter.org/article/2009/03/12/building-anti-racist-anti-imperialist-united-front, accessed November 25, 2011 (source of quotation); Eric Mann and Manuel Criollo, "Grassroots Organizing for a World Revolution," http://www.zcommunications.org/grassroots-organizing-for-a-world-revolution-by-eric-mann, accessed November 25, 2011; Tom Wetzel, "Organizing Around Transit: At the Intersection of Environmental Justice and Class Struggle," http://www.uncanny.net/~wetzel/ecoclasstransit.htm, accessed November 25, 2011.

9. Tactics shifted somewhat in 2008 when the BRU leadership worked hard for the election of Barack Obama. The underlying political analysis centered on race did not change.

10. "Hampton Roads Long-Range Transportation Plan: Visioning Survey Report," Hampton Roads Transportation Planning Organization, September 2013.

11. Peter J. Haas and Katherine Estrada, "Revisiting Factors Associated with the Success of Ballot Initiatives with a Substantial Rail Transit Component," Mineta Transportation Institute Report 10-13, June 2011, http://transweb.sjsu.edu/PDFs/research/2911-Ballot-Initiatives-Rail-Transit.pdf, accessed November 24, 2011; Weyrich and Lind, *Moving Minds*, pp. 131–142; "Transportation Finance at the Ballot Box," Center for Transportation Excellence, 2006, http://www.cfte.org/CFTE%20Election%20Trends%20Report.pdf, accessed November 24, 2011.

12. Shoup, *Free Parking*, pp. 205–223.

13. Shoup, *Free Parking*, pp. 129–141.

14. Frank J. Gruber, "Seduced by Parking," *Lookout*, June 30, 2003, http://www.surfsantamonica.com/ssm_site/the_lookout/columns/FrankGruber/FG-2003/06_2003/06_30_03_Seduced_by_Parking.htm, accessed August 3, 2012.

15. Shoup, *Free Parking*. Pasadena: pp. 238–245. Redwood City: Donald Shoup, "Cruising for Parking," *Access*, Spring 2007, pp. 16–22.

16. Henderson, *Street Fight*, pp. 87–111.

17. Thad Williamson, *Sprawl, Justice, and Citizenship: The Civic Costs of the American Way of Life* (Oxford University Press, New York, 2010), pp. 217–241.

18. Williamson's analysis of survey data reports no correlation between transit use and voting. However, he focuses on national elections, where almost everyone is aware that there is an election and few have shaken the candidates' hands. My own review of election returns in Montgomery County found that in low-turnout elections, precincts near Metro stations have much higher voting rates than sociologically similar precincts far from them.

Index